"*To those who are called, who are beloved in God the Father and kept safe for Jesus Christ: May mercy, peace, and love be yours in abundance.*"
~ Letter of Saint Jude

God in the Time of COVID-19

Reflections for these difficult times

Edited by Matthew Betts

First published by the Shrine of Saint Jude (Carmelite Charitable Trust) on 16 July 2020 - Feast of Our Lady of Mount Carmel

Shrine of Saint Jude, Carmelite Friars, PO Box 289, FAVERSHAM, Kent, ME13 3BZ
www.stjudeshrine.org.uk

ISBN 10 (print edition) 0-904849-58-9
ISBN 13 (print edition) 978-0-904849-58-5
EAN: 978-0-904849585

Edited and designed by Mr Matthew Betts

Photography: Dr Johan Bergström-Allen, TOC, Mr Matthew Betts and Fr Brendan Grady, O.Carm

Front cover designed by Miss Kerry Betts, The Happy Tea Company

Printed in the United Kingdom

Dedicated to all the supporters and friends of the Shrine of Saint Jude - past and present; and to Isabelle, Daniel, Analena, Joseph and Clara - children of the church, its future.

CONTENTS

FOREWORD
Fr Kevin Alban, O.Carm

This year has turned out to be so different from what we expected! The COVID-19 pandemic and social distancing are isolating us. But in a strange way, we are also experiencing how interconnected we are in our lives, communities, and in the world. We appreciate the fragility and gift of life and health.

The present pandemic of COVID-19 has had a profound effect on the life of the Church. In many countries, Mass and the sacraments are no longer available as a personal encounter. Not even in the Second World War were church buildings completely closed in this way. Many bishops have encouraged their priests to continue to celebrate a daily Mass alone. Many priests have transmitted the Mass from a house chapel or often from their study or sitting room. They have also taken the initiative of exposing the Blessed Sacrament and transmitting live images of the monstrance on the altar. In both cases, the priest and the Eucharist are present in a virtual way to people, making up for the lack of a personal presence.

Undoubtedly, these solutions have brought a great deal of comfort to those who feel deprived of the consolation of the sacrament and of their priest. I do wonder, however, how all those people, and there are many of them who do not have access to these virtual substitutions, are coping and what help is being offered to them. The Carmelites are trying to respond to these needs by sending out their print newsletters as usual. In this way many people will feel a connection and, I hope, a concern for their well being.

At the beginning of this crisis, I tried to offer some ways of attending to our spiritual life by drawing attention to the fact that one of the key elements in Christian spirituality is that there is a relationship in each one of us between our very self and God. While the external, communal dimension is important and necessary, nonetheless, each one of us as an individual is called to live a personal relationship with God. Saint Teresa of Avila expresses this most beautifully: *"The soul of each one is nothing else but a paradise where the Lord says He finds His delight."* I then went on to give some practical suggestions of ways of praying and reflecting.

For those of you not connected to the internet and for those of you who wish to have many of the online texts in a handy volume, this little book of articles and reflections is offered as a way of maintaining a connection and of nurturing the interior life. Here there is a wide range of styles, content and approaches to suit the widest range of readers and all tastes. Perhaps in future months and years it will remind us of what we were doing and reading in 2020. I hope you enjoy your reading.

INTRODUCTION

Mr Matthew Betts

The Shrine of Saint Jude was founded in 1955 by the Carmelite friar Father Elias Lynch, O.Carm. He was ably assisted by Brother Anthony McGreal, O.Carm. In the early 1950s Father Elias received an increasing number of petitions to the "Shrine of Saint Jude". Such a shrine did not exist, but perceiving the need Father Elias quickly developed a place of prayer and devotion to Saint Jude alongside the parish church.

Over the last few years we have developed a helpful Saint Jude online presence, whilst trying not to alienate our many supporters not able to go online. This book is one way of making sure our off-line supporters can enjoy the reflections as well as those who are able to go online.

I would like to thank each of the writers who were not only kind enough to write for the series of reflections, but have also allowed us to print them again in this book. Thank you also to the proof readers for checking this book so thoroughly. I would like to thank Johan Bergström-Allen for leading three online reflections, unfortunately I didn't have the time to write these up, but people can still view the excellent reflections on our website. Many people I have spoken to have commented on how helpful each of the 86 (so far) reflections we printed or filmed were to them. It hasn't been possible to include all of the reflections in this booklet, but I hope that I have been able to pick a varied selection.

I would also like to thank the Shrine Office team of Nic, Bev, Jilly, Debbie and Sarah for all their help in keeping the Shrine and its apostolate working over lockdown. Thank you too to the Prior Provincial, Fr Kevin Alban, for writing the foreword, and for his continued support of our initiatives. Finally, thanks to the chaplain, Fr Brendan Grady, and the Saint Jude management group for support before, now and after. It has been a very different few months to the norm, but as a team we have tried to provide good communication and service to many of the Apostle's friends.

Finally, I want to thank my wife, Terri, and our children for always being very understanding when I needed to take 'time out' each day to get the reflections online throughout March - June, and then whilst I put this book together. Thank you.

Saint Jude, pray for us all.

www.stjudeshrine.org.uk

CONTRIBUTORS

Kevin Alban, O.Carm is a Carmelite friar of the British Province. He is currently Prior Provincial and Chair of Trustees. Kevin previously served as General Secretary and General Bursar in Rome. He teaches Mariology in London and Church History in Oxford.

Matthew Betts is the lay development manager at the Shrine. In addition, he is a member of the Trust's finance commission, media group, and is also Data Lead for the charity. He is married with two children. His wife has been working in an Emergency department during the Pandemic as a paediatric nurse.

Brendan Grady, O.Carm is a Carmelite friar in the British Province. At the moment, he is parish priest at the Church of Our Lady of Mount Carmel and chaplain of the Shrine of Saint Jude. Brendan is a member of the Provincial Council and the Media Group.

Richard Green, O.Carm is a Carmelite friar in the British Province. He is studying in Rome.

Paul de Groot, O.Carm is a Carmelite friar in the British Province. He is currently Provincial Bursar for the Order in Britain. He is a member of the Carmelite community in Aylesford.

Francis Kemsley, O.Carm is a Carmelite friar in the British Province. He is currently Prior of Aylesford, but previously he was Chaplain and Shrine Director at the Shrine of Saint Jude. Francis is also a member of the Saint Jude management group.

Nicholas King, SJ is a Jesuit priest who is currently Assistant Catholic Chaplain at Oxford University. He has recently published a translation of the entire Greek Bible.

Hugh Parry is a Permanent Deacon in Portsmouth Diocese. He has been a supporter of the Shrine of Saint Jude for many years. He and his wife, Margaret, have five children and many grandchildren.

Gerard Walsh, O.Carm is a Carmelite friar in the British Province. He is part of the Carmelite community in Aylesford. Ged is a member of the province Media Group and works with the youth in Southwark.

John Warrington is a priest in the Diocese of East Anglia. He is involved in the social outreach program in the diocese and a member of Caritas East Anglia. He has worked for many years as a volunteer at the Shrine of Our Lady in Lourdes, France and travels there every year.

REST

Fr John Warrington

"And on the seventh day God finished his work that he had done, and he rested on the seventh day from all his work that he had done. So God blessed the seventh day and made it holy, because on it God rested from all his work that he had done in creation." (Genesis 2: 2-3)

In these reflections I am going to discuss 'taking time for me'. Rest is defined as *"peace, ease or refreshment."* Relax means *"to become loose or less firm, to have a milder manner, to be less stiff."* The Bible speaks quite highly of rest. It is a repeated theme throughout Scripture, beginning with the creation week. God created for six days and then He rested, not because He was tired but to set the standard for mankind to follow. God desires rest for us because it does not come naturally to us. To rest, we have to trust that God will take care of things for us. We have to trust that, if we take a day off, the world will not stop turning on its axis. The creator of the universe desires that working should be followed by rest. He created the night so that we could rest after our hours of toil.

- Are you resting enough?
- Do you take time out each day for rest?
- Try to have some time to yourself this week.

"Work saves him from the solitariness that he fears – and his fear is well founded; for when a man is alone he is really alone least of all: he is then naked in the universe; he is face to face with God; and this confrontation is formidable . . . . Modern man . . . . takes refuge in anaesthetics, and most of all the opiate of work, which keeps his thoughts away from contemplation by keeping his eyes fixed on the conveyor belt or the drawing board." ~ Arnold Toynbee

Rest and leisure are rare commodities in today's modern, technological, excellence driven society. Powerful social forces that attempt to turn each of us into human whirlwinds running in fast forward are challenging many. There's something magically refreshing about intentional down time, about stepping back, seeing the world from different angles, and getting enough space to reflect on the portion God has blessed you with.

- What do we need a break from?
- How could God be honoured in our lives by just stepping back from one activity to recharge our batteries?

*"Even youths grow tired and weary, and young men stumble and fall; but those who hope in the Lord will renew their strength. They will soar on wings like eagles; they will run and not grow weary, they will walk and not be faint". (*Isaiah 40:30-31)

When you have the time to prepare to do nothing - to sleep in; to actually read a book; to potter around; or finish what you started months ago - it will mean that your mind, body, and spirit will be rested, refreshed, and renewed, and you'll return to "real life" much more excited about what God has on your plate.

- Why not go and do something at home you have wanted to do for ages? Go and plan it, then do it!
- Is there a book you want to read and you have put off reading it for a long time? Go and start it today!
- In your busy life, why not sit down for a minute and pray to God. Talk to God about your day and what you have planned that day/week/year. Just have a conversation with Him because He likes to listen. God wants you to take that time.

Let us pray..

Oh my Jesus, I surrender myself to You. Take care of everything!
Jesus, I love You; Jesus, have mercy; Jesus, make Your will mine!
Blessed be God!
Blessed be the name of the Lord!
Divine Heart of Jesus, convert sinners, save the dying, deliver the holy souls in purgatory.
Eucharistic Heart of Jesus, increase in us our Faith, Hope and Charity.
Good Jesus, give me a deep love for Thee, that nothing may be too hard for me to bear from Thee.
Heart of Jesus, burning with love for us, set our hearts on fire with love of Thee.
Heart of Jesus, I put my trust in Thee!
Jesus I trust in You!

Reflection was first published online on 22 March 2020

Rest - Fr John Warrington

FRIENDS
Mr Matthew Betts

"My friends have come to me unsought. The great God gave them to me."
~ Ralph Waldo Emerson, Essays, First Series

This quote from Ralph Waldo Emerson is so true – we gain friendship with someone because of a random unplanned encounter – meeting someone at school, university, through someone else, at the pub, or at church. Friendship will then grow over time. God given.

Of course, all this self-isolation has meant less time with our friends and family, especially as future events become cancelled (birthday parties, etc) and we continue to stay at home.

However, there's some positives to all of this – in our self-isolation, we are making more time to call our friends (and family!) - see how they are and keep in contact. I've recently been able to enjoy two evenings with my friends online via one of the many computer programs that makes this possible. I've shared a drink and a catch-up, whilst sharing our news and, of course, our worries too.

Why not spend some time today praying for your friends and then giving one of them a call or sending them a message? We live in a time where this is easy enough to do.

Let us pray..

Dear Lord, teach me to love others the way you first loved me. As I build relationships with others, let them see you in the extent of my generosity, the authenticity of my kindness, and the depths of my love. All of those things are only possible through you, the God who abides with me and calls me friend. Amen.

Reflection was first published online on 30 March 2020

Holy Spirit - Richard Joseph King (Shrine of Saint Jude)

COMMUNITY

Fr Gerard Walsh, O.Carm

"God never asks anything from a person without giving him the strength to accomplish it".

~ Saint Teresa Benedicta of the Cross

Three of the fundamental elements of Carmelite Spirituality, which are common to many different religious charisms, are prayer, community (including family and friends) and service. Each one helps a Carmelite to focus their life in a certain direction. Prayer helps us direct ourselves to God. Community (or family and friends) help direct us to our nearest and dearest, and service helps direct ourselves to others and particularly others in most need – the anawim or little ones.

In the person of the Apostle Saint Jude, we see all three elements played out in his life and ministry and then subsequently in the lives of his early Christian communities. Saint Jude was a close follower of Jesus who from a direct exposure to the lived example of his Lord and Master was able to incorporate these values into his life as a good and faithful servant. I will be looking at each of these elements of Prayer, Community and Service.

- Think about prayer, community and service - are these three elements part of your life? Do they help you to focus?

Saint Jude would have known the absolute importance of regular conversing with God, particularly from observing Jesus regularly withdrawing from the busyness of life and the ever-growing crowds to go to his quiet place to pray. This was especially evident when a big decision needed to be made, like for example, when he was choosing his closest co-workers, the Apostles.

Saint Jude and Carmel put forward the practice of prayer as an essential act for the Christian, and that it is only through prayer that we can discern God's will for us. This is just as the Carmelite Saint, Teresa of Jesus, says: to simply spend quality time with the one we love and we know loves us. In the letter attributed to Jude, he said:

"..build yourselves up on your most holy faith; pray in the Holy Spirit; keep yourselves in the love of God; look forward to the mercy of our Lord Jesus Christ that leads to eternal life.." (Letter of Saint Jude, 20 - 22)

- Are you part of a community? Are you finding other ways to keep in contact during this Pandemic? Can you spend some quality time in prayer with God every day and pray for your community?

The importance of community is highlighted in Saint Jude's life by the communities he was instrumental in forming, especially during those early years of the infant Church. Jesus, having gathered his closest friends and followers to assist him in his mission, and then subsequently sending out the disciples in pairs for their own mission of preaching Christ and healing, would have informed Jude of the importance of being and working together and forming a community for mutual support and a common goal. This is particularly demonstrated in those early chapters of the Acts of the Apostles:

Then they gathered around him and asked him, "Lord, are you at this time going to restore the kingdom to Israel?" He said to them: "It is not for you to know the times or dates the Father has set by His own authority. But you will receive power when the Holy Spirit comes on you; and you will be my witnesses in Jerusalem, and in all Judea and Samaria, and to the ends of the earth." (Acts 1: 6 – 8)

- How can we continue the work of the Apostles in our daily lives? Can you do this through your community?

Lastly the element of service of one another and especially those on the margins of society is crucial for all Christians – for the Carmelite being in service of their sister or brother in need encompasses the act of seeking the face of the living God in them.

Jesus Christ, son of the living God, is the person at the very centre of Christian life, and therefore of Carmelite spirituality. In our Rule, the Carmelite is described as one who lives 'in allegiance to Jesus Christ', and who is expected to live devotedly in Christ, and to be whole-hearted in the service of Jesus.

Like Saint Jude who would have strived to follow the teaching of Jesus, all of us must try and find Christ in each other and especially in those that perhaps we do not wish to look upon. In many ways this element of the Carmelite charism can be the most challenging and it's only through the grace of God that we can carry this out to the full.

Although these elements have been presented separately for the purposes of explaining them, in reality they exist as a whole. We need a solid prayer life and good quality community life in order that we can be most effective in our service. Equally what we receive from our service and community is what we usually bring to our prayer. Finally, our community life only has meaning when it is supported by our prayer and our active service.

- How important is the Carmelite understanding of prayer, community, service in your life? How are they manifested, according to your personal circumstances?

Reflection was first published online on 1 April 2020

OUR RELATIONSHIP WITH GOD
Fr Brendan Grady, O.Carm

Growing up as a young boy in my native Bristol, I always looked forward to days when, as a family, we would take a trip to the sea or a holiday in Devon or Cornwall. I have always loved the sea and have found it calming, engaging and liberating. Now as an adult, I continue to find the sea, hills and mountains places of great stillness where I discover myself easily and gently becoming more conscious of the presence of God.

Saint Thérèse of Lisieux wrote, "*I was six or seven years old when Papa brought us to Trouville. Never will I forget the impression the sea made upon me; I couldn't take my eyes off it since its majesty, the roaring of its waves, everything spoke to my soul of God's grandeur and power.*" Later she likens God's love to an ocean in which she became completely immersed, knowing herself and knowing God. She writes that it was as if she "*had vanished as a drop of water is lost in the immensity of the ocean*". With such a "*transport of delight*", as John of the Cross would earlier call it, her very spirit seems to have become completely liberated by the experience.

Despite living in an enclosed Carmelite convent in Normandy, France, the spiritual experience of Thérèse did not make her aloof or disengaged from the ordinary challenges of people's lives. Her sense of God enabled her to have an even more acute awareness of the needs of those around her, as well as the incredible difficulties that faced the world of her time. It was as if she moved beyond her self-concern to an incredible empathy with struggling humanity. An essential dimension of Thérèse's spirituality was to return love for love, which involved reaching out to others with the same love that she had received.

As we move closer to Holy Week, we recognize that this Lent has been different to any Lent we as a global Christian community have witnessed. During these limiting times, when most need to stay at home, it feels as if we have been drawn into a real desert. Moses led the Hebrews from Egypt to a forty-year desert; Jesus was driven by the Spirit of God into the desert of forty days and forty nights. After a while, unsurprisingly, the Hebrews began to grumble, complain and even rebel. In his time in the desert, Jesus was tested to the core of his being. What sustained Jesus was his absolute trust and confidence in the God whose love is like a limitless ocean.

With social distancing and self-isolation, it seems that we need to drill down deep into previously unknown reserves. As we face into our deepest centre, it is possible that not only can we come to know ourselves as we truly are, but also that we can grow in our experience of God. Sometimes when I am alone at home and I cannot get out to a physical sea or mountain, I use my memory to take me to those moments when I simply knew that God is God… in the ocean, in the mountains, in the beauty…. I internalise the experiences, so that I continue to carry them with me wherever I am. Perhaps we can use this period of spending more time at home to reach into our positive memories of when we felt loved, when we loved, when others made a positive difference in our lives, when we made a difference to theirs.

Perhaps too we can explore the images and symbols that help us to think about our relationship with God. Where do we find it easiest to be aware of God? Maybe we can go to those spaces in our mind's eye or our spiritual centre and allow them to sustain us and reveal new depths to us. Those spaces can help us to know, with Thérèse of Lisieux that *"Love attracts love"*.

Let us pray..

God of majesty and tranquillity, strength and gentleness,
We thank you for so many people who have helped us to become the people we are today.
As your chosen apostle, Saint Jude, was drawn to the fascinating and liberating experience of your love in the person of Jesus, attract us to your transcendent yet ever-with-us presence.
Through your Spirit, lead us to that deepest centre where we find peace in you.
We pray in Jesus' name. Amen.

Saint Jude, pray for us.
Saint Thérèse, pray for us.

Reflection was first published online on 2 April 2020

Saint Thérèse and Our Lady of Mount Carmel
(Church of Our Lady of Mount Carmel)

WHAT DO WE ASK GOD FOR - AND WHY?

Fr Kevin Alban, O.Carm

I n times of crisis it seems quite normal for many people to turn to God, even if they do not usually think much about God or pray to Him. There seems to be something in human nature that spurs us on to seek help from some "higher power" or force. Some people would call this power "God" and in the three religious traditions of Judaism, Christianity and Islam believers are encouraged, even ordered, to bring their needs to God.

When we pray and ask God for something what are we doing and what do we believe? Do we believe that God can simply suspend the laws of nature at our request? Do we believe that God has somehow caused our crisis and we need to appease Him to make it go away? How does God cope with my asking Him one thing and you are asking Him the complete opposite? In chapter 7 of Saint Matthew's Gospel we read:

Continue to ask, and God will give to you. Continue to search, and you will find. Continue to knock, and the door will open for you. Yes, whoever continues to ask will receive. Whoever continues to look will find. And whoever continues to knock will have the door opened for them. (Matthew, 7: 7-12)

T here is no doubt about the clarity or the meaning of Jesus' words. Yet our prayer does not always receive an answer. Was Jesus lying? Was he winding us up in some way? There are, of course, all sorts of ways of interpreting that quote from the Bible and all sorts of explanations that try to fit the round peg of our experience into the square hole of the Gospel promise.

To understand our contradictory experiences, it is necessary to go more deeply into the question of who we think God is. At a fundamental level we do recognize him as the one on whom we somehow depend. He is the one whom we can turn to and with whom we can have a personal relationship. In this vision there is no place for God as a magician who can cast a spell or wave a wand – the world isn't like that. We cannot manipulate or strike a bargain with God. The Gospel story of the raising of Lazarus is helpful here.

There was a man named Lazarus who was sick. He lived in the town of Bethany, where Mary and her sister Martha lived. (Mary is the same woman who put perfume on the Lord and wiped his feet with her hair.) Mary's brother was Lazarus, the man who was now sick. So Mary and Martha sent someone to tell Jesus, "Lord, your dear friend Lazarus is sick." When Jesus heard this he said, "The end of this sickness will not be death. No, this sickness is for the glory of God. This has happened to bring glory to the Son of God." Jesus loved Martha, her sister and

Lazarus. So when he heard that Lazarus was sick, he stayed where he was two more days and then said to his followers, "We should go back to Judea." (John, 11: 1-25)

I n John's account, Jesus delays his journey for two days even though it is clear that Martha and Mary have begged him to come to Bethany. It is equally clear that Jesus has a close, personal friendship with Lazarus and his two sisters. Inexplicably, as it seems to Martha and Mary, he does not come to their aid. The key here of course, is the way in which Jesus sees these events. He wants us to understand them as an occasion for trust and faith, rather than for consolation. This is not a question of being callous or insensitive, but of embracing a bigger picture. God cannot be manipulated by us and indeed has His own plan and purposes.

We do not need to tell God what the world is going through nor what is happening in our lives – He knows already! Yet there is a great value in "telling the story" to get it off our chest. When we then reflect on how we feel after telling God our woes, it may be that something has changed within us. Maybe a new perspective has emerged? Maybe there is greater clarity? Maybe we have even found a solution we weren't expecting. Those are all "answers" to prayer but maybe not the ones we were expecting.

Prayer can reveal something significant to ourselves and help us understand ourselves better. Jesus had this experience shortly before his arrest and execution. In Matthew's Gospel (chapter 26) we read:

Then Jesus went with his followers to a place called Gethsemane. He said to them, "Sit here while I go there and pray." ... Then Jesus went on a little farther away from them. He fell to the ground and prayed, "My Father, if it is possible, don't make me drink from this cup. But do what you want, not what I want." (Matthew, 26: 36-45)

J esus is naturally frightened of what awaits him which will culminate in a terrible execution by crucifixion. He prays to his Father that he could avoid this fate (the cup). Then he realises that what he must suffer is an expression of his obedience to the Father. In a sense, Jesus appreciates that his death is part of a bigger plan. The answer to his prayer is not that he should avoid death, but that he now understands why he must die. Prayer can reveal something of our relationship with God. The real benefit of asking things from God is the deepening of our trust and dependency on him. The real answer to prayer is an understanding of the "bigger picture". Prayer can't be used to "change God's mind", but it might just change us.

Reflection was first published online on 6 April 2020

QUEENS OF ENGLAND AND SCOTLAND
Mr Matthew Betts

"The pride in who we are is not a part of our past, it defines our present and our future".

~ Queen Elizabeth II

I n this reflection, I am going to talk about Saint Margaret of Scotland, who was an English princess and a Scottish queen, and how a saint like Margaret can help us a lot. The author, George Scott-Moncrieff, wrote in his mini-biography of her: *"..a medieval queen hardly seems a person relevant as exemplar to...other saints such as Saint Theresa or of Saint Bernadette...but a queenly lady-bountiful seems to belong rather to some fairy-tale existence quite out of fashion, somebody to be confined in an ivory-tower of escape.."* However, in these days of uncertainty, I believe that a saint like Margaret can help us to find light in these dark times.

Only last Sunday, our present Queen made a speech outside of her usual Christmas message. Millions of people around the world watched the broadcast and she talked to each of us about the need to stay strong during this pandemic. In her concluding words, she said: *"I hope in the years to come everyone will be able to take pride in how they responded to this challenge. And those who come after us will say...this generation were as strong as any. That the attributes of self-discipline, of quiet good-humoured resolve and of fellow-feeling still characterise this country. The pride in who we are is not a part of our past, it defines our present and our future".* In her unique position, The Queen is stating that we should all feel proud that we are doing our bit to save countless others by staying at home, preventing the spread of the virus, and thus saving the hospitals from being overwhelmed.

As it was for Queen Elizabeth II, Saint Margaret had no inclination as a child that she would one day be a queen. She was initially brought up in Hungary, and then moved to England to be brought up in the court of King Edward the Confessor (another saint of these Isles). After the death of Edward, Margaret and some of her family took refuge from the Normans by escaping to Scotland. Here they were welcomed and protected by the Scottish king, Malcolm Canmore. He fell in love with Margaret and they were soon married. Like many wives, Margaret brought out the best in her husband!

As Queen, Margaret's mission was to *"make [the King] most attentive to the works of justice, mercy, almsgiving, and other virtues".* Margaret also sought for reconciliation in the local church, which had for a long time self-isolated from Rome because of the Viking invasions, and therefore differed slightly in how it worshipped. She carefully and kindly sought reconciliation rather than creating bitter feuds, and it worked! Saint Margaret *"also worked daily amongst the poor and diseased looking after them with her own hands"*. Margaret was as pious privately as she was publicly. She spent much of her time in prayer, and devotional reading: *"…no one [was] so wrapped in prayer [as the Queen]"*.

Observing a saint like Margaret reveals that they are just ordinary people like us – even if they also happen to be a Queen. Indeed, with this new coronavirus, we've seen that COVID-19 can infect any of us, including government officials, such as the Prime Minister, and Prince Charles. Queen Margaret used her position to better the lives of others, just as Queen Elizabeth II has done too - and countless times both Queens also put their faith and God at the forefront of their work. Our present queen often asks us to pray for her.

During this pandemic, we too have an opportunity to make life better for others: whether it's a call to a friend/family member; a donation to many of the charities that need us right now; a clap for the NHS and other key-workers; or just a chat with God about everything just as Fr Kevin suggested previously. Let us also pray for Queen Elizabeth and all leaders.

Even when lockdown ends, we'll be at home much more than we are used to, but as we have discovered, we can do so much from home!

Let us pray..

Merciful God,
you gave the holy Queen Margaret of Scotland
great love for the poor.
Lend your ear to the
intercessions of this holy woman
and help us
to live after her example
so that your goodness and mercy
becomes visible in today's world.
Through our Lord Jesus Christ, your Son,
who lives and reigns with you
in the unity of the Holy Spirit,
one God, for ever and ever. Amen.

Reflection was first published online on 7 April 2020

DISCIPLES IN THE NEW TESTAMENT
Fr Nicholas King, SJ

Saint Jude was one of Jesus' earliest disciples, but we know next to nothing about him, which makes him a good model for us, who are Jesus' obscure followers. So what I thought we might do is to look at the picture painted of the disciples in the gospel of Saint Mark, who gave us the first of the four gospels. I'm going to give you a few references in Mark, and I should like you to blow the dust off your bibles (or buy a copy of Saint Mark if you don't have one) and check out those references.

Now it is a very odd picture that he paints; because he gives us a picture of people who failed to understand Jesus, and who ran cowardly away when the chips were down. The first time that we meet them is at 1:16-20; and it is a most extraordinary story, the call of the two sets of brothers: *"come after me, and I'm going to make you into fishers for human beings"*.

- What do you think of what Simon and Andrew, and the sons of Zebedee did?
- Was it the right thing?
- Do you think they regretted it later?

The disciples do not always understand Jesus. Look at 1:35-38, when they could not understand Jesus' obsession with praying. Or look at Jesus' terrible friends in 2:13-17.

- Why does Jesus have to pray?
- Why does he have such terrible friends?

These disciples are not up to very much it seems; they can feed the crowds (6:41), but only once Jesus has done the work. They can row a boat all right, but they get frightened when Jesus walks on the water (6:45-52), and totally fail to understand Jesus' comments when they have forgotten to bring the picnic, so that he ends by saying "don't you understand yet?".

- What can you do for Jesus?
- Do you understand everything he says?

In the second half of the gospel, starting at Caesarea Philippi, they have to be taught where Jesus is headed: for Jerusalem and death. Three times (8:34-38; 9:30-37; 10:32-45) he predicts his own death; and each time one or more of them behaves in a way that makes it clear that they have not been listening to a word he says.

One disciple, however, turns out to be an absolute model of how to do it. His name is Bartimaeus, and he moves from sitting 'beside the road' to following Jesus 'on the road'. You will find this story at 10:46-52; and you might like to notice that in the verse immediately following this they are in Jerusalem – and we all know what is going to happen there.

- Do Jesus' disciples always understand him?
- Is Bartimaeus a model for you?
- Do you always understand Jesus?

For the rest of the gospel, the mood gets darker and darker, and the disciples seem to understand less and less. At the Last Supper (14:19-20) Jesus predicts that one of them is going to betray him, that all of them (14:27) are going to be *"scandalised by me"*, and that (worst of all perhaps) Peter *"today, on this very night, before the cock crows twice, you are going to betray me three times"* (14:30).

After that it gets worse, as Jesus' inner cabinet snore through his prayer in Gethsemane (14:32-42); then when the arresting party turns up, all these brave men *"abandoned him and ran away, every single one of them"* (14:52).

- What do you think of the disciples' behaviour? Have you ever treated Jesus like that?

But actually, that is not quite the end of the story. Back at the beginning, when they were first called, their main function was to be with him; and if you read the gospel through, you will find that they have managed it almost to the end (3:14); and Peter has managed that, even after the headlong flight, for he is still following Jesus *"from afar"* right into the courtyard of the High Priest (14:54). Not only that, but the women, it turns out, followed Jesus right to the end (the women almost always get it right in Mark's gospel, with one and a half exceptions); you will find the brave women at 15:40, 15:47, and 16:1-8. Not only that, but the mysterious young man whom the women find in the tomb gives them a message for *"his disciples and Peter: 'He is going before you into the Galilee. You will see him there, as he told you'."* So they are back in the group.

- Who were the *"one and a half women"* who did not get it right?
- What do you make of Jesus' disciples in this first gospel? Are they models for you to follow? Do you feel better when you read about what they did?
- Talk to Saint Jude; ask him what it was like for him.

Reflection was first published online on 8 April 2020

EASTER 2020

Fr Kevin Alban, O.Carm

Undoubtedly, Easter 2020 will be remembered as one of the strangest celebrations ever. I can hardly think of a time when all church buildings have been closed and there has been no public celebration of the Holy Week ceremonies. Even in the Second World War, Mass was celebrated publicly and people were able to participate in the liturgy. What might our reaction be to this situation?

Certainly, the lack of public celebrations, of the familiar rites of foot-washing, veneration of the Cross and the Easter fire is deeply felt by all. I am especially thinking of those who would have been received into the Church at this time and the disappointment they must feel. Even those who, for one reason or another, could not manage to attend the Holy Week liturgies, will miss the joyful and colourful Easter morning Masses. In part, this lack has been made up for by the provision of liturgies and Masses online from cathedrals and parish churches around the country. We are very fortunate to have the technological means to offer these services and liturgies. However, it would be good to spare a thought for many people who do not have access to these means. The great expansion of access via digital pathways has not been uniform and there is the real risk of creating a two-class society: those with the internet and those without.

There will be a strong sense of loss on the part of those who cannot attend Church this Easter and even more so on the part of those who have no means of watching Mass online. The feeling of emptiness and pain is not unlike that experienced by Jesus' disciples after his body had been taken down from the Cross. On Good Friday and Holy Saturday Jesus is absent. All the gospels present the primary symbol of Jesus' resurrection as an empty tomb.

The point is that "He is not here – he has risen". But the initial impact is one of loss, barrenness, desolation. In John's gospel, Peter and the Beloved Disciple race towards the emptiness and look inside. That is a powerful image and challenge. Our natural instinct would be to turn away from emptiness or seek to fill it. The two disciples embrace the darkness and the void by going inside for themselves. Do we have the courage to run towards the emptiness and to look inside our own darkness? Sometimes by acknowledging where God is not, it might lead us to where God is.

In the Carmelite tradition the figure of Elijah is helpful here. In his emptiness, fear and sense of abandonment he throws himself under a bush and simply wants to die. But God has other plans for him: he leads him up Mount Horeb for an encounter that will reshape our image of God:

Then the Lord said to Elijah, "Go, stand in front of me on the mountain. I, the Lord, will pass by you." Then a very strong wind blew. The wind caused the mountains to break apart. It broke large rocks in front of the Lord. But that wind was not the Lord. After that wind, there was an earthquake. But that earthquake was not the Lord. After the earthquake, there was a fire. But that fire was not the Lord. After the fire, there was the sound of silence. (1 Kings 19: 11-12)

God is not in the classical signs of his presence, the wind, the earthquake or the fire. Instead Elijah hears the "*sound of silence*" – a contradiction, a paradox – and understands it is the sound of the Lord. The familiar signs and symbols are sometimes emptied of meaning in order to push us towards the reality of God. And this reality is a puzzle and maybe also a challenge.

One of the greatest Carmelite writers, Saint John of the Cross, adopts the same images of darkness and emptiness to remind us that when we feel that God has abandoned us, He is in fact closer than ever. "*In the dark night of the soul, bright flows the river of God.*" (Dark Night of the Soul)

The loss, the emptiness and the lack of the familiar are not pleasant sensations as we are all discovering. But perhaps they are also pointers to where God is in our lives.

Reflection was first published online on Easter Sunday, 12 April 2020

The Crucifixion - Adam Kossowski (Shrine of Saint Jude)

BEING A DISCIPLE
Deacon Hugh Parry

Jesus Christ chose His twelve apostles. Whatever our role in pursuing our own faith, we are doing it because we are chosen by God and like Jude Thaddeus, we have chosen to say yes. The great example of saying yes was given to us by Our Lady who could herself have said no at the Annunciation of Our Lord.

There are many ways in which we can pursue our faith. Among them are Holy Orders, the Religious Life, Marriage or a life devoted to prayer. Whatever path God chooses for us, our choice must be always to fulfil it to the best of our ability. The calling we all receive is to serve, as it was for the twelve and the subsequent seven.

- What is my role in the service of God?
- How am I following in the footsteps of Saint Jude and the others in serving God?
- Am I fulfilling my calling in the way God wanted when He called me?

Saint Jude Thaddeus is less well-known than many of the other apostles, but we do know that, like the others, he was chosen by Jesus Christ. Saint Jude was chosen to go out and proclaim the Good News. He was not chosen because of his perfection; he had his failings, but he was chosen because he was a work in progress - as are we all.

At the end of each Mass, the Priest or Deacon utters the dismissal. One of the four versions of the dismissal is "Go and announce the Gospel of the Lord." This confirms our duty as a follower of Christ to spread the Good News.

- How do I proclaim the Gospel of the Lord in my daily life?
- Is it obvious from the way I live my life and love my fellows, or do I have to tell people?

The seven chosen by the disciples and approved by the apostles were not chosen to spread the word of God, but rather to support those who were. The apostles were trying to preach and pray, but as more people arrived, the Hellenists were concerned that their widows were neglected in the daily distribution of food as compared to the Hebrew widows.

The people chose Stephen, *"a man full of faith and of the Holy Spirit"* and six others. He quickly impressed everyone with his work, although there were murmurings from some who accused Stephen of blasphemy.

- Do I consider myself *"full of the spirit"* and can I see myself in the role of Stephen and his colleagues? If not, why not?

Stephen, as we know, was the first Christian martyred for his faith. His stoning was conducted in the presence of Saul who, it is said, *"was consenting to his death."* Despite the pain he would have suffered, at no time did Stephen condemn his accusers. Instead, he prayed *"Lord Jesus, receive my spirit."* Shortly afterwards, he cried in a loud voice: *"Lord, do not hold their sin against them,"* whereupon, he *"fell asleep."*

Saul continued his persecution after this event until, on the road to Damascus, Jesus asked *"Saul, Saul, why do you persecute me?"* As we know, the transformation from Saul to Paul saw a dramatic change of direction with Saint Paul becoming as powerful an advocate for Jesus as he had been a persecutor before.

- Could I submit to torture and death as did Stephen to protect my faith?
- Are there times in my life when I have stood there and watched while others are persecuted rather than remembering my call to be a servant of God?

Let us pray..

Saint Jude Thaddeus, servant of God, you were one of the twelve called by Our Lord Jesus Christ to spread His Word. As one of the twelve, when the disciples were increasing in number so rapidly, you approved the appointment of seven men "of good repute, full of the Spirit and of wisdom," to assist in your work.

We ask that you walk with us as we fulfil whatever task God asks of us. Help us to follow in the footsteps of the twelve and then the seven, while understanding that no task is too arduous or humble when it is carried out for the Glory of God.

Amen

Reflection was first published online on 17 April 2020

Whitefriars gardens (Shrine of Saint Jude/Our Lady of Mount Carmel church)

MY LORD AND MY GOD
Fr Brendan Grady, O.Carm

As we each do our best to live within the necessary restrictions that the current situation demands of us as responsible and caring people, there seems to be among many, a real renewed appreciation of our need for one another. We are so filled with gratitude, especially expressed on Thursday evenings when many join in clapping for our dedicated NHS and other key staff, as we recognise the tremendous generosity, selflessness and sacrifices that are being offered for the common good.

We acknowledge that at this time, even though for us Christians we are in the Easter season, much effort is needed to sustain our sense of balance, rhythm, inner joy and hope. If we find ourselves lacking motivation, we know we are not alone and can only do our best to be faithful to what matters most. Just like the early disciples just after the crucifixion and death of Jesus, for so many this has proven to be a "heavy" time, but perhaps we can take some little courage in knowing that eventually it will pass. Just as Jesus was raised from the tomb on the third day, so we too will rise.

During the Easter Vigil last year, Pope Francis said:

"Each of us is called...to rediscover in the Risen Christ the one who rolls back from our heart the heaviest of stones...Do not fear, then: the Lord loves your life, even when you are afraid to look at it and take it in hand... Jesus is a specialist at turning our deaths into life... Easter teaches us that believers do not linger at graveyards, for they are called to go forth to meet the Living One."

Can we use this long but temporary period to do our best to keep our inner lives nourished though prayer and reflection on the scriptures?

After the resurrection of Jesus, there seem to have been a variety of responses to the news that he is transformed, risen and present in a new way. In Mark's Gospel, Mary of Magdala is the first to acknowledge with faith that he is indeed risen. In John's Gospel, when Peter and the Beloved Disciple run to the empty tomb, Peter seems to be dumbfounded while the Beloved Disciple sees and believes. The two disciples walking to Emmaus are somehow blinded to the presence of the Risen One until he sits with them and breaks bread. And Thomas... he wasn't with the other disciples, including Jude, when Jesus appeared to them and finds great difficulty in believing simply because of their word. He must see, reach out and touch the wounded yet transformed person of Jesus to come to faith. The officials of the Jewish religion try to stop Peter and the others proclaiming this astonishing news.

As we reflect on the different reactions and the ways in which the early Christians come to encounter the Risen Christ, we may be drawn to reflect on how we ourselves have arrived at the point of having a deepening relationship with this Lord of life and communicator of hope.

P erhaps I was fortunate, or perhaps things were made easy for me, by being raised in a family where the teaching of Jesus and the practice of faith went unquestioned. Prayer, participation at Mass and the other sacraments, engaging with different aspects of the Church's mission and ministries were taken for granted. Until.... well, until I myself began to delve more deeply into what had been passed on to me. I came to a moment when I was no longer content simply to accept everything blindly. Although there has always been something of a rebellious spirit in me, neither was it enough for me merely to reject what I had been taught and shown. I felt the urge to understand and to assimilate, interiorise and integrate it for myself. I wouldn't talk in terms of conversion, for that can be radical for many people. Rather, my eyes and heart were being opened to a deeper mystery that called for an acceptance in faith that would begin a very different journey, yet one that has already had a certain direction set.

Now, years later, as a committed Christian, as a most willing disciple of Jesus, as a Carmelite friar and as a still-developing human person, I find myself re-interpreting my life story. I am tremendously grateful for the foundations that my parents, sister, brother and others laid for me; I rejoice at the good teachers I had who enabled me to question without arbitrarily dismissing the most important things that have become central in my life. I offer gratitude to God for divine patience, relentless calling and amazing forgiveness and compassion.

Was I a "doubting Thomas"? He needed evidence. He needed a personal encounter. He needed an opportunity to have a love that had been crushed in his life with the death of Jesus to be resurrected and transformed. He needed the Wounded Healer. As I look back I can trace key moments when God most certainly seemed to be at work, gently beckoning, persistently pursuing and constantly stirring my searching heart. I can see the development of my understanding of the scriptures, the gentle and sometimes earthquake-like moments of prayer, the shining and heroic examples of dedication, especially to those who are suffering or on the fringes of our normal experience, of people whose energy and compassion reflect a divine empathy that transforms not only themselves but those around and beyond them.

Perhaps we can spend some time during this Easter period calling upon God to shake up our taken-for-granted faith and our doubt in the midst of convincing lived testimony. Perhaps we can ask God to grant us the missionary zeal of an apostle like Saint Jude and the perceptive contemplative glance of the Beloved Disciple.

- As we look back at our own personal history, how has our individual and personal faith been tested, purified and deepened?
- How might we describe our relationship with the Risen Christ?
- Where do we need to invite God to transform our unbelief into trusting belief and faith?

Let us pray..

God of light, shattering the darkness and removing fear,
we offer thanks for the tremendous joy of coming to know Jesus.
We thank you for all who have
formed us in his Way,
led us in his Truth
and shared with us his Life.
With Saint Thomas, may we call out: "My Lord and my God".
With Saint Jude, may we become beacons of hope for others.
With the Risen Christ,
and fired by his transforming Spirit,
may we become agents of transformation
in our families, our society and our world.
Amen.

Saint Jude, pray for us.
Saint Thomas, pray for us.

Keep safe, keep well, keep praying... and keep sane!

Reflection was first published online on 19 April 2020

Whitefriars gardens (Shrine of Saint Jude/Our Lady of Mount Carmel church)

CAULIFLOWER CHEESE
Br Richard Green, O.Carm

In Matthew's Gospel, there's a point where one of the religious scholars asks Jesus a question:

"Teacher," he asked, *"which is the greatest commandment in the Law?"* Jesus answered, *"'Love the Lord your God with all your heart, with all your soul, and with all your mind.' This is the greatest and the most important commandment. The second most important commandment is like it: 'Love your neighbour as you love yourself.'"* (Matthew 22:36-40)

As I write this, it's 46 days since I last left the house. I'm locked down in Rome, in a Carmelite house which is full of friars, most of whom are doing further study at one of the universities in the city. It's a roomy house, and there is plenty of company, so we're in better conditions than many people, but it has still been a very strange Easter.

One of the things I'm grateful for is that this is an age when there is easy communication. I can phone my family, and know that they're OK, I can 'meet' online with friends, and see them and we can share photos of our Sunday lunch. When I do this, people ask me how things are in Italy, and what's happening, and I have to answer that I don't have the faintest idea. Just like everybody back home, all I know is what I see on the television and in the newspapers. I know more about the cauliflower cheese that my friend had with her lunch 1,200 miles from here, than I do about what's happening at the end of my road.

This is part of the strangeness of this situation. There are so many situations that I see, or read about where people are in need, or they are suffering, and there's nothing I can do. The need to do something to help, even if it's something very small, is really deeply embedded in the way we live our lives. We've heard so many times about how words without actions are meaningless, and suddenly so many of us can't act. We don't have the skills needed, or we can't leave home, or there is some other barrier in the way. And this helplessness feels horrible.

Even if we can't do anything else, we can still love. And as Jesus made clear when he was asked that question about the most important commandment, that is the most important thing. The concern that we all feel when we watch the news is a sign that we really do love our neighbours. Even if we can't express this love in any practical way at the moment, it's still real. It's still there. Even in our isolation, even if we can't help, we can still follow Jesus in some way.

Reflection was first published online on 22 April 2020

STATUES OF SAINT JUDE
Fr Francis Kemsley, O.Carm

I am always surprised at the number of statues of Saint Jude that can be found in Cathedrals and Shrines. I still remember the fine statue of the apostle in the cloister in Barcelona Cathedral. His relics are preserved in Saint Peter's, Rome. They can be seen in one of the side chapels dedicated to Saint Joseph. There, in the same chapel, is a confessional used by the Carmelites.

The Carmelites have long had a devotion to Saint Jude. There is a famous shrine to the saint in the Carmelite Church, Whitefriars Street, Dublin. When I lived in the city in the 1980's the church was full on a Tuesday evening for mass and devotion to Saint Jude.

The Cloister Chapel at Aylesford is often called the Saint Jude's Chapel. For many it is their favourite place of prayer at Aylesford. The first statue was rather simple; it was made from a mould from the pottery. It is now upstairs in the Community house on a window sill.

The present statue of Saint Jude was created in ceramic by Adam Kossowski in the early 1970's. The artist was commissioned to create a similar one in white for the Shrine of Our Lady and the Forty Martyrs, Hazlewood, the Carmelite retreat and pilgrimage centre in North Yorkshire. When it closed in 1996, the statue found a fitting home in the Shrine Information Centre at the Shrine in Faversham.

Saint Jude is known as the patron of difficult cases due to him being the forgotten apostle as he was often confused with the one who betrayed Jesus.

We know very little about Saint Jude. He may have been a relative of Jesus. He was one of the twelve. There are many traditions about him after Pentecost, including one that he was clubbed to death.

Saint Jude is a reminder that when we feel our situation is hopeless and pointless, God has the last word.

Reflection was first published online on 6 May 2020

Statue of Saint Jude - Adam Kossowski

HOW SAINT JUDE CAN HELP US TO COPE WITH COVID-19

Fr Kevin Alban, O.Carm

You might be forgiven for thinking that Saint Jude doesn't have much to tell us about COVID-19 and the pandemic it has caused. After all, he lived nearly 2,000 years ago in a very different society and neither he nor any other of the apostles had any medical knowledge, as we would understand it. However, maybe a fresh look at the letter in the New Testament which bears his name might prove fruitful for us today.

No one knows for sure whether the apostle Jude who appears in the gospels is the same person that wrote the letter of Saint Jude. In one sense, that doesn't matter because the belief of the early Church was that Jude of James or Jude Thaddaeus was the author, so for the sake of argument, let's go along with that. Jude speaks only once in John's gospel in chapter 14 when Jesus tells the apostles he will make himself known to those who obey his commands and understand that Jesus comes from the Father and is in the Father. This is part of Jesus' mission to the world as messiah and Jude wants to go deeper into the question to understand what Jesus means. Jude asks him *"Lord, how will you make yourself known to us, but not to the world?"* In other words, how can the traditional image of a 'globally recognised' messiah be squared with Jesus' own statement that he will make himself known. So, Jesus' identity will not be self evidently clear to all, rather he will choose those to whom he wishes to reveal himself. Jude's question receives a clear answer from Jesus: *"All who love me will obey my teaching."* The practical following of Jesus by obeying his commands will be recognised by the Father who together with Jesus will come and live with these loyal disciples.

I have spent a little time discussing these two verses from John 14 because Jude's question helps to understand what he writes in his letter. Looking through the New Testament to find the Letter of Jude you might easily miss it if you flick through too fast. It is only 25 verses long! Yet concentrated in these few lines are some precious teachings which could illuminate our present predicament in 2020.

Jude's opening remarks are addressed to exactly the same people Jesus mentioned in John 14: those chosen by the Father and protected by Jesus. Yet there is something amiss: Jude had wanted to write a letter of encouragement about salvation, but he feels compelled to deal with the realities of the present circumstances. What seemed so simple and straightforward has become complicated and even a struggle – does that ring any bells today? The changes we are living through prompt us to talk of a "new normal", so profound and far reaching are the effects of this pandemic. Naturally, we can feel disturbed and even agitated by the prospect of these unknown developments.

Jude reminds us that the true Messiah, Jesus, keeps people safe. *"I want to encourage you to fight hard for the faith that God gave his holy people. God gave this faith once, and it is good for all time."* The capacity for faith and the ability to believe are at the heart of discipleship. They provide a bedrock for our confidence that God does take care of his people, but not in some theoretical or abstract way. God's protection is seen in practical and concrete ways from his dealings with the people of Israel. Very often we are not conscious of God's positive involvement in our lives until after the event. Sometimes we are so busy asking and telling God what we want that we don't hear the answer! As a demonstration of his concern, Jude alerts his congregation to the various ways over history that God has led, protected, guided and shaped his people. Jude also reminds his listeners that God's people have always struggled to achieve their destiny, so the people must contribute something to the divine plan as well.

So, tranquillity and peace of mind are to be found not among the latest fads, suggestions and, dare I say, fake news. Rather it is the demonstrable facts of history that gives Israel and us confidence. Jude offers a whole series of examples drawn from the Old Testament which I am not going to reproduce or comment on here. Instead, may I suggest that this might be a good point for each of us to reflect a moment on those times we have felt God at work in our lives or maybe, after the event, realise that's what it was. Strangely, our map going forward is based on previous experiences. We don't have to re-invent God's protection or presence in our lives.

That almost insignificant figure and that briefest of letters have much to teach us in terms of realism, constructing a solid basis of faith and relying on God's protection. Seen in this way, maybe the "new normal" won't look so different from the past experience of God's love.

"God is strong and can keep you from falling. He can bring you before his glory without any wrong in you and give you great joy. He is the only God, the one who saves us. To him be glory, greatness, power, and authority through Jesus Christ our Lord for all time past, now, and forever. Amen". (Jude 24-25)

Reflection was first published online on 8 May 2020

TRIBE OF THE FREE

Mr Matthew Betts

There is a well-known science fiction novel by Brian Aldiss called "Non-Stop". I won't spoil it by revealing too much of the plot or the big reveal at the end, but a quick summary would be useful: curiosity is discouraged in the Greene tribe. Its members lived out their lives in cramped quarters, hacking away at the encroaching ponics (which they eat). As to where they were – that was forgotten. Roy Complain decides to find out. With the renegade Marapper, he moves into unmapped territory, where they make a series of discoveries that turns their universe upside down.

Now I am not suggesting that after lock-down, we are all going to forget where we are, but the novel rings a bell for me in some ways. On my street, before we were told to lock down, if we saw a neighbour, we would always give them a courtesy greeting, but say no more. Now that we are forced to stay at home and are only allowed outside once, we decided it might be useful to have a WhatsApp group to keep in touch with each other whilst we self-isolate. This has changed everything, and we all know each other much better and enjoy the communication. Quite often, one of us gets shopping for the other, or will provide some milk when a neighbour runs out. Now and again a neighbour has surprised us with a beautiful picture, or cookies, or chocolate to give us all a boost. And it works - we get a bit of joy from good neighbours in a difficult time.

However, we shouldn't fear the unknown and love and compassion is not an unknown. It is from God.

"And so we know and rely on the love God has for us. God is love. Whoever lives in love lives in God, and God in them." (1 John 4:16)

Are you discovering more about yourselves in these times? What can you do to make lives better outside your home? Is the self-isolation making you 'think outside the box (house)'?

Let us pray..

Lord, help me to be the person that you intended for me to be. Help me do what is right by my family and my friends. Help me see what is right and do what is best for the greater good of those around me. Help me to better cope with life when things don't necessarily go the way I may have liked them to. And lastly, help me to take better care of myself so that I can be a rock that my family can lean on. In Jesus' name, Amen.

Reflection was first published online on 7 May 2020

CHATTING WITH GOD
Fr Kevin Alban, O.Carm

During this time of lockdown, social distancing, closed churches and a great yearning for familiar forms of worship, there is a tremendous opportunity to explore other forms of communication with God. In an earlier reflection, I mentioned that while the external, communal dimension is important and necessary, nonetheless, each one of as an individual is called to live a personal relationship with God. In the Easter season, the gospel of John is used extensively in the liturgy. In chapter 14, Jesus explains the relationship between the Father, the Son, and each one of us: *"The Father lives in me, and he is doing his own work. Believe me when I say that I am in the Father and the Father is in me."* (vv. 10-11) So there is complete unity between the Father and the Son, without removing the distinction between them. This unity is shared by each one of us: *"He [the Father] lives with you, and he will be in you."* (v. 17) and *"You will know that you are in me and I am in you."* (v. 20)

Saint Teresa of Avila expresses the same idea most beautifully: *"The soul of each one is nothing else but a paradise where the Lord says He finds His delight."* So, we have the Lord himself within us, or perhaps better, the Lord has chosen to live in each one of us.

This points to an intimate connection with God which again Saint Teresa describes in simple terms: *"We need no wings to go in search of Him but have only to look upon Him present within us."* Finding God does not mean exalted flights of imagination, not hours of silence, nor focusing on some object like our breath, but it is an interior process of discovery. The search for God is the search for our true selves, and finding our true selves means finding God. Put in basic terms, when we discover that the centre of our lives, of our selves is love, then we have discovered God. When we are able to let go of our self-centred, selfish attitudes, then we can focus on others. She writes, *"One needs no bodily strength for mental prayer, but only love and the formation of a habit."* The driving force then is the desire to find love for others within and the best example of this is in God.

Saint Teresa also likens the relationship between God and humanity in terms of friendship: *"Contemplative prayer is nothing else than a close sharing between friends; it means taking time frequently to be alone with him who we know loves us."* She is not the first writer to use this image: Aelred of Rievaulx, a monk who lived in Yorkshire in the 12th century, wrote a work entitled Spiritual Friendship, for example. But arguably, Teresa's phrasing is the more striking since it seems to go to the very heart of the matter and is very much in line with Jesus' words in John's gospel.

What are the implications or the consequences of looking at prayer as an expression of friendship? It's not possible here to explore all the various answers to that question. However, I would like to point out maybe two ways that thinking about our relationship with God as friendship changes our approach to prayer.

Friends are there to listen to anything we have to say. We can get things off our chest with a good friend. But even with our closest friends, we sometimes avoid controversial topics that would cause strong disagreement, or even anger. We try not to 'push people's buttons'. The beauty of our conversation with God is that he has no buttons to push! Saint Paul had an elegant way of putting this:

"Yes, I am sure that nothing can separate us from God's love—not death, life, angels, or ruling spirits. I am sure that nothing now, nothing in the future, no powers, nothing above us or nothing below us—nothing in the whole created world—will ever be able to separate us from the love God has shown us in Christ Jesus our Lord". (Romans 8:38-39)

Sometimes I like to make a slight change from *nothing* to *no thing* to make the point more forcibly. There is no thing that we can say or do that will turn God away from us. Put positively, we can say anything we like to God. There is no approved list of topics, no off-limit subjects, no emotion that cannot be expressed openly and honestly. This is the liberating aspect of prayer seen as friendship. We are totally free from all inhibitions, all taboos, all blockages.

The second way our approach to prayer can change is related to the first. If there are no topics off the table or prohibited, then there is a freedom in the way that we pray. Better perhaps, anything that brings God to mind and draws our attention to Him, is a way of praying. Many people who would like to pray, wonder how they can begin. Many people who do pray, wonder if they are doing it correctly or if there is a better way. It is true that there are methods and techniques that can help us to pray. There are measures we can take to facilitate our relationship. Finding space, time and silence are very helpful. But there is no 'magic' method or sure-fire way that we must follow before entering into this conversation.

This aspect of seeing prayer as friendship is also very liberating: we do not have to worry if we are "doing it right" – there is no right way. Anything that makes us think of God and consciously turn towards Him and begin to talk to him is a way to prayer. A sunset, a flower, a child, but also fear, doubt and anxiety...so many ways to God. How could the infinite God confine himself to one method of discovering him? That's why I've called this piece "Chatting with God". When we talk, we don't follow a script or get in the right posture or frame of mind to speak to our friends. We just pick up the phone and get on with it. In the same way, we can chat with God and that's prayer...

Reflection was first published online on 15 May 2020

THE EARLY CHURCH
Br Richard Green, O.Carm

Over the last few weeks we've been hearing about the very early church in the first readings, which have been from the Acts of the Apostles. One of the things that has struck me very deeply is how hard they worked to avoid having divisions within the community of people who followed Christ.

This was difficult to do, because they were trying to bring together Jewish people, and those from non-Jewish backgrounds into the same community. The Jewish law tried to keep Israel separate from the other nations: a Jewish person staying in a non-Jewish house, or eating at the same table as non-Jews would be made "unclean".

This meant that when the first non-Jews joined the group of Jesus's followers, it was very difficult for them to do anything together. In fact, there were even questions as to whether it was possible for non-Jews to join the movement at all.

At the time there were some non-Jews who were sympathetic to Jewish religious ideas. They thought that there was only one God, and spent time praying to God. They were generous to their Jewish neighbours and some of them supported their local synagogue. We hear about one of these in the book of Acts: *"He was a Roman centurion called Cornelius, who sent messengers to Peter, to ask Peter to visit him, so that he could hear more about Jesus"*.

If Peter was going to follow the strictest Jewish law he would have to turn these messengers away - he couldn't be a guest of Cornelius without becoming "unclean". However, just before these messengers arrived he had a vision. He saw a collection of all sorts of animals and birds, both types of animal that the Jews were allowed to eat and the forbidden types, and he heard a voice telling him to eat. He saw this, and heard the same voice three times (Peter seems to have needed to be told everything three times!). Peter took this as a sign that he shouldn't call anyone profane or unclean. He went with the messengers, and spoke to a large group of people at Cornelius's house, telling them about the things that Jesus had done, and about Jesus's death and resurrection. He said:

Then Peter began to speak to them: "I truly understand that God shows no partiality, but in every nation anyone who fears him and does what is right is acceptable to him. You know the message he sent to the people of Israel, preaching peace by Jesus Christ—he is Lord of all. That message spread throughout Judea, beginning in Galilee after the baptism that John announced: how God anointed Jesus of Nazareth with the Holy Spirit and with power; how he went about doing good and healing all who were oppressed by the devil, for God was with him".
(Acts 10. 34-38)

Peter was the most important of the apostles, and when he acted like this a lot of those who had been sceptical about allowing non-Jews to become followers of Jesus changed their minds. His example meant that both Jews and non-Jews could gather together to worship God, and especially that they could share the meal of the Eucharist together. And it's still a message for us today.

We can act towards some people as though they were "unclean", but we should always remember that they were made in God's image, and that God has made them clean.

Let us pray..

I believe in God, the Father Almighty, Creator of Heaven and earth;
and in Jesus Christ, His only Son Our Lord,
Who was conceived by the Holy Spirit, born of the Virgin Mary, suffered under Pontius Pilate, was crucified, died, and was buried.

He descended into Hell; the third day He rose again from the dead;
He ascended into Heaven, and sitteth at the right hand of God, the Father almighty;
from thence He shall come to judge the living and the dead.

I believe in the Holy Spirit, the holy Catholic Church, the communion of saints, the forgiveness of sins, the resurrection of the body and life everlasting.

Amen

Reflection was first published online on 18 May 2020

Part of the list of Apostles - Adam Kossowski (Shrine of Saint Jude)

PRAYER AS FRIENDSHIP - WHAT DIFFERENCE DOES IT MAKE?
Fr Kevin Alban, O.Carm

I n my last reflection I explained that when we look at prayer as an expression of friendship with God, it means that we can say whatever we want, in whatever way we want to say it. This freedom of expression and of content creates a space within us. It is a space which is safe because we are not worried by what we are saying nor by how we are saying it. There are friends, maybe one special friend, to whom we can speak in complete openness, and this produces a feeling of great security and safety within us.

Very often I have had the following experience: someone asks to speak with me to get advice or help. They then spend the next 10, 20 or even 30 minutes telling me all their problems. I say very little, maybe a nod, an um or an ah. Then as the "conversation" draws to an end, the person says something like, "Well thank you very much. You've been a great help." I haven't said anything at all, or very little. What has happened, and it's very important, is that person has found a space to express themselves. It doesn't matter really what I said. They were able to talk though their problem and felt better for it. That's what prayer can do for us when we feel that safe space and able just to chat with God about our problems.

Of course, you may say, God knows our problems, feelings and fears already, so why bother to tell him? That's true from God's perspective: he does know everything. But it's the good it does us to verbalise our feelings and problems that is important. This approach finds a parallel in the technique called "echoing" in counselling and therapy. The counsellor or therapist repeats back to us what we have told them: *"What you are saying then, is…"* is the phrase that's often used. The counsellor or therapist isn't only checking that they have understood their client, but also letting the client hear what their words sound like on the lips of another. It can help us focus and reflect on what we have said. Telling God what He already knows, as it were, helps us to be attentive to and concentrate on what we are experiencing.

In this respect, the lack of prescribed method is also important here. We do not have to possess a "prepared script" of what we want to say. Most of our daily conversations would look pretty disjointed and incoherent if we were to transcribe them on paper. "Rambling" would be a good way to describe most of our interactions! This is what we can do with God without any inhibitions or embarrassment. Prayer and meditation are not sleek, well-organised conversations, or worse, monologues. They are meandering and circular discourses – rambling with God.

Our sense of security and safety are also relevant here. Some of our friends, and many others besides, sometimes get impatient when we witter on aimlessly, jumping from subject to subject. Not so God...He doesn't mind rambling or wittering. That's so comforting and so reassuring.

There are other consequences here of great importance. When we are able to focus on and attend to our experiences with God, then this reveals our weaknesses, slips, negative attitudes and bad behaviour to us. Perhaps we even recognise our... sin... to use an unpopular word. I don't mean a sort of morbid self-absorption or narcissistic introspection, but just the realisation that we don't have all the answers and that we make mistakes. Prayer reveals our incompetency to us in a very honest way. Prayer reveals our need for God.

The realisation that we have been unthinking and unkind can be a learning experience and help us to show compassion and understanding to others. We realise that our own self-centredness is often at the root of interpersonal difficulties. We also realise that our own vulnerabilities are part of who we are. This learning process can, paradoxically perhaps, help us to accept and live with unkindness and heartlessness from others. Since we are unaware of the impact of our actions on others, we can appreciate better that those who treat us badly are not conscious of their actions and attitudes. This realisation can also help us to be more tolerant and understanding of others. It can take the sting out of the frictions and tensions of daily life.

Ultimately, prayer brings us face to face with the challenge of establishing a relationship where our incompetence and thoughtlessness are not the product of psychological or personal problems. Rather we are confronted with the "other" whom we do not really know. Our challenge in prayer is relating to someone who by his very nature we cannot truly understand. Even if the image of God as friend is, I believe, a very helpful one, God is not just a friend like another friend, he is beyond our human friendships. I don't mean that in a 'when we pray what we do not know', then the real search begins.

Reflection was first published online on 25 May 2020

Pilgrims and a friar at the Shrine of Saint Jude

PENTECOST AND THE PANDEMIC

Fr Kevin Alban, O.Carm

As we gradually come to the end of lockdown, there is an uncanny parallel with the situation we read about in the early Church. The first Christian community is gathered in prayer, as it has been since the time of Jesus' ascent to heaven. The disciples, men and women, have self-isolated for a short period as they prepare themselves for the gift of the Spirit promised by Jesus.

"When the day of Pentecost came, they were all together in one place. Suddenly a noise came from heaven. It sounded like a strong wind blowing. This noise filled the whole house where they were sitting". (Acts 2: 1-2)

It is important to bear in mind that the Jewish feast of Pentecost occurred 50 days after the Passover, that seminal festival of liberation which recalls the escape of the people of Israel to a new life. On that 50th day, Moses goes up Mount Sinai (ascends, if you like), has his experience of the Lord, and comes down with the framework or key points for a new way of life, that we call the Ten Commandments or the Law. Moses' descent from Sinai also marks a new relationship with the Lord. The Law is not simply an imposition, or an obligation placed on the people. It is also the sign of a mutual relationship: *"You will be my people and I will be your God."* (Exodus 6:7). So the celebration of Pentecost is full of meaning for Israel, and by extension, for the early Christian community. As we emerge from lockdown, we can readily identify with that sense of freedom from constraints, of a changed way of life (the "new normality") and with that sense of a deepened relationship with God, forged in the period of isolation that we have experienced. Israel's period in the desert was the time the nation discovered its identity as the recipient of mercy and love. So too I believe many people have discovered or deepened their relationship with God in the period of lockdown.

I would like to draw attention to two more aspects of Pentecost as it might relate to our current situation: the restoration of unity and the birth of something new. Saint Luke's account of the scene in the Upper Room underlines the power of the Spirit, in wind and fire. It also stresses that the disciples begin to speak in a new way.

"They were all filled with the Holy Spirit, and they began to speak different languages. The Holy Spirit was giving them the power to do this". (Acts 2:4)

The text is quite clear that they were not speaking gibberish or babbling, they were speaking different languages. The two commonest languages in Jerusalem at this time would have been Aramaic and Greek. Luke wishes to describe a new development here. There is a miraculous acquisition of new linguistic ability.

Perhaps our own experiences over the last ten weeks have helped us to develop a new language of relationships, of community, of prayer? Luke illustrates this newfound capacity for language when he describes the emergence of the community from the house where they have been meeting.

There were some godly Jews in Jerusalem at this time. They were from every country in the world. A large crowd came together because they heard the noise. They were surprised because, as the apostles were speaking, everyone heard in their own language. (Acts 2:5-6)

In the context of the experience of Israel, this incident is the flip side of the punishment given to the people for their pride and arrogance in the Old Testament:

There was a time when the whole world spoke one language. Everyone used the same words… Then the people said, "Let's build ourselves a city and a tower that will reach to the sky. Then we will be famous. This will keep us together so that we will not be scattered all over the earth." Then the Lord came down to see the city and the tower. The Lord said, "These people all speak the same language. And I see that they are joined together to do this work. This is only the beginning of what they can do. Soon they will be able to do anything they want. Let's go down and confuse their language. Then they will not understand each other." So people stopped building the city, and the Lord scattered them all over the earth. That is the place where the Lord confused the language of the whole world. That is why it is called Babel. (Genesis 11: 1-9)

Pentecost reverses Babel. Jesus Christ reverses Adam. Mary reverses Eve. More than this, however, confusion gives way to order and intelligibility. Misunderstanding is replaced by comprehension, and fragmentation is healed in unity. The Christian community must, by its very nature, be able to communicate the experience of Jesus to others and this requires a specific language. One of the fundamental beliefs in our Christian faith is that God does communicate with humanity in order to teach us and to guide us. So, directness and clarity are basic to the Christian mission to bring the relationship enjoyed with Christ to others. Jesus Christ is, of course, the best and highest communication of who God is, being God's own son. As Saint John of the Cross puts it, *"For, in giving us, as he did, his Son, who is his one and only Word, he spoke to us once and for all, in this single Word, and he has no occasion to speak further."*

The final point I would like to make relates to the way the Pentecost event is depicted as the birth or beginning of the Church. Leaving aside the question of whether this is the only way of looking at the start of the Church, it is clear that in Luke's description there is something new here.

The images of fire and wind sweeping through the place where the disciples gather bring to mind someone cleaning or sweeping out a room! The action of the Spirit is to create, to inspire, to bring life, to jolt, to stir up. The birth of the Church implies a new creative force in the world and a new perspective on reality.

I have wandered away from the theme of the pandemic a bit, however, I hope you can appreciate the connection with Pentecost. As we come back to life in society, we bring a new force, a creative spirit, and a renewed framework for living.

Let us pray..

Come Holy Spirit and Come, Holy Ghost, fill the hearts and minds of Thy faithful servants and enkindle in them the fire of Thy Divine love.
Send forth Thy Spirit and they shall be created.
And Thou shalt renew the faith of the earth.

Reflection was first published online on 31 May 2020

Pentecost - Adam Kossowski (Shrine of Saint Jude)

HOPE IN THE NEW TESTAMENT
Fr Nicholas King, SJ

What do you hope for in this strange time of lockdown? Hope is a strange Christian attitude, but incredibly important. It places us between the now and the not-yet. Can you remember all the way back to Pre-Virus, when we had never heard of Corona (or Zoom, for that matter)? Do you recall how simple things were then, in contrast to this extraordinary moment when it is suddenly no longer possible to plan, and all we can do is live one day at a time? So "hope" is what gets us through the darkness; and it is not the same as being "optimistic". Our source of hope is not the gloomy insight that "things can't possibly get any worse; so they must get better". Rather it is the entirely cheerful certainty that God has raised Jesus from the dead, so everything is all right, no matter how dark things may appear.

Paul is the go-to person here. The word "*hope*" appears four times in the very first of his letters, 1 Thessalonians. Twice (1:3; 5:8) it appears as part of his great triad of "*faith, hope and love*"; and you may remember the same pattern at 1 Corinthians 13:13 ("*there remain faith, hope and love, these three…*") and a rather more elaborate version at Galatians 5:5-6 "*by the Spirit, as a result of faith, we are waiting for the hope of justification…which works through love*". And he is able to see grounds for hope, at the moment of Jesus' coming, in the very fact of the Thessalonian community: "*who is our hope, or joy, or crown of boasting – isn't it you people also?*" (2:19). The connection with Resurrection is made absolutely clear in the fourth use of the word in 1 Thessalonians, at 4:13, where he wants the Thessalonians "*not to be ignorant about those who have fallen asleep – you are not to grieve like the others, who have no hope*". Here we are clearly talking about life after death.

Paul comes back to the idea in Romans 5:1-5 and 8:23-24; the grounds here are what God has done for us: "*we have been justified as a result of faith, and we have peace with God, through our Lord Jesus Christ*", before he speaks of our ability to "*boast in the hope of God's glory*", and therefore even to put up with "*tribulations, knowing that tribulation brings endurance and endurance brings calibre, and calibre brings about hope, and hope is not ashamed because the love of God is poured out in our hearts through the Holy Spirit that was given us*". Here, once again, hope is a matter of recognising what God has done in Christ; and the same is true when we come to the end of this section, when Paul points to the idea of hope deep in God's creation: "*We know that the whole of creation groans together, and is in labour pains together, right down to the present moment*"… and we share the groaning, but in fact "*we were saved by hope; but hope that is seen is not hope. (For who hopes for what they can see?). Now if we are hoping* for what we cannot see, then we are eagerly awaiting in endurance". The point, then, is that hope comes because of what we have glimpsed about God. That is what Abraham does, according to Paul (see Romans 4:18-21), "*hoping against hope*"; and it is all about what God does and has already done in our lives. That is, according to Paul, what Scripture gives us: "*it was written for our teaching, in order that through the endurance and comfort that the scriptures give we might have hope*". And hope gives us a cheerful and generous confidence: "*So since we have such a great hope, we have huge confidence*". It is all about the sense of God at work in our lives.

During this plague of the virus, have you felt God at work in your lives? And has that given you hope?

Let us pray..

Heavenly Father, I am your humble servant, I come before you today in need of hope. There are times when I feel helpless, There are times when I feel weak. I pray for hope. I need hope for a better future. I need hope for a better life. I need hope for love and kindness.

Some say that the sky is at its darkest just before the light. I pray that this is true, for all seems dark. I need your light, Lord, in every way. I pray to be filled with your light from head to toe. To bask in your glory. To know that all is right in the world, as you have planned, and as you want it to be.

Help me to walk in your light, and live my life in faith and glory. In your name, I pray, Amen.

Reflection was first published online on 6 June 2020

Statue of Saint Jude - unknown artist (Whitefriars)

HOW SAINT ISIDORE BECAME THE PATRON SAINT OF THE INTERNET
Fr Gerard Walsh, O.Carm

One of the gifts of the lockdown of 2020 has been the application of the internet into Church life. This can be seen particularly in Church circles where many priests have taken the bull by the horns and got out there on the airwaves posting daily Masses and reflections online via Facebook or YouTube or one of the other social media platforms. Likewise at the Shrine of Saint Jude, we have had our daily reflections, and now weekly reflections.

When we began the lockdown late March, and in early April the Church celebrated the feast day commemoration of Saint Isidore of Seville on 4 April – what has this 6th Century Spanish Saint and Doctor of the Church got to do with the pandemic lockdown and the live streaming of religious services?

Well, in 1997, Pope Saint John Paul II nominated Saint Isidore the Patron Saint of the Internet (although the Vatican have yet to make it official, he is widely recognised today). It may seem a strange choice to name a saint who died over 1200 years before the advent of electricity and over 1300 years before the internet itself was invented to be its patron saint, but if we dig a little deeper we can say that Isidore is a fine choice.

Saint Isidore of Seville (c.560-636) was born in Seville in about 560 and after his father's death he was educated by his brother Leander, Archbishop of Seville. He was instrumental in converting the Visigothic kings from the Arian heresy, which asserted the belief that Jesus Christ is the Son of God who was begotten by God the Father at a point in time, a creature distinct from the Father and is therefore subordinate to him, but the Son is also God (i.e. God the Son).

Isidore was made Archbishop of Seville after his brother's death; and he took a prominent part in the Church councils at Toledo and Seville. The Council of Toledo, in particular, laid great emphasis on learning, with all bishops in the kingdom commanded to establish seminaries and to encourage the teaching of Greek and Hebrew, law and medicine. He promoted the study of the philosophy of Aristotle, long before the Arabs discovered him and centuries before 13th Century Christian philosophers discovered him through the Arabs.

Isidore embarked on the project of writing an encyclopaedia of universal knowledge but did not live to complete it. Perhaps this has now been realised with a certain search engine beginning with G or an online encyclopaedia beginning with W. In my Carmelite community, in Aylesford, we often ask obscure questions during meals and recreation and frequently the response is: 'There are no unanswered questions!', as the smartphone is removed from the pocket and consulted.

Two weeks ago, we celebrated the Ascension of Jesus into heaven, forty days after His resurrection at Easter. In the Gospel for that feast Jesus instructs Saint Jude and the other Apostles to:

"Go therefore and make disciples of all nations, baptising them in the name of the Father and of the Son and of the Holy Spirit, and teaching them to obey everything that I have commanded you. And remember, I am with you always, to the end of the age."

In other words, go and spread my Good News and gather and instruct my followers throughout the world and throughout time.

With the lockdown and social restrictions, this command of Jesus has been impossible to continue face-to-face, as it has been achieved over the last almost 2,000 years, but through the internet and the social media platforms, under the patronage of Saint Isidore and through the intercession of Saint Jude, the patron of hope, many have been able to partake in the Mass in various services. Even those without access to the internet have been able to participate through the media of television and radio.

So, this obscure saint of the 6th Century is really a saint for our times! At the time of writing this the churches are beginning to open up for private prayer and the day when we can worship together once more is looking more and more hopeful even though there are new restrictions in place.

I call on the intercession of saints Jude and Isidore in hopeful thanksgiving to God, for the gift of the internet and making evangelisation in these trying times possible.

Reflection was first published online on 19 June 2020

Statue of Saint Jude - Philip Lindsey Clark (Shrine of Saint Jude)

COVID-19
Br Paul de Groot, O.Carm

Stay at Home - Protect the NHS - Save Lives

when did we get Brexit done?

Shielding

the Queen at Windsor Castle

Self-Isolating

Johnson at Chequers

Home schooling

with your family in a Tower Block?

Stock Piling

has the Food Bank had to close?

On Furlough

but enough to meet the bills?

The Signs of the Times:
absent family, absent friends...
sleepless nights, acute anxiety...
irritation, violence...

loving partners, helpful neighbours...
the kindness of strangers...
shared tasks, bursts of laughter...
shared moments of delight...

Plus ça change, plus c'est la même chose.

Rosary Way (Shrine of Saint Jude)

My Lord God,
I have no idea where I am going.
I do not see the road ahead of me.
I cannot know for certain where it will end.
nor do I really know myself,
and the fact that I think I am following your will
does not mean that I am actually doing so.
But I believe that the desire to please you
does in fact please you.
And I hope I have that desire in all that I am doing.
I hope that I will never do anything apart from that desire.
And I know that if I do this you will lead me by the right road,
though I may know nothing about it.
Therefore will I trust you always though
I may seem to be lost and in the shadow of death.
I will not fear, for you are ever with me,
and you will never leave me to face my perils alone.

~ Thomas Merton, 1915 - 1968

A prayer for those with COVID-19

Dear Lord,

in your ministry, you healed and cared for everyone regardless of age, sex, creed or position in society.

Be with all the people who need you because of COVID-19. Protect those who will feel isolated whilst they are in quarantine or whilst receiving treatment.

Help all those who look after the sick. Give them strength for this selfless service, enabling them to give hope to those they are called to serve.

Help people to work together rather than individually, just as Jesus did with his Apostles.

Saint Jude, saint of hope, pray for us.

Amen.

www.PraywithJude.co.uk

Prayer written by Matthew Betts

Although originally an engineer, I have a Doctorate degree in Education from the University of Lincoln and, an MBA degree from the University of Humberside. I am now a semi-retired, management, business and education consultant with a passion for history, especially local history. Since 'retiring' I have undertaken several history related research projects and given talks on aspects of the social history of Grimsby, which I now see as my third career.

SEARCHING FOR WALTER

The Story of My Family's Journey from Tydd St Mary
to War Hero via Grimsby

This book is dedicated to my mother Grace Mary Bloy, née James, (1916- 1983), in recognition of the desperately short time, which was frequently interrupted by his war service, she had with my father Walter, before his tragic fatal accident. It acknowledges how she kept his memory alive through the box of 'treasures' she had kept hidden for many years, which provided me with a rich source of information and the inspiration and motivation to write this story.

Dr Stephen Bloy

SEARCHING FOR WALTER

The Story of My Family's Journey from Tydd St Mary
to War Hero via Grimsby

AUSTIN MACAULEY
PUBLISHERS LTD.

A CIP catalogue record for this title is available from the British Library.

ISBN 978 184963 356 7

www.austinmacauley.com

First Published (2013)
Austin Macauley Publishers Ltd.
25 Canada Square
Canary Wharf
London
E14 5LB

Printed and Bound in Great Britain

Acknowledgments

I also thank and acknowledge those members of my family who helped me to tell the story by contributing their recollections, photos and family records they had available; without which, the story would be lacking in depth and interest.

Contents

Chapter One

Why Did I Write The Story?

This is the story of my search into the history, fate, fortunes and lifestyle of my extended family from the late 18th century until the latter part of the 20th century. The inspiration to write this account was prompted by a desire to get to know my father. 'Searching for Walter' is both a metaphor and the story of my personal and at times, emotional quest, into the short life and untimely death in 1947 of Walter Bloy at the age of 35. Although writing this story was a cathartic journey for me, because of the wealth of information I discovered during the research, it became something far greater and much more rewarding. I recognised that I wanted to be able to tell, not just Walter's story, but that of my ancestors also. And, I wanted to do it in such a way that it would appeal and be of interest from a social history perspective, to a far wider audience.

I grew up not knowing my father or very much about him or his family. Walter had been killed in tragic circumstances, whilst I was still only a baby, not two years old and barely walking. In truth, during my childhood and early adult life, for reasons that will become clear, I never really looked that hard to find out more about him. Walter was just an ordinary, unremarkable man who had been my mother's husband and, I am sorry to say, he meant nothing to me. Being a young child, it wasn't important nor mattered enough to try and make a connection to him. Now, with the benefit of wisdom and hindsight that comes with age, my personal values about what really matters and what is valuable have changed. I have become more reflective and now view my family and my family heritage from a totally different perspective. My father and my ancestral origins are now more important to me.

As the research, which I undertook progressed, my desire to find out more developed. I soon recognised that, I really did regret not knowing more about my father during my childhood and youth. I needed to know who Walter Bloy was, what had he done, what had he achieved and, what sort of life he had led. Finding out the answers to these questions about his life, from his birth in 1912 until his tragic death whilst still a young man, I appreciated, would give me some personal closure. But why did I start to research my father's life in the first place? The initial purpose of undertaking the research, which this whole story is now based upon, was to gather enough information to be able to claim any medals to which Walter may have been entitled from his service in the Merchant Navy during World War II. Nothing else! The reasoning and rationale behind that particular purpose, I will explain shortly. It was never my original intention for this to be an in-depth search into my extended family history, or to be presented, as I now do, in a book. Far from it, nothing could have been further from my mind. I have learned however, throughout my life, that quite often our good and original intentions don't always go to plan, which is certainly what happened once I started to investigate and research Walter's life and family.

Through my investigations, I started to find out many fascinating details about Walter and his extended family, which made me realise that I wanted, and more importantly, needed to know more. Subsequently, the exercise, which had started out as a confined bounded piece of research focussing just on Walter's life, expanded into a very comprehensive research into the life, history and ancestry of both my father's and mother's families, and now covers a time span of over two hundred years. Furthermore, the story of my search for Walter, which I am now able to relate, within the social history and context of the times, became a more enriching and emotionally fulfilling experience for me to write. What has changed? I am now fast approaching what is politely referred to as venerable old age, and have become much more contemplative and philosophical with the passage of time. I now appreciate that, for several reasons which will form part of the story, I have probably been 'Searching for Walter', for most of my life.

Growing up in the late 1940s and early 1950s was not, for a variety of reasons, the most comfortable. I was raised by my mother, Grace Mary and my step-father, Stanley Shreeve, who would later become one of the most successful trawler skippers sailing from Grimsby. However, as a child, the 1950s weren't an easy period of my life. The country was recovering from the war and for many, my family included, times were hard and money was very scarce. In addition, fierce and deeply upsetting arguments caused by my step-father's heavy drinking were an all-too-often feature of our family life. When he was sober, he could be a nice and generous man, but, in drink, which was every time he was home from sea, he was very frightening and threatening. I came to resent him coming home and looked forward to him going back to sea. It wasn't until I was old enough to understand why my elder sister and I had a different surname from our two younger siblings that I really appreciated we had different fathers. I confess, I didn't like to be different and envied my younger brother and sister and my school pals, who had a mother and father with the same name.

Though perhaps not always deliberately intended, children can be intolerably cruel to each other. What seems harmless enough as a nickname, or a childish taunt in the school playground, or within your 'street gang', can be very hurtful, especially if it becomes a daily occurrence. My different and unusual surname, and the ginger hair I had as a child, which I now know came from my father, often led to taunts and bullying that, to this day, left their mark on me and caused me great distress. There are periods of my childhood that, for the most part, I now prefer to forget, because at that time, I could not draw comfort from knowing who my father was and where my name had come from.

In our family home, as far as I can recall, Walter was never really talked about in any depth; there were no photographs of him on display. It was as though he hadn't existed. Unfortunately, my step-father was a very jealous man, particularly when he was in drink. To keep the peace, our mother deliberately kept any references to Walter to a minimum. My elder sister, Pamela, was more fortunate than I; being five years older, she was nearly seven years old when Walter died, so she had actual memories of the time she spent with our father – not so I. My only real recollection of people referring to Walter in those days occurred when as a child, my mother, my brother, sisters and I, along with several aunts and cousins on my mother's side of the family would often meet on a Saturday at my granny's house for fish and chips and, a 'nice cup of tea'. Many of us crammed in the kitchen, sitting wherever we could. That's what people did in those days - the extended family regularly coming together. With the number of adults and children all talking at once in a very crowded room, it was always bedlam, chaotic and like a madhouse, but good fun. The kettle seemed to be permanently singing on the hob. Occasionally, one of my mother's sisters, particularly the youngest, my Aunt Edna, who I think had a crush on Walter, would comment *'what a nice man Walter was'*, or *'he would do anything for anyone'*, or something similar. Beyond that, nothing much else was ever said about him, at least not to me. In truth, Walter really was a complete stranger to me!

Why I knew very little about my father or my father's family during my early childhood can be easily explained, but not so easily understood. After he died, for several years Walter's mother, my Grandma Alice, didn't want anything at all to do with my mother after she had married my step-father. It appears that Grandma was so put out and angry that her son's wife (who I believe Walter had married in defiance of his mother in the first place,) had remarried now that she was a widow. Grandma chose to ostracise my mother, my sister Pamela and me for several years. I was nearly 12 years old before I discovered I had a paternal grandma, aunts, uncles and cousins. After contact had been made with this 'lost' part of my family, my sister and I began to visit and I started to find out more about my father and his life through photographs and stories. Unfortunately, this was not enough at that time, to fill me with an overwhelming desire to find out more. When I look back now, I really regret not asking more questions about him.

But, as the saying goes, *'you can't put a wise head on young shoulders'.*

For me, these visits to my newly-discovered grandma became a real chore and not something I looked forward to. Unlike my granny (my mother's mother), I found my grandma very distant, cold and hard to warm to. Dressed in our Sunday best and, against our wishes, our mother made Pamela and me go to see her. My reluctance to visit became stronger when I entered my teen years and started to pursue my own life and plan my career path in the Merchant Navy, which coincidently, had some similarity to my father's life. Furthermore, I also began to understand what had happened when my mother, my sister and I were ostracised. Not surprisingly, I became more than a little resentful that I was being made to visit a 'stranger', who for so many years it seemed, had not wanted to know, or have anything to do with Pamela or me. Like most people, as I grew older, my view of what was really important to me changed. Curiosity became a need to find out more about Walter.

Over the years, and bit by bit, I started to piece together a picture, albeit very sketchy, about his life. I now recognise that part of me had always wanted to know more, but didn't acknowledge it at the time. Moreover, on reflection, the desire to research and write this story had always been there. It was lying dormant. I just needed the proverbial kick up the backside to galvanise me into action. The inspiration to put pen to paper would come from an unlikely source. In October 2009, a television documentary about the role of the Merchant Navy and the North Atlantic convoys in World War II was broadcast prior to Remembrance Sunday. This documentary was the catalyst I needed to get me started on a very emotive and revealing journey of discovery into the history of my family. A journey, I was soon to discover that would embrace joy and happiness, un-imaginable sadness and tragedy, frequent infant mortality, insanity, two murders, repugnant immoral behaviour, bigamy, a social scandal, robbery, deportation to the colonies, time spent in prison, and provide many other surprises as the story unfolded. Once I started to record and organise my findings, it didn't take long to realise that I had opened a Pandora's Box of surprises and emotions. Each new revelation, I now liken to the peeling of an onion, with layer after layer revealing more underneath.

It was no real revelation to discover that some of my paternal and maternal ancestors had arrived in Grimsby from rural East Anglia in the middle of the 19th century. This was not at all unusual during the industrialisation of Victorian England. Throughout the country, many families left agricultural labouring in the countryside and moved to the towns in search of more prosperous work. In Grimsby's case, the town started to grow and prosper, from the middle of the 19th century onwards, through the development of the emerging fishing industry. By the 1860/70's much of the population of Grimsby was made up of people who had migrated to the town, not just from the countryside, as was the case with Walter's ancestors, but also from other fishing ports such as Barking and Greenwich on the River Thames or Brixham on the south coast, among others. For reasons that will become more obvious later in the story, it is impossible to separate the rapid growth of Grimsby from the fate and fortunes of Walter's antecedents and those of the family of his wife Grace Mary, my mother.

For instance, during the latter half of the 19th century, adequate living accommodation did not keep pace with the rapid growth of the population of the town. Inevitably, the arrival of so many people led to horrific overcrowding, unsanitary and unhygienic conditions in which the newly arrived had to live, and contributed significantly to the frequent cases of infant mortality, which my ancestors and so many others had to contend with. Overcrowding brings very specific social problems. The stench from sweat, urine, vomit and human and animal excrement, particularly in the heat of the summer months, in the squalid overcrowded parts of the town, must have been overpowering. Poor health was inevitable; outbreaks of cholera and other virulent diseases associated with poor sanitation and lack of personal hygiene were frequent and deadly occurrences. One particular outbreak of cholera in Grimsby in 1893 killed 246 people.

In addition to being able to paint a picture of the contrasting social conditions between the rich and poor, which my ancestors had to contend with, what I also discovered and will be narrated within the story in a more light-hearted manner, was the number of 'characters' and petty criminals on all sides of the family. Documented court and newspaper reports of the crimes they committed, the penal sentences they served and in some cases, how they got away with it, will add more colour to the picture I paint. Unfortunately though, I also found some terrible and much darker episodes in the history of Walter's family, which resulted in at least one 'wilful murder' and two cases of insanity and morally unstable behaviour. This was very disquieting for me, as it was a little too close to home. Thankfully, I am able to offer a balance in telling the family's story; the origin of my status as Freeman of Grimsby and the connection through the extended family trees to some great people of local and national importance, provided a welcomed counterpoint.

I have explained why I have written this story, but how did I finally get started on this journey of discovery? To answer that, I need to return to the television documentary about the North Atlantic convoys. This proverbially, 'kick-started' the research and the subsequent writing of the 'Searching for Walter' story. The documentary made it abundantly clear to the viewer that the sailors of the Merchant Navy performed a vital role in keeping the British war effort going, often in appalling and terrifying circumstances. The Merchant Navy loss of ships and sailors through German submarine U-boat action, was extremely high. Millions of tonnes of shipping and tens of thousands of men were lost. For quite some time, because of the success of the German submarine offensive, it was doubtful whether these losses could be sustained. Many people, including the British government, openly questioned whether the war was actually winnable if Britain could not be kept supplied by Canada and the United States, who had not yet entered the War.

At that stage of the conflict, the German Admiral, Karl Doenitz, who masterminded what became known as the Battle of the Atlantic, had Adolf Hitler's total support for the strategy of using groups of submarine U-boats, which became known as wolf packs, to hunt down, torpedo and sink the supply convoys. Unfortunately, as the convoys could only travel at the speed of the slowest ship, which for some was only 8-10 knots, for the captains of the attacking U-boats, it was like, *'shooting fish in a barrel'*. For the convoy ships, death and destruction could come at any moment, silently and without warning. And, for many it did! Amidst this carnage of the Atlantic convoys, it isn't difficult to appreciate the considerable bravery and not inconsiderable fears of the Merchant Navy sailors and their families. Most likely, they wouldn't have considered themselves anything special; just ordinary men and women doing their job for King and country, when in reality, to a man, they were all heroes.

As I watched the documentary, my eyes were frequently drawn to a photograph of Walter, which I have hanging in my living room. He was just a boy then, aged about 15 and probably not even started shaving yet, but trying to look all grown up in his Merchant Navy apprentice's uniform. Since I had no memories of shared experiences with him that I could refer to, I had no emotional attachment to him at all. At that time, although I knew he was my father, in reality, Walter, as I have already said, was a complete stranger. He was just a person in a few old photographs, who had briefly been referred to by my mother and her sisters. Although, thanks to my sister Pamela, who had obtained them, I did have an understanding from old Grimsby Evening Telegraph newspaper cuttings, of how he had died in a dreadful accident, shortly after the end of the war. And I also knew, but didn't know very much, that he had been an officer in the Merchant Navy during World War II and had served in the North Atlantic. Knowing that this young man had served on the North Atlantic convoys added a poignant factor to the documentary I was watching, especially when I took into account that almost every convoy lost several

Walter Bloy in his Merchant Navy Uniform – 15 years old

ships. Walter would most certainly have seen other ships being sunk and fellow mariners dying.

Through the powerful and evocative imagery of the documentary, I began to see Walter in a very different light. I was left in no doubt whatsoever, about how dangerous the role of the officers and sailors of the Merchant Navy had been during the war years. It wasn't too testing therefore, to recognise and appreciate, through the catastrophic losses being sustained by the ships and sailors, that chances of survival at times were extremely slim. This led me to thinking how fickle fate can be! How could Walter have survived all that, only to die, crushed to death by his own motor vehicle shortly after the war, just as he was building a prosperous life for my mother, my sister Pamela and me? If Walter had died on the convoys, I would not have been born and this story would not have been written. This encouraged me to think how much of our history is down to chance and survival.

From that moment on, how I saw Walter, my father, irrevocably changed. The documentary added a dimension and perspective to his young life which I had never really considered in any depth previously. The all-too-graphic depiction and images of sinking ships and men drowning in the oily and icy waters of the North Atlantic Ocean, illustrated the horrors of war at sea. These images left a lasting and, I have to confess, moving impression on me. Ironically, I was suddenly very proud of this stranger, whose picture hangs on my wall. Walter had changed from being just a photograph and a few brief, sketchy and, perhaps unreliable memories told by others. He had become the father I was proud of and wanted to know.

As the television documentary was being broadcast as a part of the lead-up to Remembrance Sunday in 2009, I wondered whether my father had ever claimed any medal entitlement for his active service in the Merchant Navy during the war. My intention was to claim the medals if he had not, or to obtain replacements if he had. Although, as I have already said, I had no previous emotional attachment to him, watching the programme made me realise what he, and many young men like him, had gone through. Obtaining his medals and then wearing them with pride on Remembrance Sunday would be my way of saying thank you, not only to Walter, but also to the other 30,000 or more sailors who had died in the Atlantic waters. You are not forgotten and will be remembered. Admittedly, this was not an entirely original idea, as I had seen a friend do just that with his own father's medals. I thought how appropriate it would be to honour my father in this way. My journey of discovery had now begun.

Neither my sister nor I had any recollection of seeing any medals during our childhood and, as our mother was dead, I had to start from scratch by researching his Merchant Navy career and records. Through gaining access to the National Archives, I quite easily and quickly found my father's war record, which indicated his medal entitlement and confirmed that his medals had never been claimed, these being: the 1939-1945 Star, the Atlantic Star, the Defence Medal and the War Medal 1939-45. Further research directed me to the Registry of Shipping and Seamen, based in Cardiff, to whom the claim for his medals would have to be made by my sister Pamela, as she is Walter's eldest child. On our behalf, I undertook to put the claim together and to gather the evidence needed to support the claim, which is where my research started. From the collection of documents and papers my sister and I had available, the necessary evidence required for the medal entitlement, such as Walter's birth certificate and death certificate were found.

Unexpectedly and quite surprisingly though, when sorting through several boxes of papers, letters and documents, I found a wealth of information about Walter's life, which for the reasons previously mentioned, had been purposely kept hidden away by our mother. I also realised that all this material, which I didn't know even existed, had most probably never been read by anyone other than our mother since Walter's death. While studying and mentally cataloguing the information, it occurred to me that here was a story waiting to be told, if only for the interest of the immediate family. Every family has a story to tell if we only bother to take the time to look. Armed with all this new information, I set out to find all I could about the short-lived life of my father. If truth be told, at this stage of my life, I also felt a little cheated that I hadn't been made aware of the existence of this rich source of information. I could have known so much more about my father many years before. From his birth certificate, apprentice seaman indentures, Merchant Navy Continuous Certificate of Discharge book, letters, personal references and inscriptions on the backs of old photographs, I started to unravel and document his life story.

Before long, I could tell the story of Walter's life from the age of 15, when he entered the Merchant Navy, until his tragic death, just ten days before Christmas in 1947. Amongst other things, I found out where he went, what he did, what ships he sailed on and when he got married, some of which was captured on old family photographs. However, the bigger picture, metaphorically speaking, was still incomplete, as I could not produce any details at all about his early childhood or school days. I wanted answers to questions such as: what schools did he go to, what did he excel at and did he have a happy childhood? To answer these questions, my search included gathering whatever information, anecdotal or documented, that I could from other members of the Bloy family, such as my two first cousins. In addition, I also rummaged for information from various census documents, parish records and the birth, death and marriage registers that are held within the local, county and national archives and local and county reference libraries. I certainly hadn't planned for what I began to find out; it was as though a light had been switched on. It certainly was a real *eureka* moment!

My investigations began to reveal a wide range and depth of family and relevant societal-related information that, to the best of my knowledge, had never been previously assembled, analysed or documented by anyone in my immediate family before. Frequently burning the midnight oil, it became a real exciting and all-consuming challenge. Other important aspects of my life, which I really should have been dealing with at the time, just had to wait. I was peeling the metaphorical onion. Each new discovery and disclosure expanded the storyboard and my lines of enquiry to the point where I became able to relate, in a coherent chronological narrative, from the 18th century until the middle of 20th century, the life and lifestyles, of several generations of the ancestors of both my father and mother. With each new revelation, it was inevitable that the focus of the story would change. It was no longer just a search for Walter. Nor could it be just a family tree, a collection of faceless names. As I researched, wrote, edited and re-wrote, the story took on a much more human-interest perspective: a perspective which included uncovering extremes of family misfortune, success and joy and social injustice within the context of the society, mainly Victorian and Edwardian, in which it occurred.

It is easy to become obsessed with finding out more, as I did. Clearly a case of the more you know, the more you want to know. The current popularity of television programmes such as *'Who do you think you are?'* and the growth of ancestry and heritage-tracing web-sites, appears to indicate that unearthing our roots and antecedents has become a widespread pastime for many. Given that my professional background was in academic research and, having the time to do it, this was a 'project' I mistakenly thought I could easily and dispassionately undertake. I emphasise the word dispassionately though, because inevitably, new knowledge has the tendency to shape our perspective and realign our thinking. The more I found out, the more my perspective and particularly my personal motivation and emotions changed. Consequently, the further and deeper I went with the research, the project stopped being a project *per se* and became a fascinating, extremely moving and occasionally distressing journey of discovery about my family; how they had prospered and the trials and tribulations they had faced. My search for Walter became a personal mission.

Though I originally intended to focus solely on Walter's life and family through the Bloy ancestry on his father's side, I realised that this would produce an incomplete story. Alternative and contrasting family perspectives needed to be included. Consequently, my study was expanded to include the history and lineage of Walter's family on his mother's side, who are the Smiths. This was, although not earth shattering, a surprise. Like so many other things prior to undertaking this investigation, I was not aware that I had ancestors on my grandma's side who were called Smith. Once I did discover I had a grandma, to me she was always a Bloy or Grandma Stephen, which was her third husband's surname. Rather ironically, my grandma's third marriage, in 1940, added a significant, contradictory and hard-to-understand dimension to Walter's story.

To complete the search of Walter's extended family and provide a balance when narrating the story, I felt it was important that my mother's family was also included. For a few short years, Grace Mary James had been such an important and cherished part of Walter's life, especially as I believe, and will demonstrate, he had defied his mother to marry her. In my opinion, grandma was a social snob; she saw herself as middle class and my mother's family as very poor working class, which I have to agree with, and say with no shame at all, they certainly were. When I reflected on key dates and events, I found it sad and a little heart-breaking to think that my mother and father had less than eight years together as a couple before he died. And, as the country went to war not long after they met, Walter would have been away at sea serving his country for approximately five of those eight years. This is considerably less than the ten years or so it took for grandma to decide that she wanted to see my sister and me again!

On a brighter note, my exploration of the history of Grace Mary's ancestry through the Nelson family tree on her mother's side, and the James family tree on her father's side, added several interesting and colourful characters to the story. In addition to which, an absolutely astonishing and exciting connection to one of the most famous men in English history was uncovered in this part of the research. Who was this famous person? There is a clue in the names above, and I can say with my tongue in my cheek, I am not referring to the actor and comedian Sid James! The discovery of this family link goes to show that no matter how desperately impoverished a current generation of a family may be, if the search goes back far enough in time, connections to people of wealth and importance can sometimes be found.

It was relatively easy to identify initially what I wanted to find out, which in research terms, are often referred to as the known unknowns. Meaning, you have some idea of where you want to get to when building up the story of your family history. Most likely you will have a reasonably good idea about what questions to ask and where to go to find that information. Not surprisingly, in this case, the objective of my search changed. It changed from just finding out about my father's schooling and childhood, to a much larger and expansive objective, of building up the history of the family tree, discovering who my forebears were, identifying where and how they had lived, wondering what they had done and, establishing what type of life they had led. Had they fared well? The joy of undertaking family and social research of this nature and, focusing on the Victorian and Edwardian period of history, is that information may emerge, which had never previously been considered or taken into account. In research terms, these are the unknown unknowns, better expressed as *'I didn't know that'*, the unearthing of which can tend to alter the shape and overall direction, as it did in my case, of what you are actually trying to find out. The story of my search for Walter and his family, which now has clear direction and purpose had begun in earnest.

Chapter Two

Starting The Journey – What Did I Really Know?

My search of my family's history started with: what did I know already, or perhaps more importantly what did I think I knew! What, amongst the muddle of information that I had mentally gathered over the years, were actual facts and, what were family myths, legends, interpretations or misrepresentation of the actualité. The passage of time can often filter and distort our recollections and fundamentally alter what we believe to be true. As some would say, *'nostalgia isn't what it used to be'*. When we refer to the 'good old days', was that the reality, or what we preferred to believe? For example, where does the name Bloy come from? Although I knew very little about my father, I have always had an interest in the origin of the name Bloy, especially as it was a source of my childhood bullying. I suppose, the number of times people have remarked, *'that's an unusual name I've not heard it before, is it foreign?'* also stimulates one's interest in finding out more. For that reason the story I began to research and relate was initially considered from the Bloy family perspective.

At some point when I was in my twenties, I began to suspect that the name Bloy was of French origin. Even now, I am still not sure why I thought this. But with the English Channel, which separates England from France, being only 30 km wide at its narrowest, it's hardly surprising that many people in Britain actually claim French ancestry; their evidence being that they have a surname which suggests that their ancestors came from places in France. In my case, there is a City called Blois, which is the capital of Loir-et-Cher department in central France, situated on the banks of the lower River Loire between Orléans and Tours. The name Bloy is most certainly French, or to be more accurate Norman. It has several alternative spellings such as Bloys, Bloye, and in France today it is Blois. Whenever I have made visits to France, my name is always pronounced as the phonetic spelling 'Blwah', which is also how Blois is pronounced. Furthermore, there are many other derivatives of the name such as Bliss or Bleys, the reason for which I shall discuss shortly.

The ancient chronicles of England reveal the earliest records of the name Bloy(e) as a Norman surname which ranks as one of the oldest and is still in common use today in Normandy and Brittany. Although many alternate spellings can be found in the archives, they typically link to a common root, usually one of the Norman nobles at the Battle of Hastings in 1066. It is possible, but most unlikely, that my ancestors were among William the Conqueror's followers. It is relevant to acknowledge that people came to England from France over the centuries for a variety of reasons and not just to make war and conquer. Some came for trade purposes or as servants, and there are those who were driven out of France by religious or political persecution.

It was also not unusual for changes in the spelling of family names to frequently occur, even between father and son. Very few of the 'common' people and only some of the nobility could either read or write. The scribes of the day would record and spell the name as it sounded – regional accents could influence what the scribe heard and so affect how the name was spelled. It was therefore possible that a person could be born and baptised with one spelling, married with another, and buried with a headstone or marker that shows another spelling of their name. Consequently when tracing the family history, the further back in time one goes, the more difficult it starts to become. This became abundantly clear to me after I had obtained a copy of the marriage certificate of Walter's great-great-grandfather, William Bloy.

Early records show William's surname as Bloye, not Bloy. However, when he married his wife Elizabeth in 1815, both he and Elizabeth made their 'mark' on the wedding register, as neither could read or write. As it happens, the Reverend Metcalf who completed their marriage details on the Parish register did spell their names correctly, but omitted the 'e'. Being illiterate, neither William nor Elizabeth would have been any the wiser and, the new alternative spelling would then be there for perpetuity, or until the next 'scribe' got it wrong.

Though the family name Bloy (e) is believed to have descended originally from the Norman race, historically it would be more correct to say they were probably of Viking origin. The Viking King Rollo, a fierce warrior who was rumoured to be so large that a horse would struggle to carry him, after raiding parts of Scotland landed in northern France about 940 AD. The French King, Charles the Simple, to avoid further bloodshed when Rollo laid siege to Paris, granted Rollo parts of Northern France and he became the first Duke of Normandy. William the Conqueror, who invaded England in 1066, was a direct descendent of the first Duke Rollo of Normandy. After the battle of Hastings, and once he was enthroned as the King, William ordered the taking of a census of most of England in 1086, which was recorded in what became known as the Domesday Book. A family name capable of being traced back to this document, or even to Hastings, would be a signal honour for most families during the Middle Ages, and even to this day.

The Chronicles reveal that the surname Bloy(e) emerged as a notable family name in England in the counties of Worcestershire and Leicestershire where the family, originally from the City of Blois in Normandy, were granted lands by King William the Conqueror. By an ironic twist of fate this ancient family name may have even become the Royal family of England had not King Stephen, Count of Blois, perished with his wife Adela, the daughter of William the Conqueror, in the wreck of the 'Blanche Nef' in 1119, leaving no issue. So, the only King of England to be called Stephen was 'Stephen of

Bloy'. Although I have no delusions of grandeur and make no claim to royalty, I find that piece of English history a source of amusement, particularly as Stephen, by some accounts, was not a very effective King.

An alternative and, in my family's case the more likely route into England, occurred about six centuries later, when the Calvinist Huguenots in France began to be persecuted for their religious beliefs. Huguenots were the largest group of the French people that came to Britain, driven out of their country because of their refusal to convert to Roman Catholicism. To escape the persecution, countless numbers fled to the Low Countries of Northern Europe to the area we now know as Holland, Belgium and Luxembourg. From there, they then migrated across the North Sea into the Fenland area of Lincolnshire, Norfolk and Cambridge, the part of England we refer to as East Anglia. Immigration records indicate that, although several Bloy families settled in the area, many others left England and migrated to the United States of America and Canada during the 19th century.

The first influx of Huguenot migrants came in the last half of the 16th century, but a greater number arrived between the 1680s and the middle of the 18th century, which is where we will pick up the story of the Bloy family. Parish records, the National Archives and census documents among other sources, all indicate that during the late 18th and early 19th centuries there was a thriving Bloy community in those adjoining counties. It is reasonably safe therefore, to conclude that many Bloy families must have made that journey across the North Sea into the Fenlands via Holland or Belgium. The research for this story will reveal that my allegorical search for Walter has its origins and roots in the East Anglia region.

Returning to the question, what did I know already; from the moment I met my grandma and started to get to know that side of the family, it became abundantly clear that, in material wealth and lifestyle terms, Walter's home life and upbringing, had been very comfortable in comparison to that which his wife (my mother), Grace Mary James, had experienced. The quite marked differences in their respective upbringing and family fortunes reflected how wide the social divide, between those aspiring to be middle class and the working classes, actually was at this time. This was evidenced by where and how they lived, the work they did and the lifestyles they enjoyed. For some, Walter's mother included, during the first half of the 20th century, social status was still very important. Although, there would be a major sea-change in attitude and perception of social class during the 1960s and beyond, when I first met my grandma in 1958, the distinction between the middle and working classes still very much existed.

Whilst writing this section of the story and being reflective, I couldn't help thinking about the daily struggle my mother had had to clothe and feed my brother, sisters and me during the 1950s. Although my step-father would become a very successful Trawler Skipper in the 1960/70s, during my early childhood, money was very scarce and times were certainly hard. It really was the austerity years. My younger siblings and I were regularly dressed with clothes our mother bought at jumble sales, which was an acute source of embarrassment for us.

Frequently, food and other essential items were bought from the local corner shop on 'tick' or on the 'slate', which was how 'buy now and pay at the end of the week' was then called. When sent to the shop on errands, I hated having to say when it came time to pay, *'my mother says can you put it on her slate?'* One particular incident which I caused, I recall so clearly because of the distress it gave my mother. On this occasion, she gave me two shillings (10 pence in today's money), to go to the shop to buy some corned beef, with which she was to make a 'corned beef hash' for the family dinner. It was all the money she had in her purse. When I got to the shop, my mind was obviously elsewhere, I asked the shopkeeper for 'cooked beetroot'. I spent nearly the whole two shillings. My mother's response when I got home, besides giving me a 'clip round the ear', was to burst into tears. What was she going to give her children to eat for dinner? Beetroot was not a meal. I'll never know whether they were tears of anger, frustration or even despair.

Though I have never told anyone about this, the memory and the sight of my mother crying has stayed with me for nearly 60 years. Coincidently, this episode occurred round about the time I discovered that I had a relatively wealthy middle class grandma! I thought long and hard before deciding whether to relate the incident of the corned beef. I eventually chose to include it in the story by way of an insight and explanation of my personal attitude and also to add some tangible contrast in the background and lifestyles of both sides of my immediate family.

Leaving the financial considerations and social differences aside for just a moment, the further I went with my exploration, I found there was a common thread of catastrophes, heartbreak and misfortune with both Walter's and Grace Mary's immediate families. Rather sadly, there were unfortunate parallels during the first half of the 20th century; each family had to come to terms with tragic and serious accidents, which were so grave that they would have a lasting influence on the family fortunes and lifestyles. Understanding what had happened and the subsequent consequences illustrated how providence had contributed to the wealth and materialistic differences of both families. It is a remarkable ill-fated coincidence that the Bloy family had to come to terms with two fatal tragedies through motoring accidents. Whereas in Grace Mary's case, the primary cause of her family's misfortunes, poverty and distress were not fatalities, but two serious industrial accidents, both of which involved her father.

Before I examine the origins, ancestors and history of each family in greater detail, it seems appropriate to reflect on what destiny had in store for the Bloy family. Appreciating what happened to Walter and his father Walter Sidney Bloy provided a suitable point from which I could progress the story of my search for Walter and his ancestors. The corresponding and, no less unfortunate, aspects of Grace Mary's life will be explored in greater detail when her family's background is discussed later in the story.

Walter's father and mother were Walter Sidney Bloy (b.1886), and Alice (nee Smith) who was also born 1886. They had married in September, 1909, and in addition to Walter, produced two daughters: Lucy, who was the eldest of the three children and, Alice Irene, hereafter referred to as Irene, the youngest. Walter didn't really get the chance to know his father. Scarcely two weeks after Walter's fourth birthday, Walter Sidney Bloy, was killed on the 19th June 1916 in a motoring accident on the Brigsley Road, (now the High Street), in Waltham, which is on the outskirts of Grimsby. He crashed his motorcycle and sustained head injuries from which he never regained consciousness and died. The death certificate wrongly stated his age as 32. Walter Sidney Bloy was just 30 years old. Details of the accident and the Coroner's inquest were reported over three consecutive days in the Grimsby Evening Telegraph, as:

19th June 1916 (Latest edition) '**ACCIDENT NEAR WALTHAM**'

> *Last night a serious motorcycle accident occurred near Waltham. A machine ridden by Mr W. S. Bloy residing in Clayton Street apparently struck a stone heap and Mr Bloy and his wife who was accompanying him, were both badly hurt. They were taken to the Grimsby Hospital and we understand that Mr Bloy is in a serious condition.*

20th June 1916 '**FATAL SEQUEL TO MOTOR-CYCLE ACCIDENT**'

> *We regret to say that Mr Walter Sidney Bloy, coal merchant late of 60 Clayton Street, died at the Grimsby and District Hospital on Monday afternoon as a result of injuries he sustained on Sunday in a motor-cycle accident at Waltham. Mr Bloy was travelling along the Brigsley road*

on his motorcycle, his wife being on the carrier behind, when he lost control of the machine, which dashed on to the grass at the side of the road and bumped into a heap of stones about 100 yards from the Waltham crossroads. The machine jumped three or four feet into the air and Mr and Mrs Bloy were thrown off, the deceased falling with his head on the grass. Both Mr and Mrs Bloy were removed to the Grimsby and District Hospital but the latter was able to leave after receiving treatment. An inquest will be held tomorrow morning by Mr T. Mountain the Borough Coroner.

21st June 1916 'MACHINE TURNED A SOMERSAULT – EVIDENCE BY AN EYE WITNESS'

Grimsby Motor Cyclist's Death - Inquest into Waltham Fatality

A verdict of 'Accidental Death' was returned at an enquiry held by the Grimsby Coroner (Mr T. Mountain) this morning, concerning the death of Walter Sidney Bloy (30), coal merchant of 60 Clayton Street, who was fatally injured in a motor -cycle accident on Sunday. The deceased's wife who was with him at the time was rendered unconscious but was not otherwise injured. She was however too unwell to give evidence today. Walter Bloy senior, the father of the deceased, living in Garden Street, identified the body.

Mr Tom Chapman, a cattle dealer of Mavis House Waltham, gave evidence to the Coroner. On Sunday night he was on the Brigsley Road. About 9.30pm he saw the deceased riding a motorcycle with a lady on the seat behind him. The motor- cycle was proceeding from Brigsley towards Waltham. When the witness was about 100 yards from the Waltham crossroads the two motorcycles passed and another with a sidecar. The deceased got past these machines. He must have been travelling at 40 miles per hour. He then seemed to lose control and then ran onto the grass for about 15 yards. The machine struck a stone. As it did so it jumped into the air from four or five feet. The machine dropped about eight yards beyond the stone and when it struck the ground turned a complete somersault. The deceased man fell on his head. His wife went over him and lay about six yards beyond. Witness found the deceased lying unconscious face downwards. Dr Mc Kane was sent for and the injured man was conveyed on a motor lorry to the Grimsby Hospital. His wife was also unconscious but came round and was able to say where they came from.

The Coroner: *Did he appear to easily overtake the other cyclists on the road?*

Witness: *Yes.*

In reply to a juror, the witness said there was a slight dip in the road at this point. The road was in good condition.

Dr Dunn, house surgeon at the Grimsby Hospital, found the deceased quite unconscious when he arrived at the Hospital. He died about 2 o'clock on Monday without ever regaining consciousness. In his judgement death was due to concussion and laceration of the brain. His jaw was also broken.

The Coroner said in his judgement: a motorcycle was rather a dangerous vehicle but when it came to be ridden at a speed of 40 miles an hour, in his opinion it became very dangerous.

The legislature had fixed the maximum speed of these vehicles at 20 miles an hour. That being so, if a cyclist drove a machine at twice that speed it was quite obvious it was very dangerous indeed. The young man had only himself to blame and, it was a merciful dispensation of providence that his wife was not killed also.

I am sure the Coroner meant well, but his concluding remarks, *'merciful dispensation of providence that his wife was not killed also'*, in my opinion, were insensitive and, would have been cold comfort to his wife Alice and other members of the family.

Despite my rhetoric in the opening chapter, I am not sure when I first became aware of how my father, Walter had died. Most probably, it would have been around about the same time that I found out about my grandma's existence when I was eleven or twelve years old. It was however, quite a long time later before I discovered that my grandfather, Walter Sidney Bloy had also died through a motoring accident in 1916. And, until I found these newspaper reports during my initial research in 2010, I had few details of the accident. Moreover, when I discussed our grandfather's accident with my two cousins, who are the surviving members on this side of the Bloy family, I was surprised to discover that neither of them was aware that Grandma Alice had also been on the motorcycle at the time of the accident and that she was lucky to survive. Another example of the intervention of fate and providence! I find it rather ironic, after all those years of not knowing, I now regularly drive down Waltham High Street past the spot where the accident happened and my grandfather died.

Why did the accident happen? I often try to picture the event and, find it not too difficult to imagine what Walter's mother and father may have been doing prior to the accident. It was 9.30 pm on a warm summer's Sunday evening and would have still been light. The young couple, Walter Sidney and Alice were returning to their home in Clayton Street, Grimsby after having a ride out into the country. Where they had been will never be known. But, as they were returning on the Brigsley Road, it is a reasonable assumption to think they may have been to Ravendale Valley, which is only about 4 miles down the road and was a popular beauty spot for young courting couples to go and picnic. Walter Sidney, I have no doubt, like all young men, would have been very proud of his motorcycle, especially as there were not too many about in 1916; not all could afford them. Owning one, being a visible expression of material wealth, would have given him status. The motorcycle would have been his pride and joy and moreover, perhaps gave him a chance to show off. When he saw the other motorcycles, what was he thinking as he sped past them? Was it male machismo to try and impress his wife and the other motorcyclists? Was his wife actively encouraging him to go faster as she sat behind with her arms wrapped round him, urging him onwards? Or was she clinging on in abject terror. I prefer to think the former. Although we'll never know, it is not unreasonable to pose these questions to try to gain an insight as to what actually happened.

At this stage of the story of my search for Walter and his family, when I learned the date of the motorcycle accident I realised, Walter had never really got to know his father; just as I too never got to know my father because of his death when I was a baby. So, how did Walter Bloy die?

Walter was born on 3rd June 1912, at 89 Newmarket Street, Grimsby and, at the age of 35, just ten days before Christmas, on 15th December 1947 he was killed in a terribly tragic accident. Walter was crushed to death on the R.A.F. Base at Binbrook, in Lincolnshire, by his own brand new Bedford Van, (registration AEE 960), which he had only owned for four days. He left a wife, Grace Mary and two children, Pamela Diane who was nearly 7 years old and me, aged 1yr 10 months. And, just as his father's fatal accident, some 31 years before, was reported in the Grimsby Evening Telegraph. Walter's accident and subsequent death was also featured in the local paper. The following are extracts:

Wednesday 17th December 1947 'KILLED BY VAN AT BINBROOK'

Walter Bloy, aged 32, a greengrocer living at 181, Cooper Road, Grimsby, well known throughout the Wold area, died yesterday following injuries received when he was crushed between his van and a garage wall at R.A.F. Station Binbrook. Mr Bloy was delivering produce at the R.A.F station and on returning to his van saw that it was running backwards down a slope. He got behind the van in an effort to stop it, but was trapped against the garage wall. He died two hours later.

Thursday 18th December 1947 'CRUSHED TO DEATH AT BINBROOK'

A tragic story of the death of Walter Bloy (32), a green grocer, living at 181 Cooper Road, Grimsby, was told to the Louth District Coroner (Capt. R.H. Helmer) at an inquest held at Binbrook R.A.F. station last night. Evidence was given that, on Tuesday Bloy was delivering produce to R.A.F. officers' houses near Binbrook airfield when his van commenced to run backwards down an incline. Trying to stop it by pushing it from the rear, he was crushed against the door of a garage. A VAIN EFFORT - Arthur Smith- Dales, a baker's roundsman of Tealby, the only witness of the accident said that when he saw the van was running backwards he joined Bloy in an attempt to stop it, but this was impossible, and it crashed into a garage door, Bloy being pinned in between. He called for help and Bloy was taken away by ambulance. P.C. Baumber said that Bloy's van was a new one, the brakes and all equipment being perfect. Human hair was found on the garage wall. Dr Arnold D. Charnley, Medical officer of health at Binbrook R.A.F. station said Bloy's condition when he saw him was consistent with his having fractured his skull. The Coroner found this was the cause of death and, returned a verdict accordingly; expressing sympathy with the relatives.

How strangely coincidental that, Walter and his father both died from a fractured skull sustained in accidents with motor vehicles, which were 31 years apart.

With Walter's accident, it is not too challenging to be able to paint a fairly accurate picture of what may have happened. Walter was becoming a successful business man. In addition, to owning a greengrocer's shop and 'Wet-Fish' business in Grimsby, he delivered provisions, on a regular basis, to the villages and R.A.F. bases in rural Lincolnshire. On this fateful day, he would have been full of Christmas cheer and bonhomie as he delivered food and supplies to his customers, who were the officer's families that lived at the R.A.F. Binbrook aerodrome. It is also most likely that he would have been rushing to get back home to his own wife and children, who would be happily and excitedly preparing for Christmas. As Walter made his deliveries, he would have been frequently getting in and out of the Bedford van as he moved around the family homes on the R.A.F. base. And, as was reported to the coroner, there was nothing wrong with the vehicle's brakes one can only assume that, having parked the van on the incline, he did not fully apply the handbrake. When he saw the van rolling backwards he tried to stop it, which resulted in the devastating consequences. Sadly, Walter would never go home again. At the age of 31 and, just 10 days before Christmas, my mother, Grace Mary, was left widowed with two very young children.

Even now, I still find it difficult to read these newspaper reports without thinking, for an intelligent man, what an incredibly stupid thing he did! He reacted instinctively, concerned for the new van and all the stock it contained, which was his livelihood. Walter was not a powerful man; he was only slight built and just 5ft 9ins tall. What on earth was he thinking? The catastrophic outcome was inevitable. But who is to say that they would not have done something similar in the same circumstances? It is all too easy to be critical. Learning how both my father and grandfather had died from similar injuries as a result of dreadful accidents when barely into their thirties, whilst still a young man myself, certainly made me speculate what fate may have in store for me.

Much of what I have written, thus far, has been a sketch to provide the reader with a basis and contextual framework to aid their understanding of the search that I undertook. And, why I did it. As well as the narrative being purposely anecdotal, it tends to reflect what I have referred to as the known knowns. From here on in, the narrative will become a more comprehensively detailed and personalised telling of all that I discovered during this very moving and at times poignant journey. I make no apologies for the personal comments I make, as they reflect my understanding interpretation and perspective. Recognising that this became a cathartic road I travelled, I am mindful of the often-used expression, *'you can't make an omelette without breaking eggs'*. I do not deliberately intend to malign or offend anyone. At times however, when putting pen to paper to relate my family's history, I felt like I was walking a tightrope between mawkish sentimentality, the rewriting of my family's history and impartiality. The acknowledgement of this led me to question whether my narrative was a fair and accurate presentation of the facts or, was it being skewed by a personal subliminal agenda. At the outset, it was not my deliberate intention to lay a few ghosts to rest, I just wanted to claim Walter's medals, or did I! But, I suppose, because of the nature of what I was writing about, that the development of a personal agenda was inevitable.

Chapter Three

Who Were Walter's Proximate Ancestors?

Though I am writing this story from a personal perspective and specifically talking about ancestors of my extended family, by revealing a series of very human stories, with all their joy and sadness, hopes and expectations, located within the social framework of the time, I intend to go far beyond just documenting a family tree. As I discover and explore the factors that influenced the fortunes and fate of the family members, I will provide a personal commentary of the times, which others who read this story may be able to relate to in respect of their own family. In addition, it is not my intention to present this story of my search for Walter and his family as a dry and dusty history lesson, but without interrupting the narrative, it does seem appropriate to provide a historical contextual *'canvas background'* of what is known already, onto which some of the story can be overlaid. Therefore, throughout the narrative, I will use little vignettes of history to locate this story into the events of the time.

After documenting the death of his father, Walter Sidney, my search for Walter's ancestry from his father backwards in time took on a renewed sense of urgency and excitement. However, when researching the family's history and looking for particular individuals, I soon discovered that the regular use of the same forenames would start to confuse the story. Frequently, in my search I found myself, metaphorically speaking, being sent up blind alleys. It was far more customary for parents in the 18th and 19th century, to name their children after themselves or their parents, than is the practice today. In this next part of the story for example, we have three consecutive generations of Bloys, all called Walter. For initial clarity, the abridged family tree below illustrates our Walter's immediate ancestry. A more comprehensively detailed and expanded family tree will be discussed shortly.

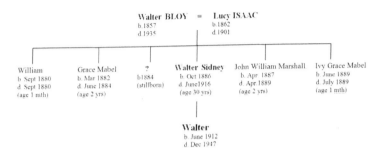

As I began to identify other members of the extended Bloy family, William was also a name which cropped up very frequently within the family throughout the 19th century. Grandfathers, fathers, several uncles and cousins were named William. For example, Walter's great-uncle William (b.1840), who made the journey to Grimsby in the 1860s and features in this story, was named after his father and grandfather before him. And, my father's grandfather, as can be seen from the abridged family tree above, also named his first-born son William. Then as now, children's names appeared to follow the trends of the day. When naming their children, parents would have most probably been influenced by what was fashionable. Adopting the names of royalty and prominent personalities of the times is really no different from parents of today being influenced by the cult of celebrities and, whatever is 'flavour of the month'. During the early part of the 18th century, William III had been King of England and William IV would later become our King in 1830, which may offer an explanation as to why William was such a popular name. With the naming of daughters, Mary or Mary Ann (e) and Sarah, these were also names that regularly occurred. I have no doubt at all that future historians won't have any problems explaining why, after the Royal Wedding in 2011, the names William and Catherine became popular again in 2011/12. How future historians explain the popularity of names such as Chardonnay and Jordan will be interesting!

For clarity, the chronological summary below shows the immediate ancestors of Walter, to whom I will frequently be referring, and indicates the extent and limits of my search for the Bloys' ancestry which features in this part of the story. Parish records that are available become fairly sketchy the further back in time one goes. Therefore, it is not my intention to look for any ancestors further back than Walter's great-great-grandfather William Bloye, who was born in 1780. In telling the story of my search for Walter, the focus will be mainly, from about 1800 onwards:

Walter's parents - Walter Sidney Bloy (b. 1886) and Alice Bloy (nee Smith) (b. 1886)

Walter's sisters - Lucy Bloy (b.1909) and Alice Irene Bloy (b. 1915)

Walter's paternal grandparents - Walter Bloy (b.1857) and Lucy Bloy (nee Isaac) (b.1862)

Walter's paternal great-uncles - William Bloy (b.1840), David Bloy (b.1844) and John Bloy (b.1850)

Walter's paternal great-grandparents - William Bloy (b. abt.1816) and Mary Ann Bloy (nee Hume) (b.abt 1818)

Walter's paternal great-great-grandparents - William Bloye (b. abt.1780) and Elizabeth Bloy (nee Rocket) (b. abt.1790)

Returning to the naming of children just for a moment, we can see from the above that Walter [my father], had been named after his father and grandfather. His elder sister Lucy was named after their grandmother, and sister Alice Irene was named after their mother.

What is the Bloy family story? Walter's grandfather, also called Walter Bloy, was born in 1857 in Tydd St Mary, a small village in the southeast corner of rural Lincolnshire. He was the youngest of four surviving children produced by William Bloy and his wife Mary Ann (nee Hume). And, full of hopes and expectations of a better future that most young men have, Walter left Tydd St Mary's and moved to Grimsby in the late 1870s to seek his fortune. His eldest brother William (b.1840) moved to Grimsby much earlier and established a successful Marine Stores Dealer business in the 1860s. The two middle brothers of the four siblings, David (b.1844) and John (b.1850), did not fare very well at all. Both were involved in the most deeply disturbing series of incidents, including murder, which my research revealed. The extraordinary and serious nature of what they did, and the outcome of their actions, warrants them being dealt with separately. Consequently, the discomforting details of their story will be told as a discrete chapter.

When Walter reached Grimsby, he met and allegedly married Lucy (nee Isaac) in 1879. I say allegedly married, because although Lucy appears on consecutive census documents 1881-1901 as his wife, no matter how I searched, I could not find any record of Walter's marriage to Lucy Isaac. So I gave up looking. Couples living together and claiming to be married when they were not, was not uncommon in Victorian England. I will however, give them the benefit of the doubt and refer to Lucy as his wife. From the census records, it seems that, as a child and young girl, Lucy had lived with her uncle, Thomas Isaac and his wife Francis, on their farm at Grainsby, Lincolnshire. Several other nieces and nephews also lived on the farm under the care of Thomas and Francis, who appear to have been childless. Their farm must have been doing well, because in addition to their nephews and nieces, it also supported a young female servant aged 13 and four male 'live in' agricultural labourers, which reflects aspects of the comments I make later regarding agricultural labourers 'living in' on the farm that employs them. Living in became increasingly rare in the latter part of the 19th century.

Walter Sidney Bloy, the father of Walter, the initial focus of my story, was born in Grimsby in 1886, one of five children that I know of for definite who were born to Walter and his 'wife' Lucy. Closer examination of the dates and the frequency Lucy gave birth to her children, suggests to me that a sixth child, who was still-born or didn't survive, may have been born sometime during 1884/5. With contraception being practically non-existent, it is most unlikely that Lucy would not have fallen pregnant again during the four-year period 1882 to 1886. Still-births and miscarriages were common enough for Victorian mothers!

I soon discovered that Walter, and his 'wife' Lucy, who was only seventeen when they 'married', experienced more than their fair share of misfortune. They would be no strangers to frequent family anguish and upset, not only with their own immediate family, but also in Walter's case, with his two sibling brothers, David and John. Rather distressingly, my research revealed, although this Walter would initially prosper through the Coal Merchant's business he established in Grimsby, he would outlive his wife Lucy and all of their children, before he too died at the age of 78 in 1935. Lucy though, would die much earlier at the age of 39 in 1901; but not before seeing at least four of her children, which does not include the still-born child, die and not reach maturity; one of whom, Grace Mabel, died a particularly horrific and harrowing death. Not only did Walter, my father's grandfather (my great-grandfather), have Lucy's death from pneumonia to come to terms with; all his children, bar one, also died whilst infants and never reached adulthood.

Just when you think his misfortune couldn't get any worse, his only child to reach maturity, Walter Sidney Bloy, was killed in a motorcycle accident when just 30 years old. How devastating this must have been for great-grandfather Walter, having outlived his wife and four of his children; his sole surviving child is killed in an accident. As a father, I cannot begin to imagine how dreadfully painful and heart-rending it must be to bury not one, but all of your children. To lose one child is traumatic enough; to lose all your children must be so overwhelming. We expect our children to bury us, not the other way round.

When I discovered that all my great-grandfather Walter's other children had died whilst still infants, I tried to imagine how he must have felt after Walter Sidney's death in the motorcycle accident. The picture that came to my mind is one of a shattered old man, nearly 60 years of age, being led into the morgue at the hospital, trying to remain steadfast and dignified, as the sheet that covered his son's body was pulled back. What thoughts must have been going through his mind as he identified the bruised and damaged remains of his last surviving child, who at the time of his death, was working with him in the family Coal Merchant's business? Any dreams that great-grandfather Walter had of leaving his business to his son vanished that warm summer night on the Brigsley Road! Further research evidence indicated that, alas, this would not be the end of the misfortune that Walter, by now a lonely old man, had to face. The census of 1911 indicates that after Walter Sidney married Alice in 1909, his father, who by then was a widower, was living alone and would do so for the remaining 24 years of his life.

Great-grandfather Walter's wife Lucy and their children are registered as being buried in the Ainslie Street Municipal Cemetery in Grimsby, which opened in 1855 and was closed in 1943. It is no longer a cemetery; it has become an open recreational park area for all the community to use. People walk their dogs and children now happily play there. Regrettably, all the grave stones and markers have now been removed; to where, nobody appears to know! Consequently, there are no remaining visible signs of where Lucy, her children and many others are actually buried.

The entries in the cemetery register, which records the children's death, makes for poignant reading. William, the first child born in 1880 to Walter and Lucy, only lived for one month before dying from diarrhoea on the 3rd September 1880. Diarrhoea was a common cause of infant mortality in Victorian England, just as we can see that it still is today in many parts of the third and developing world, such as Ethiopia and other parts of Africa. Even more disturbing, and dreadfully upsetting, is how Walter and Lucy's second child Grace Mabel died from accidental burning, when only two years old. The Coroner's inquest, which was reported in the local newspaper, The Grimsby News on 6th June 1884, stated:

'FATAL RESULT OF BURNS IN UPPER BURGESS STREET'

Mr Alderman Moody, J.P., the coroner for the district, held an inquest on Wednesday, at the Hope and Anchor Inn, Victoria Street, on view of the body of Grace Mabel Bloy, two years and three months old, daughter of Walter Bloy, 12 Burgess Street. On the 10th May, the mother left the child in bed while she went out to procure the dinner for the family. During Mrs Bloy's absence the child set her clothing on fire with a match, and on Tuesday last she succumbed to her injuries. A verdict of "Accidental Death" was returned.

Words cannot convey how Lucy must have felt, when she returned home and walked through the door to find her daughter screaming in agony, as she was literally burning to death with her clothes on fire, or just the smouldering remains of clothes stuck to her charred skin. Lucy must have been inconsolable and beside herself with grief! What did she do, how did Lucy get help? What could she do? How long did it take to get some medical attention, or for the child to be taken to the hospital, which was situated about two miles away from where the family lived? There was no ambulance service or motorcars in 1884, just horses and carts! Somehow, they got her to the hospital and, astonishingly, the child clung on to life for over three weeks before she died from her injuries. It doesn't bear thinking about, but the poor child must have been in agony during the last days of her short life.

Clearly, had she survived, there is no doubt that Grace Mabel would have been horribly burnt and disfigured. This made me wonder what sort of life she would have led. How normal would it, or could it, have been? Would she have ever found employment or got married? Would she have gone out into public view, or would she have become a recluse, hiding her disfigurement away? Again I pose more questions than answers. I do so because I am mindful that Victorian society at that time may not have been as tolerant and understanding of people who were different, as we are today. It helps to put Grace Mabel's hypothetical situation into perspective when we remember that this was a period in our country's social history, when circus freak shows were very popular. Disfigurement through burns, and in particular facial disfigurement, causes people, even when they don't intend to, to recoil in horror. I couldn't help thinking, was Grace Mabel's ultimate death an act of God's mercy?

We'll never know how Lucy came to terms with this tragedy; it is worth remembering that she was a young woman only 22 years old when it happened. In the years that followed, how many times must she have blamed and tormented herself for leaving a two-year-old child unattended with matches lying around for the child to pick up and 'play' with? We'll also never know how Walter reacted to the accident. Grace Mabel, his only daughter, was also the only child of the family at that time; their son William had died two years before. Most probably, she would have been the apple of her father's eye. I can picture him, sat in his favourite armchair in front of the fire playing with her and bouncing her about on his knee. And, I am sure that he would have looked forward to giving her a big hug when he got home from work, like most fathers do with their children. After the accident, did he blame Lucy and perhaps more importantly if he did, could he forgive her? What effect did it have on their marriage? Walter and Lucy had only been married for five years when this accident happened. Although we will never find the answers for these questions, it helps us put the incident into perspective to ask them. What we can safely assume, is that the horror and nature of this accident will have lived with Lucy for the remainder of her days. She will have carried a sense of guilt with her to the grave.

After Grace Mabel's death, Walter and Lucy remained childless until Lucy produced Walter Sidney in 1886 and, John William Marshall, just eight months later in 1887. Not surprisingly, I am somewhat sceptical about the accuracy of this fourth child's date of birth, especially as records of child birth then, if kept at all, were not as reliable as they are today. In those days, children would have been delivered at home by the local midwife and, whether birth dates were accurately recorded or not, is a matter of speculation. Many people, perhaps including the midwife, could barely read or write at that time. As I reviewed the dates of the birth of these two children, I was still drawn to the conclusion that Lucy would have most probably fallen pregnant some time in 1884/5, and either miscarried, or the child was still-born.

The Ainslie Street cemetery records indicated that, after the birth of John William Marshall in 1887, Lucy had not yet finished her child bearing. Rather poignantly in June 1889, she gave birth to another daughter, whom they named Ivy Grace Mabel. Why they chose that name, suggests to me how much the death of Grace Mabel in 1884, had affected them. It was as though the naming of their second daughter in this manner would keep the memory of the first Grace Mabel in their minds. Regrettably, Walter and Lucy's distress didn't end with William's death in 1880, Grace Mabel's death in 1884 and, the birth of a stillborn child soon after. Their fourth child that survived childbirth, John William Marshall, died on the 23rd April 1889 from whooping cough when just two years old. At the time of his death, Lucy was seven months pregnant with Ivy Grace Mabel. And, unbelievably heart-rending, just one month after she gave birth to Ivy Grace Mabel, this child also died.

It is widely acknowledged that infant mortality was high, due to poverty, poor sanitation and unhealthy living conditions in the latter part of the 19th century, which is why they are often referred to as the 'Mortality Years'. The vast majority of children of the poor working classes never reached their fifth birthday! Even so, how heartbreaking it must have been for Walter to lose his wife and all his children. Although the cemetery records indicate that Lucy had died in 1901, age 39, from pneumonia, it is my belief that she would have been both mentally and physically exhausted from having, and then losing her children. I am convinced that these frequent traumas would have contributed to a gradual worsening state of health and her pneumonia was the tragic outcome. After Lucy died, great-grandfather Walter was not immediately left alone; his son Walter Sidney was still alive and would live with him until he got married in 1909. Walter Sidney did not die until 1916, another 7 years later; then Walter senior was alone!

Great-grandfather Walter's bad luck and misfortune didn't end with the death of his wife and children. Just seven years after his son Walter Sidney's death, in October 1923, the Coal Merchant's business, W. Bloy and Son Ltd, that he had established and originally prospered with, went into 'official receivership' with debts of £220-8s-10d.   Although this is conjecture, I couldn't help but wonder how much the death of his last child (Walter Sidney), and he being left all alone, affected his state of mind and interest in running his business. We'll never know. Discovering this latest calamity to befall Walter, also made me question how Grandma Alice, his son's widow, reacted to the news of this latest misfortune. By 1923, as we shall see when I examine Alice's story, she was married to her second husband and was, to coin a modern phrase, 'socially upwardly mobile'. From the moment Alice remarried, she was financially secure and would not have to worry about money. I'm fairly sure she would have been none too pleased with the public shame, in a small town like Grimsby, of seeing her former father-in-law being declared bankrupt.

The records of administration and receivership, and a statement in the London Gazette appear to show that great-grandfather Walter's creditors would receive £0-1s-0¾d (approximately 6p in new money) in the pound. Somehow, he must have found a way to satisfy the official receivers and wind the business up, because in December 1924 he was discharged from receivership. Further research in the local trade directories indicated that he was still trading at the time of his death in 1935 as a Coal Merchant, albeit this time as W. Bloy and Co Ltd.

Whilst writing this section, I couldn't help being terribly moved by all the sadness and tragedy my great-grandparents had to come to terms with. They are, after all, my ancestors of only a couple of generations ago. Like so many other things I was to discover on this journey, neither I nor my sister Pamela had any idea of these tragedies. Walter and Lucy had ceased to be strangers, but part of my family I had at last got to know. Being a parent myself, I could feel their pain and grief at the loss of their children.

I found myself hoping that great-grandfather Walter, in his final years, had not become a lonely and embittered man. I wanted to think he was able to draw some comfort and joy from his three grandchildren, which Walter Sidney and his wife Alice had produced. All of whom, my father Walter and my aunts, Lucy and Irene, we know reached maturity. As Walter senior didn't die until 1935, he would have seen his grandson, Walter, go into the Merchant Navy as an apprentice officer in 1928. He would have also seen his granddaughters Lucy and Irene grow up, and in Lucy's case, get married: something we know he didn't see with his own two daughters who had died young. Were these grandchildren a source of pride for him? I really wanted to think so. Alas, my research and anecdotal evidence suggests this wasn't the case.

After Walter Sidney died, there is no doubt that Alice initially struggled to support her three children. Irene, who was just a baby went to 'stay' with one of Alice's sisters; leaving Lucy, still only a child herself, to stay at home and look after Walter, while Alice was doing whatever work she could get to keep the children clothed and fed. All of which indicated, for Alice money was initially tight, and implies that great-grandfather Walter did not offer much financial support at all. Assuming that he could, and that he wanted to! I really wanted to think well of great-grandfather Walter. From my research, I am now able to say what happened to him, but what I cannot say is what type of person he was. There is no anecdotal evidence to indicate whether he was a nice, kind- hearted, caring man or not. He may well have been a mean, hard, cold-hearted man. Again we'll never know. I do know though what type of determined person Grandma Alice was!

Once Alice had met and married her second husband in 1922 and began to prosper, I am drawn to the conclusion that, Walter did not feature at all in his grandchildren's lives. Alice, with her new husband, had 'moved on'. This seems to be borne out by the fact that, although I found many family photographs from the 1920s, I didn't find any which showed great-grandfather Walter with his grandchildren, or indeed, any photographs of him at all. And although he didn't die until 1935, surprisingly, he does not appear on any of the group photographs that were taken when his eldest grandchild, Lucy, married in 1933. I don't think he was at the wedding! When I discussed this matter with my cousins Sandra, Aunt Lucy's daughter and Maureen, Aunt Irene's daughter, neither had any recollection whatsoever of their mothers ever referring to time spent with their grandfather Walter. Sadly, I can only conclude that my great-grandfather Walter lived a lonely and probably a miserable life in his final years. I am absolutely certain this would not have featured in his hopes and dreams when he made the journey from Tydd St Mary to Grimsby, some fifty-odd years before.

Chapter Four

Discovering The Bloy Family Ancestry from
1780 Onwards

As I continued my search of the Bloy family ancestry, in addition to finding that despair, anguish and misfortune were frequent occurrences for the family during the 19th century, I also found two cases of insanity, one of whom was a committed murderer. Therefore to provide readers with a framework for following my discussion regarding some rather interesting and unsavoury individuals within the family, I have drawn below a simplified version of five generations of the BLOY family tree to cover the period from 1780 to 1947.

With so many ancestors having the same forename, either William or Walter, regular reference to this family tree will need to be made to follow and perhaps, make sense of my narrative of the Bloy family history and their fortunes. Although, the primary focus of this story was my father Walter and his immediate forefathers, I have also highlighted his great-uncle William (b.1840) in the family tree, because he was the first Bloy to arrive in Grimsby from Tydd St Mary. His fate, fortune and misdemeanours added another interesting dimension to the overall story of how he and his brother Walter fared as they tried to make their way in the rapidly developing town. William's son, George (b.1874), will also be referred to in the chapter where I tell the tragic story of brothers, David (b.1844) and John (b.1850), who were both certified as lunatics. More recent generations of Walter's extended family are included in the family trees, which I use to discuss the family history of his mother Alice Smith and his wife Grace Mary James.

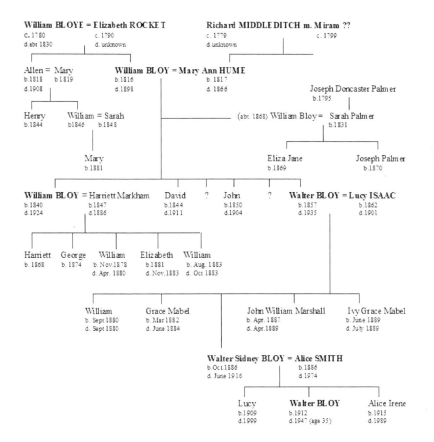

For this next part of the story, my search into the Bloys' ancestry refers back to Walter's great-great-grandfather William Bloye, which is as far backward as I intend to go within the Bloy lineage. William Bloye was born about 1780; 'Mad' King George III, who some blame for the loss of the American Colonies in the War of Independence of 1775 - 1782, was on the throne and would remain the kingdom's monarch for another 40 years: a fact I mention to provide readers with an historical perspective of the family timeline I am now referring to.

William Bloye lived and worked all his life as an agricultural labourer, in the area around the village of Tydd St Mary in the Fenland area of southeast Lincolnshire where it borders with Cambridgeshire and Norfolk. Genealogists contend that almost everyone will have an agricultural labourer or two in their family tree. My family in this story are no different. I found many ancestors, throughout several branches of the extended family tree, of both my father's and mother's lineage, who worked as agricultural labourers. For that reason alone, I believe it is worth taking a moment to consider; what exactly did agricultural labourers do? What were their working conditions like? Did they stay in one place or did they move around to find work? How were they paid and where did they live? What sort of life did they have?

In the 18th and the early part of the 19th century, prior to the impact of the industrial revolution, the vast majority of the population worked in agriculture. At the beginning of this period, life for the smallholder and labourers without land, though not a bed of roses, would not have been too bad. Common land was still plentiful, where the 'commoners' could grow their own vegetables, raise and graze their animals and gather fuel for their fires. All this however, would dramatically change. With the continuation of enclosure, the common land was gradually being handed over to single landowners, who then rented the land out to tenant farmers, who in turn hired casual labourers to work for them. This, (together with a down- turn in the economy at the end of the Napoleonic Wars in 1815, when Napoleon's new army had been defeated at Waterloo by the Duke of Wellington, and the course of European history changed; along with the surplus of labour generated by the return of the ex-servicemen), meant that life was becoming more precarious and a daily struggle for our agricultural labourers.

It is clear to see that it wouldn't have been an easy time for William who, at the age of 35, was married by the Reverend John Metcalf to Elizabeth Rocket on the 20th November 1815, in the parish church of St Mary in Tydd St Mary. According to the wedding certificate, William was a widower and Elizabeth, who was younger than William by about 10 years, a spinster. Obviously William had been married before. However, as I could not find any record of William's first marriage or whether it produced any children and, it having no relevance for this story, I looked no further. In these difficult times for agricultural labourers, William now had a wife and would soon have the first of his children, William (b.1816) and Allen (b.1818), to support. Several other children were born to William and Elizabeth, but as they too are not relevant to this story and to avoid digressing too much, no further comments about them will be offered.

In addition to the economic situation and the surplus of agricultural labour, the increasing mechanisation of farm life, through such wonders as the threshing machines, would irrevocably change the nature of farm work for ever. Matters were made worse because the threshing machine took away valuable winter work from the labourers, where they would thresh the corn and wheat by hand. So much so, that in the 1830s, the so-called 'Swing Riots' broke out in the counties of England which had been most affected by the continuing enclosure. The rioters demanded a minimum wage, the end of rural unemployment, and tithe and rent reductions. The riots, which took the form of vandalising the new machines, arson, meetings and general unrest, were the first demonstrations of agricultural unrest and, would continue for some time after the passing of the 1834 Poor Law Amendment Act. For many rioters, a dire consequence of the unrest was that they were arrested, tried and deported to the penal colony of 'Van Diemen's land, which is what Tasmania (Australia) was then called. It was during these turbulent times that William, and subsequently his sons, tried to find work.

Bearing in mind that the situation for agricultural labourers was not an easy one, how did our ancestors find work? Some may have been born in tied cottages on farms where their parents were already working. Consequently, they grew up on the farms and would progress from simple jobs suitable for children, to more skilled work as they grew older. They may have even taken over the tied cottage from their fathers after they died and raised their own families on the same farm. Most probably, their wives and daughters would have worked in the dairy, in the vegetable plots or in the house. Although their lives may have seemed secure and comfortable, they were always at the mercy, and the benevolent nature, or not, of their employers; who could, without any notice, lower their wages or even turn them out of their cottages if they felt they could no longer afford to employ them, or if they had become too old or too sick to work. Being 'turfed' out from the farm would not have been uncommon.

For our ancestors, there was another route for gaining agricultural work, the 'Hiring Fairs'. These would be held bi-annually in Spring and Autumn and were the place where the more mobile farm workers would hope to find jobs. The hiring fairs had their historical roots in England's medieval history, as they came into being after the Black Death. The Black Death was a bubonic plague pandemic, which reached Europe in 1347 and spread to England in 1348 and killed between a third and more than half of the nation's inhabitants. Consequently, during the Middle Ages, agricultural workers were hard to come by. They became an itinerant workforce moving about to where the work was. The hiring fairs adopted a loose form of regulation. In order to stop desperate farmers offering excessive wages to find workers it was decided that they should be hired in public and that each worker should carry an emblem of his trade to ensure that workers were hired at the correct rate for the job. Thomas Hardy, in his novel, 'Far From the Madding Crowd' describes a hiring fair as:

> 'At one end of the street stood from two to three hundred blithe and hearty labourers waiting upon chance. Among these, carters and waggoners were distinguished by having a piece of whip cord twisted round their hats; thatchers wore a fragment of woven straw; shepherds held their sheep-crooks in their hands; and thus the situation required was known to the hirers at a glance'.

Although Hardy paints a very colourful scene, one I am sure my ancestors of William's era c.1800, would most certainly recognise. It must have been a little overwhelming and daunting for the younger workers, some as young as 12, who were also hoping to find work. This system of travelling to the hiring fair and from there to the farm provides an explanation of the sometimes surprising mobility of our ancestors.

Workers hired at these hiring fairs, if they were single, were sometimes taken on as farm servants, usually for a year, meaning that they would 'live in' on the farm and share the farmer's table at mealtimes. Casual labourers would be hired from the neighbouring villages on an 'as needed' basis, to supplement their work. Whilst at the farm, if a worker met and fell in love with a farm servant from another village and decided to get married, they were then obliged to live out and would have to find lodgings in the surrounding area. Hiring fairs and the system of 'living in' gradually died out during the 19th century and, by 1900 it was virtually unheard of for a farm servant to share the farmer's house. I have already commented that, within the Bloy family history, at the farm of Thomas Isaac where Lucy Bloy (nee Isaac) was raised in the 1870s, four 'live-in' labourers were employed.

In respect of those agricultural labourers who had families to support and/or no specialised skills to offer, these would be hired on a casual basis for specific tasks. It is easy to see with casual labour that, in some cases, there would not have been the continuity of regular employment and, more importantly a regular wage. This may well have been the situation for William after he married Elizabeth and they started their family! I could not establish whether they had the relative security of a tied cottage on a specific farm, or whether William had to seek his employment through the pot luck and chance of the hiring fairs or casual labour. All the records I could find relating to William refer to him as a labourer; I have no way of knowing whether he had any specific skills. Then as now, casual labourers would only be paid for the work they did, and would receive nothing if they were sick or if the weather was too bad for them to work. Added to which, wages were, in general, very low and unemployment due to a surplus in the labour force was very high. With so much uncertainty, it would not have been an easy life.

For many agricultural labourers, their comfort and survival depended on poor relief to help them through the frequent difficult times. Even this couldn't be relied upon, as changes in the poor laws took place during the 19th century. Before 1834, poor relief, which had its basis in the early 17th century when it was introduced as a way to alleviate distress and to ensure public order, was dealt with at parish level. The Poor Law Guardians decided who was eligible for help and, as they often knew the recipients, it could be a fair system, although, I do recognise that local knowledge, as well as being fair, also has the potential for abuse of the system. Labourers could ask the Poor Law Guardians for 'outdoor' relief to supplement their loss of wages due to illness or unemployment. However, by the early 19th century, public attitudes to the poor had begun to change. Being poor started to be seen as the person's fault and the payment of poor relief was believed to only encourage people to ask for help rather than to seek work, or work harder. Isn't it coincidental that this point of view has so much similarity with views that are frequently expressed nowadays regarding state benefits and the unemployed!

The Poor Law Amendment Act of 1834 aimed to do away with outdoor relief and make the workhouses (unions) the only way of accessing help. It was intended that this would act as a deterrent to ensure only the genuinely destitute would apply. Being sent to the workhouse was seen by many as a source of shame. This change of poor relief provision is particularly important and relevant for this story. During my research into the Bloy family ancestry, I discovered that the Holbeach Union Workhouse in 1860 provided the setting for the most distressing and disturbing chapter of my family's history I was to find.

As the 19th century wore on the condition of our agricultural labourer ancestors and the way they were perceived by the more fortunate parts of the population gradually deteriorated. They were badly paid and their 'cottages' were often small and in a sorry state of repair. They were seen as idle, unskilled and unintelligent. However, the range of farm work that these 'unskilled' people were expected to undertake, shows just how incorrect the perceived view of the time was. In the summer agricultural labourers were employed to do harvesting, which was done by hand with a sickle at the beginning of the 19th century and with a scythe in the second half of the century. The wives of the harvesters would sometimes be employed to rake the cut corn into rows ready to be tied into sheaves. Images of this type of work look very appealing and rewarding on classic fine art paintings, the reality was, it was back-breaking, hard dawn-to-dusk grafting. Before the advent of threshing machines at the beginning of the 19th century, winter work would consist of threshing the corn and sieving it to separate the grain and chaff. Agricultural labourers would sow and tend to the various crops on the farm as well as caring for the farm animals, milking cows, feeding pigs, herding and shearing sheep and looking after the poultry. Their work also consisted of trimming and layering hedges and maintaining the farm buildings, fences, gates, farm tracks, ditches and ponds.

Industrialisation of working practices in Britain during the 19th century would irrevocably change country life forever. Although the living conditions were difficult and life expectancy much lower due to the insanitary conditions and over-crowding, work in the towns and cities was plentiful and wages were much higher. There is little wonder then, that many agricultural workers moved to the new industrialised towns to seek their fortune, which is exactly what William did in the 1860s and Walter in the 1870s. This important point has now brought us, albeit in a roundabout way, back to the main purpose of our story. I now know that it is from the lowly beginnings of William Bloye (b.1780), the agricultural labourer and his wife Elizabeth, that all the Bloy family members, who can now be found living in Grimsby, have been descended. From these humble roots, I shall now go on to discuss how fate and tragedies influenced the family fortunes and will explore in more comprehensive detail the journey that the two brothers made out of Tydd St Mary to Grimsby.

During the search for accurate information to build up the story, I found the further I tried to go back on the timeline looking for Walter's ancestors, the more difficult the research became. I believe this may be typical when researching the history of poor 'working class' families, who most likely, the further back in time one goes, would be illiterate. If details could not be found in parish records, who then would record and document the family members and its history. Therefore, with the Bloy family I chose to look no further than William and Elizabeth, who were born in the latter part of the 18th century and are my ancestors to whom I previously referred who could neither read nor write. Being illiterate in the 18th and early 19th century wouldn't have any stigma attached to it at all.

Many working class children in early Victorian England never went to school and more than half grew up unable to read or write. Instead, out of necessity, they had to start work at a very young age, to earn money for their families. If they were not working on the land, children as young as twelve years old and perhaps even younger, were often indentured as apprentices to work in the emerging and developing industrialised towns. The conditions that apprentices lived and endured, for example in the Grimsby fishing industry and the mills, mines and factories of other parts of the country, were very dangerous, unhealthy and harsh and certainly claimed their casualties. In Victorian Grimsby, fishing casualties at sea were high. It is well documented that many hundreds of apprentice fishermen lost their lives through drowning after falling overboard, or even, after being thrown overboard. Now, that is another astonishing story! It is common knowledge and often stated, almost to the point of becoming a cliché for all that was wrong during this period of our country's social history, that to earn a pittance children, some as young as seven or eight years old, were forced to climb up inside of chimneys to clean them. Education for the working classes was not a high priority. Only the upper and middle class children regularly went to school, although some more fortunate poorer children may have gone to Sunday schools which the churches ran.

Despite all that I have just said, during the 19th century, the situation did start to improve; many schools were actually built in the Victorian era, between 1837 and 1901. In the country, some barns were converted into schoolrooms and increasing numbers of children began to attend. Several kinds of school for poorer children started to emerge; the youngest might go to a 'Dame' school, run by a local woman in a room of her house, whilst the older ones went to a day school. In Tydd St Mary, there was a free school, which had been founded in 1740 by Dame Martha Trafford, though not all children attended. Other schools were organised by churches and charities. Among these were the 'Ragged' schools, which was the name commonly given after about 1840 to the many independently established 19th century charity schools that provided education for orphans and very poor children. In addition to entirely free education, in most cases, food, clothing, lodging and other home missionary services for those too poor to pay were given. Often these schools were established in poor working class districts of the rapidly expanding industrial towns.

Of particular relevance to this story is the fact that education was not compulsory at that time and, would not be so for many decades yet to come. It wasn't until the 1880s that schooling became mandatory and all children had to attend a school until they were 10 years old. In 1889, the school leaving age was then raised to twelve, and in 1891, the school's pence fee was abolished and schooling became free. It would be nearly thirty more years before the Education Act of 1917 made schooling compulsory until the age of 14. Although I have digressed, I believe that the lack of compulsory schooling adds an interesting social dimension to the life and times of our forefathers, especially as several ancestors to whom I refer throughout this story were illiterate.

Returning to the story of Walter's family lineage: the parish records of St Mary's church in Tydd St Mary indicate that Elizabeth bore William at least two children. According to census information and parish records, William, their first child, from whom my Bloy family line is directly descended, was born in Tydd St Mary's about 1816. Their second son, Allen, was born two years later in 1818, presumably also in Tydd St Mary, as both William and Allen were baptised by the Reverend John Metcalf at the parish church on 13th October 1816 and the 30th August 1818 respectively. When William Bloy was 23 years old, on the 30th July 1839, he married Mary Ann Hume in the Parish church of Tydd St Giles in Cambridgeshire. Mary Ann, who was 22 years old, originally came from Braintree in Essex. Rather interestingly, the records indicate that her mother, Miram Middleditch, was only 16 years old when she gave birth to Mary Ann. And, not surprisingly, given all I have previously said about work, according to the copy of the wedding certificate I obtained, Mary Ann's father, Richard Middleditch, was described as an agricultural labourer.

I found his surname interesting. Somewhere in his family history, presumably, somebody must have lived close to a middle ditch in the fields or fens and was known through the location where he dwelled, which eventually led to it becoming the family surname. However, his daughter, Mary Ann, was described on the wedding certificate as a spinster and not a widow. Consequently, I can offer no explanation for the differing surnames between father and daughter! William and his brother Allen may have attended the 'Dame' school in Tydd St Mary, because it does appear that they could both read and write; William had signed the wedding certificate, whereas Mary Ann only made her mark. Brother Allen, and his new wife, who was also called Mary were the witnesses to the wedding. I appreciate that the frequent use of the same names, William, Walter and now Mary Ann, does make the narrative confusing and difficult to follow at times!

It had been a day of double wedding celebrations. Allen, who would live to the ripe old age of 90 and will not feature much further in this story, had married Mary Rigalle on the same day that William had married Mary. During the research however, I was interested to discover that Allen and Mary's son, Henry (b.1844), a first cousin of the brothers William and Walter, became the Police Constable in the Lincolnshire village of Digby. When he wasn't policing, Henry was certainly kept busy at home because, after marrying Mary Ann Garner in 1870, (yes, another Mary Ann,) together they produced eighteen children, one of whom, George Henry Bloy, became an 'Old Contemptible' soldier in the British Army in the Great War. But that is yet another story! William (b.1816), (whom I am discussing, and would also live a long life; he died in Grimsby in 1898 at the age of 82,) returned Allen's favour. He was the witness for Allen and Mary Rigalles's wedding. William had married earlier in the day in the parish church of Tydd St Giles, in Cambridgeshire, which is just a few miles down the road from the parish church in Tydd St Mary, where Allen had married. When these two brothers William and Allen got married, I think that their father William was dead and no further trace of their mother Elizabeth could be found.

According to census information Walter's great-grandparents, William and Mary Ann had at least four children together, all boys, William, David, John and Walter. As the census was taken every ten years and only recorded people that were alive on the census date, it is most likely, and highly probable, that other children may well have been born and died as infants, or perhaps had been stillborn, between the consecutive census dates. In which case, they would not be listed on the census and, if they had been stillborn, perhaps not recorded on the Parish records. With William and Mary Ann, the gap of six years between the birth of David (b. 1844) and John (b. 1850), and then the seven year gap between John and Walter's (b. 1857) birth, does seem highly unusual for the time, as contraception would most certainly have not been used. Their cousin Henry's eighteen children provides convincing evidence of that. Furthermore, William was still sexually active and capable of producing children. We can see from the family tree that within two years of his wife Mary Ann dying in 1866, William married Sarah Palmer, a spinster who was 15 years his junior, and then fathered two children in quick succession with her.

Just like his father and father-in-law before him, William, was also employed in the Tydd St Mary area as a 'farm labourer'. According to Whites Lincolnshire Directory (1872), Tydd St Mary is described in such a manner that encourages readers to picture it as a typical pleasant idyllic English country village of several hundred people. Having visited the village and St Mary's church, during the research for this story, I can say, it is exactly what you would expect. What is implicit and important about White's observations is, if you didn't have a trade, such as a blacksmith, thatcher, carpenter, wheelwright or tanner and if you didn't own the land, you probably worked, on a tied or casual basis, for someone that did own the land. To reiterate what I have previously said, until people migrated to the developing towns during the 19th century, agricultural labouring was still the main source of employment. Central to the story of my search for Walter is the fact that two of William and Mary Ann's children, William (b.1840) and Walter (b.1857), gave up their life of scraping a living through working on the land to make the journey to Grimsby to seek their fortune, which is where our story will eventually take us.

Although they were poor and had humble origins, being the offspring of a farm labourer, their lifestyle in Tydd St Mary's would have been relatively healthy compared to what they would find and experience when they first arrived in

Grimsby. Life expectancy in the countryside though impoverished, was considerably longer than in the squalor, overcrowded and unsanitary conditions of parts of Grimsby. Living in the country, however lowly and desperate their financial well-being, the family would most probably have eaten relatively well. In addition to fish, rabbits and game birds that they could catch, or maybe poach, they would probably have kept chickens, maybe even had pigs and also have a readily available supply of fresh fruit and vegetables, which they would grow for themselves. Being 'labourers', they would have also benefited from the physical aspect of working outdoors in the fresh air of the countryside. Although these are my assumptions, they seem to be well founded. One of William and Mary Ann's children, their third son John, when admitted to St John's Mental Hospital in 1867, was described as 'well-nourished and in general good health'. Regrettably, a closer examination of this episode of the family's history revealed yet again more wretched and shocking misfortune: a hereditary and alarming mental condition, and another disturbingly mysterious sequence of events. Rather than discuss the details now of why John was admitted to St John's Mental Hospital, because of the extreme nature of the circumstances, as I have already said, I will return to these unsettling events and those concerning John's brother David in a separate chapter.

According to the census of 1851, William and Mary Ann were living with their children, Walter's great-uncles, William, David and John at Broadgate in Tydd St Mary. When I visited the village, the verger of St Mary's church in the village explained that in the 18/19th century, Broadgate wasn't really the name of a road, but more a description. It literally meant that the road was wide enough for two horses and carts going in opposite directions to be able to pass each other in safety. Street and road names of the 19th century were often descriptive and indicative of activities that took place in the locality. For example, Slaughter House Lane and Skinners Lane are names that I am aware of in rural Lincolnshire that shouldn't really require further explanation. The following census, ten years later in 1861, indicates that William and Mary Ann were still living at Broadgate, but now only with sons William, John and Walter, who had been born in 1857. Their son William, who by then was 21 years old, left home shortly after the 1861 census and headed to Grimsby, where he established a business in about 1865. The business, which started out as a marine stores dealer, is now among other things, a scrap metal merchant. Despite an early setback, it became very successful and is still thriving today nearly one hundred and fifty years later and, quite rightly, is proud to promote the date, when it was established.

For William and Mary Ann, the 1860s would prove to be an unbelievable and eventful decade. Not only did their children start to leave home; in the space of ten years, in addition to having to cope initially with exceptional family shame and harrowing tragedy, William would lose his wife Mary Ann and within two years take a new wife and become a father again to two more children. Sadly, for Mary Ann, she lived long enough to see her second-born son, David (b.1844), feature in some of the most disturbing series of acts that I found in the whole of my research. Even now, I can hardly believe it and find it hard to comprehend. Because he was not listed on the 1861 census document, I originally assumed David had died. Child mortality being what it was then, it was the easy option for me to take. The simple fact was, David was no longer living at home. Quite by accident, I found him again in the Criminal Records and then the census documents from 1871 onwards. David Bloy, my father's great-uncle, at the age of twenty had been incarcerated in 1864, as inmate number 156 into 'Broadmoor Criminal Lunatic Asylum', where he would remain for the next forty-seven years of his life until dying in 1911. David Bloy was, purportedly, a murderer!

As if David's insanity and incarceration for murder weren't enough, fate proved to be unkind yet again in a very tormenting way for William. Mary Ann, when only 48 years old, and just two years after David's incarceration, died on the 8th December 1866, allegedly from pneumonia. Mary Ann was buried at the parish church of Tydd St Mary. Sadly, there are no visible signs left today of where Mary Ann or any other Bloys from this period are buried in the parish church grounds. The verger suggested, although they would have most likely been buried there, being 'paupers', the cost of an engraved headstone would have been beyond their means. A wooden cross, which has long since rotted away, is most likely to have been placed at the grave at the time of the funeral. William's wretched misery and despair would soon continue.

Mary Ann's death created an episode and explanation I still find hard to understand or moreover accept. The entry on the copy of her death certificate I obtained does not seem quite right. Mary Ann was certified dead by a neighbour! I said 'allegedly' when referring to the pneumonia, because I suspect that their third son, John, was somehow involved in his mother's death. Although there is plenty of circumstantial evidence, I cannot find the actual hard evidence I need to confirm my suspicions. Mary Ann's death left me asking questions, but struggling initially to find the answers.

After Mary Ann died in December 1866, and John's committal six weeks later to St John's Hospital in Lincoln, William Bloy was left alone with his youngest son Walter, who being only nine years old, was still living at home. William certainly didn't appear to waste any time living as a widower. Within two years of his wife's death, at the age of 51 he married again. His new wife, Sarah Palmer, who was fifteen years younger than him, was from the Palmer family who, according to the 1861 census, were the next-door neighbours of the Bloy family in Tydd St Mary. How very convenient for the old rogue to court and romance the next door neighbour! From what I discovered when researching John Bloy's medical history, I don't think he was too happy that his father had remarried. He frequently made his displeasure known to William and his step-mother Sarah. Nevertheless, Sarah bore William two children, Eliza Jane (b.1869) and Joseph Palmer (b.1870). After their marriage, they continued to live at Broadgate with Walter and the new children, Eliza Jane and Joseph Palmer and also Sarah's father, Joseph Doncaster Palmer (b.1795). It was not uncommon in those days for elderly parents to live with their children. Within a few years of his father remarrying, Walter, when in his early 20's, would also leave Tydd St Mary and travel to Grimsby to seek his fortune and make his way in the world, which is where our journey will next take us.

Sometime during the 1880s, Walter's great-grandfather William, by now an old man of 75 years, had left Sarah and their daughter Eliza Jane in Tydd St Mary to come and live with his son Walter and his family at East Street in Grimsby. For patriarch William, this move to Grimsby would also bring him closer to his eldest son William who had made the journey from Tydd St Mary thirty years before. Quite why William had left behind his wife Sarah and his daughter Eliza Jane, by then a young woman aged 22, is not really known. I have my suspicions that it may have had something to do with William's son John's violent behaviour, which I will be discussing shortly. William and Sarah's son, Joseph Palmer Bloy, who was then in his twenties had also left Tydd St Mary's and was living in Croydon, Surrey, as a 'boarder'. According to the census ten years later in 1901, when she was 70 years old, Sarah had also moved and was living in Croydon with her son Joseph Palmer and his wife Emily, where she remained for the rest of her life.

When I reviewed John Bloy's case history file, it seems from correspondence contained therein that in 1910, he was still able to torment Sarah, even though he had been dead for six years. The explanation for this strange turn of events will be revealed presently. For the record, William, Walter's great-grandfather died in Grimsby in 1898 at the age of 82; whatever happened to William and Sarah's daughter Eliza Jane is not known.

Chapter Five

Murder, Mania and Mayhem!

At this point in the story, it is appropriate to examine and try to understand the sequence of events concerning Walter's great-uncles David (b.1844) and John (b.1850).The fact that these events are so serious and involve two brothers who were born consecutively is not in doubt. But why they happened is a cause for concern, given that their other brothers William and Walter did not display the same characteristics and behavioural traits as them. Quite the opposite in fact! To be able to tell this part of the story, in addition to newspaper articles, I drew extensively from the medical case files for David and John Bloy that are held in archives for St John's Lunatic Asylum in Lincoln, and Fair Mile Lunatic Asylum and Broadmoor Criminal Lunatic Asylum, which are both in Berkshire. To narrate these events authentically, articles, correspondence and reports from the case files will be used verbatim, except where the sentence construction and grammar needs slight amendment to be able to make sense of what is being said. For ease of explanation, I will also refer to the above Lunatic Asylums as St John's, Fair Mile and Broadmoor.

David Bloy's medical problems, which were the primary cause of his behaviour, began early in his life. He was epileptic and had started having violent epileptic fits from the age of eight years old. His *'attacks would sometimes last an hour, sometimes for a day'*. During these attacks, he was considered *'dangerous to others and himself'*. His epilepsy had supposedly been triggered by; *'Fright by a man in a white gown which he supposed was a ghost'*. David had had some schooling. The admittance statement for his incarceration, as inmate number 156, into Broadmoor in 1864, indicates that he could *'read and write imperfectly'*. His general health was described as good and, he was considered to be temperate in his habits.

Although David was described as a farm labourer, it seems that he had been unable to find casual work under the hiring fair system. The fact that he was, according to one doctor's consideration, of low intellect and suffered from epileptic fits and had done so since a child, may have made farmers very wary of employing him. Nevertheless, as the family were really paupers, David from the age of 12 onwards, maybe even earlier, would have had to somehow start earning a living to contribute to the family wellbeing; being epileptic, this would not have been easy for him. The records don't indicate at what age he actually left home, but taking into account what I have discovered about those times, when he was 14 or 15 years old is the most likely. David would have been struggling to find work, not living at home and had no other means of subsistence. Consequently, in accordance with the Poor Law Amendment Act (1834), in 1860, at the age of sixteen, David was recorded as being an inmate of the Holbeach Union, the workhouse which served the local area including Tydd St Mary's. I believe he had been there for some time. While residing in the workhouse he murdered a fellow inmate, Simon Cote, by stabbing him in the neck with a knife. The Broadmoor admittance statement for David Bloy records this entry:

> *Stabbing one Simon Cote, in the Holbeach Union House on the 3rd day of December 1860; this occurred a short time previous to one of the epileptic fits and at that time Bloy was insane. He was removed to the County Lunatic Asylum on the 4th day of December 1860 and remained at that establishment until the 24th June 1864. He was handed over to the police and committed to the Castle of Lincoln for trial charged with murder at the Assizes on the 2nd July 1864.*

I found it very disturbing that after the murder had been committed, David was held without trial in a County Lunatic Asylum for nearly four years. In addition to feeling quite angry, I was left wondering whether being imprisoned in a Lunatic Asylum, at the age of 16, contributed greatly to a rapid worsening of his mental state.

David eventually stood trial for 'wilful murder' at the Summer Assizes for the County of Lincoln on 26th July 1864. The trial was reported on two occasions in the Lincoln Chronicle newspaper. On the 29th July 1864, the newspaper report focused on the directions the LORDSHIP was giving to the Grand Jury regarding cases to be heard at that Summer Assizes:

> *He trusted the gentlemen of the Grand Jury would be seated. The first charge of wilful murder was against David Bloy, and he thought it would not give them much trouble in investigating it, for they would find early that wilful murder was undoubtedly committed. There was every reason to believe that the unfortunate man who committed the murder was at the time labouring under insanity. That however, would be investigated and it would be more prudent if that investigation took place in open court.*

For me, this reads like the Judge was already telling the Grand Jury what their verdict should be before the trial had even started and any evidence had been heard! The second article, which appeared in the Lincoln Chronicle on the 5th August 1864, provided a comprehensive account of the trial and was reported thus:

WILFUL MURDER AT FLEET

> *David Bloy, 20, labourer, was charged with the wilful murder of Simon Cote, at Fleet, on 3rd Dec.*

1860. Mr KYME appeared for the prosecution; the prisoner was undefended.

It appeared from the evidence that the prisoner and the deceased were inmates on the Holbeach workhouse in Dec. 1860, both being in the infirmary. About half past eight o'clock on the night of the 2nd Dec, Bloy was carried to bed and soon afterwards he got up, saying he was going to the cupboard for a drink. There were knives in the cupboard. He got in bed again and about an hour afterwards got out and went to the night stool, and while sitting upon it he put his arm around Simon Cote's neck and cut his throat. Bloy immediately afterwards fell into a fit. Cote jumped out of bed and said, "That boy has cut my throat". Jas Clarke, the nurse, then got up and saw the prisoner on the floor, and sent for Richard Watton, another pauper nurse, who dressed Cote's wound. He was bleeding profusely. The knife with which the wound was inflicted was an ordinary dinner knife. Bloy was lying insensible at the time.

Dr Harper, surgeon, was sent for early in the morning, and found an incised angular wound on the right side of Cote's neck about four inches long –such a wound as might be caused by an ordinary table knife. The patient had a fatal illness upon him at the time, he was admitted for chronic diarrhoea of many months standing, and was in a very weak state. The wound went on satisfactorily for several days, but on the 18th Dec. it put on an unsatisfactory appearance, and on the 19th erysipelas supervened, commencing at the wound, and extending over the head and face. This caused his death on the 22nd Dec.

Dr Harper had known the prisoner for nearly eight years, and up to the 3rd Dec. he was under his care in the infirmary. For several years he had *returned him to the Lunacy Commissioners, every quarter as person of weak intellect, but he had always been of a harmless nature up to that period. He had been subject to epileptic fits for many years, but had only shown violence on one occasion, when he tore his blankets and bed clothes to pieces. Bloy was sent to the Lunatic Aylum after the murder, Dr Harper still considering him of unsound mind. On the 24th June 1864, Bloy was apprehended at the Asylum by police-sergeant Groom on the charge of murdering Cote. He said, "I have heard I murdered him, but was unconscious at the time". Clarke said there had never been any quarrel between the prisoner and the deceased.*

His LORDSHIP summed up, remarking that there could be no doubt the acts of the prisoner were such as in a sane man would amount to wilful murder. The question for the jury to consider, however, was whether the prisoner was at the time in a state of mind to know what he was about. He had long been the subject of epileptic fits, and Dr Harper had periodically returned him as being of unsound mind. If they thought that the prisoner was not a responsible agent, it was competent for them to return a verdict of not guilty on the ground of insanity, and for him (the judge) to order him to be kept in proper custody during Her Majesty's pleasure.

The jury returned a verdict of not guilty on the ground of insanity, and his LORDSHIP ordered him to be detained during Her Majesty's pleasure.

Although there is no doubt that David inflicted the wound that led to Simon Cote's death; there is much about this case that causes me unease. This is a twenty year old man we are talking about, who had been kept in a lunatic asylum since he was sixteen. For example, why was David undefended at his trial? Had the judge not directed the jury to consider David's sanity, he may well have been found guilty and sent to the gallows! Why wasn't the wound considered serious enough to call the doctor on the night that it happened and not the next day? Simon Cote did not die until twenty days later. And he was already described as a very weak man with a fatal illness; consequently his resistance to infection would have been low. Once Erysipelas, which is a superficial infection of the skin that typically involves the lymphatic system, occurred, Simon Cote's death was inevitable. Erysipelas also known as St. Anthony's Fire, because of the intensity of the rash, was a feared disease in those pre-antibiotic days and can be caused by an inciting wound such as trauma, or some other break in the skin that precedes the fiery infection. Yes, David inflicted the wound, but nowadays, with modern antibiotics, it is most likely that Simon would not have died; and as David's epilepsy and general mental health would have been treated very differently, the attack most likely would not have happened. But this was Victorian England!

After the trial, David was initially imprisoned at Lincoln County Gaol, from where he was transferred on 16th August 1864 to Broadmoor, which had only opened in 1863, originally for women and had just started admitting men. Hence David's relatively low admissions number of 156. On his transfer from gaol to Broadmoor, the Surgeon to the Lincoln County Goal wrote:

> *I certify that David Bloye [sic] is in good health, free from any infectious disease, and fit for removal from Lincoln County Gaol to the Criminal Lunatic Asylum at Broadmoor, Berkshire. The man is the subject of very violent epileptic fits and at those times is dangerous to himself and others if not especially watched.*
> *Ed. Farr Broadbent,*
> *Lincoln Castle - August 15th 1864*

The warrant for the reception of David Bloy into Broadmoor was issued by The Right Honourable W. George Grey Bar, one of Her Majesty's Most Honourable Privy Council, and Principal Secretary of State; given at Whitehall on the 8th day of August 1864 in the 20th year of Her Majesty's Reign.

Unlike his brother John, who caused problems in all the prisons and lunatic asylums in which he served time, David's time spent in Broadmoor is remarkably uneventful. From David's incarceration in 1864 until his first petition to the Home Secretary in 1883, for his release, I could find no records or correspondence at all, though I do believe he had been visited by John several times during this period. With respect to David's petition for release, on the 19th January 1883, the Home Office wrote to the Superintendent of Broadmoor:

Sir, A.Liddell requests that the Superintendent of the Broadmoor Lunatic Asylum will inform David Bloy that his petition has been fully considered by the Secretary of State for the Home Department, who sees no ground to justify him in recommending compliance with the prayer thereof.
Home Office, Whitehall

Two years later, David petitioned the Home Office again, only to receive, on the 20th March 1885, the same response. He was not deterred by this setback and, on the 26th May 1885, David wrote to Dr Orange at Broadmoor:

Dr Orange, Will you please allow me to see the Council of Supervision on Friday next? You informed me on the last occasion that they met the week previous to my application. I trust I am early enough to see them this time. D. Bloy

David was seen by the Council on the 29th May 1885; it did not however, secure his release. He wasn't to know that he would never be released and, he would live in Broadmoor until he died in 1911. Forever hopeful, David never gave up trying and petitioned again in 1887, 1896, 1901 and 1904, by which time he was 60 years old. The case file revealed through correspondence in 1886, from his father William and stepmother Sarah, though I suspect it was Sarah who wrote both letters, there was a grave concern that his brother John, after escaping himself from St John's in Lincoln, was trying to make his way to Broadmoor to effect David's escape. These letters also suggest that stepmother Sarah lived in fear of John.

Letter rom Sarah and William Bloy to the Superintendent at Broadmoor:

7th June 1886

*Sir, I beg to inform you that John Bloy, David's brother has escaped from Lincoln Asylum and we are afraid he should make his way up to David and get him out. He is in the habit of picking locks and David has been wanting [sic] us to ask leave for him to come home for a holiday. But we do not wish he should we cannot do anything with him so if John should come please take care of him and send him onward to Lincoln at once you will...*the next part of the sentence is unclear.
    Yours faithfully
    Sarah and William Bloy

Letter dated in response from the Broadmoor Superintendent to William Bloy:

9th June 1886

Dear Sir, Having been informed that John Bloy (a brother of David Bloy an inmate of this asylum) has escaped from the Bracebridge Asylum, I write to say that John has written here requesting his brother

David to send him some money to be addressed to him at the General Post Office, Nottingham, till called for.

PS

David Bloy writes enclosing 2/6 today to his brother John at the address given opposite; but the letter shall be detained until I hear from you.

Reply from Sarah Bloy to the Broadmoor Superintendent:

12th June 1886

Sir, I thank you very much for the information given reflecting John. I hope they will be able to secure him and that you will be very careful about the letters that come too and go from David they are such a crafty family it is hard work to find them out they keep everything so close to themselves. John has escaped 5 times he picks locks with a bent nail. I took it out of his pocket the last time he came home. I know by their way of ???? what they mean. John is trying to ???? David away. David he ask me to ask for him to be sent to Lincoln some time back. I wrote and told him I should not think of such a thing and he sent his bible that he wished for so much to his brother Walter at Grimsby. I thought it very strange a while back he said would I ask for him to come home for a bit. But I have not answered that I do not wish for him to come I have so much trouble with those I have. I trust you will keep him but do not let him know I have written to you as he will tell John who has threatened to kill me if he can.

Yours
Sarah Bloy

It is worth bearing in mind in 1886, when these letters were exchanged that, William was 70 and Sarah was 55 years old. And, despite all that I said in a previous chapter regarding compulsory education, Sarah's letters are reasonably articulate. The underlining of the last part of Sarah's letter emphasises, for me, that she didn't want to be part of stepson David's welfare and was certainly very frightened of John.

In the 'Reports as to the condition and circumstances of a Criminal Lunatic' required by the Criminal Lunatics Act 1884, which was part of the petition for release, David's state of mental health can be seen to be changing with each new petition. 'Unsound', 'naturally of weak intellect', 'suffers from melancholia' and 'enfeebled' were the phrases being used to describe him. Surprisingly for an enfeebled man of low intellect, I found the following letter and poem, which David had written in October 1891 deeply moving. And though I cannot reproduce David's spidery handwriting, I present it in the same manner that David wrote it:

Rev. Mr Morgan
Sir, The following poem enclosed now intended for
"All Saints Day" was composed many months ago
with the exception of two lines revised. If you think
it worthy of a place in the parish magazine, I should
like to see it appears next month if space permit.
>   *Yours respectfully*
>   *David Bloy*

*On the word **"Resurrection"***
"All Saints Day"

Rejoice ye Saints! Your jubilee is here
Earth and sea gives up our friends most dear
Sweet is our happy meeting! O blest day!
Uniting tender loving hearts, for aye!
Ransom Great! Millions upon millions stand,
Round our father's throne at his right hand.
Echoes long resound from that mighty throng,
Chanting to their Redeemer's praise their song
The angels take up the strain at His command!
Inexpressible joys, dwell in that land
O bright new earth from sin and sorrow free
<u>*Now*</u> *"Peace, goodwill to men". Glad Jubilee*

David had obviously given this poem a lot of thought. I can picture him sat by candlelight, or maybe gaslight, writing this poem with a goose-quill pen. Sadly there is no indication whether or not it was included in the parish magazine.

During the late 1890s David's health starts to deteriorate and his behaviour radically changes. For example, a log book entry for May 1897 reports, *'D. Bloy slept in the dormitory. He, Bloy has been very restless at times. Baxendale, a fellow inmate, says the night previous to Bloy being removed from the block, he was moaning and crying nearly the whole night and frequently out of bed'* A further entry from October 1897, states that, *'Bloy on returning from chapel ran into the ....room and threw his arms around the neck of the boy Pither and kissed him'.* I offer no comment! Shortly before David died in 1911, his nephew George Bloy, who was the son of his elder brother William, wrote to Broadmoor requesting to see his uncle. I don't think this visit happened as the letter was not answered! On the 15th July 1911, David Bloy died on the Broadmoor cricket field. There are two incident entries in David's case file:

*'David Bloy on going to the cricket field appeared
in his usual health and quite cheerful and told me it
was cooler going out of the block. On the cricket
field he became suddenly very ill and was at once
seen by Dr Fullerston and returned to the block. On
his arrival he was examined by Dr Fullerston and
found to be dead at 4.20 pm. He was carried from
the cricket field by A.Lorick and A.Smith. Dr.
Fullerston, being present'.*

*'At about 3.30 this afternoon in the cricket field,
Att. Wilkins came to me and said D Bloy
complained of pain in the chest. I went and saw him
at once. He said he felt a little better took a drink of
oatmeal water, walked about for a time then sat
down on the grass resting his back against the seat,
shortly after he gave a kind of shout. Att. Wilkins
(who was close by) loosened his shirt collar and ran
for Dr Fullerton (who was fielding at the time). He
was with Bloy within a few seconds and was
removed to Block 3 on a stretcher with Dr Fullerton
in attendance'.*

At the age of 67 David Bloy was dead. An inquest held at
Broadmoor on 17th July 1911, recorded the cause of death as
'Sycope', which is fainting or sudden loss of consciousness
from which the patient usually quickly recovers; whereas
another document assigned the cause of death as Epilepsy.
David's father, William, had died in 1898, so his nephew
George Bloy was informed of his death. Because of the
distance from Grimsby to Broadmoor, it is unlikely that
anyone attended the funeral; no family members were there to
mourn his death.

From the events with David and medical reports which I
obtained for John Bloy, it appears that insanity (epilepsy) and
associated anger and violence were a hereditary family trait?
That however, is where the similarity between David and John
ends. Scrutiny of the case files for John suggests that he was,
and I am sorry to say this about my great-great-uncle, a deeply
disturbed and vile man. To examine John's story, I have to

return to the death of his mother Mary Ann in December 1866, a death with which, having now seen his case file and some correspondence concerning John, I am more convinced he had something to do.

John must have been very close to his mother, as his grief over her death, according to St John's records, apparently became too hard for him to bear. He was struggling to cope with it and his behaviour became very erratic, very violent and unpredictable. Or, I ask myself, was he really struggling with the burden of guilt from somehow, maybe accidently, being involved in her death. On the 17th January 1867, just over a month after his mother's death, John, at the age of 17 whilst employed as an apprentice shoemaker, was committed to St John's Hospital, a lunatic asylum, at Bracebridge Heath in Lincoln. The admissions record, (number 1792), for John's entry into St John's indicates that he was committed as a 'pauper lunatic' on the authority of the Reverend Charles Benjamin Lowe, who had been instituted as the Rector of Tydd St Mary a few months before in August 1866, and Richard Winfrey, whom I believe to be a local magistrate. John was described as *'well-nourished and in general good health suffering from mania and subject to epileptic fits'*. The cause of John's 'lunacy' is stated as the death of his mother!

This is indeed tragic as most likely, prior to his mother's death, John would not have been totally imbecilic. He was employed as an apprentice shoemaker, an occupation that requires both cognitive and motor skills, which an imbecile would probably not possess. John, like his brother David, suffered from epilepsy or another form of mental illness, medical science of the time had not yet identified, which caused occasional bouts of unstable violent behaviour. John's actual case records from St John's, do however add a more darkly disturbing perspective to aspects of John's character and nature. It states as the cause of his mania, *'excitement at the death of his mother'*, which in my opinion is very strange wording indeed. When I considered this, in conjunction with other 'expert' opinions of John's behaviour I found in the case files, it encouraged me to think that my original assumption could be correct. For example, in 1891 when a case was being made for John's incarceration into Broadmoor, where he eventually ended up, the Medical Superintendent of Lincoln County Asylum gave an account of the behaviour and character of John Bloy of whom he said, *'He was about the worst lunatic, morally, that I have known here'*. And points out the danger of keeping such a man in a pauper asylum, and he should be kept at Broadmoor.

After John was committed to St John's in 1867, although, he was not considered suicidal he was certainly considered a threat to others. It is recorded that: *These attacks, which sometimes continues for several hours reoccur frequently: At the time he is highly dangerous and during the interval he is an imbecile.* And, goes on to add;

> *...during the last attack he has been especially lurid with convulsions and he invariably threatens those about him. They believe he would murder them as he says he will do. The Rector of the Parish, the neighbours and his own relations has told this to me.*

There is clearly some acute mental instability in John's behaviour. The comment, *'he would murder them as he says he will do'*, is both interesting and, perhaps, revealing; and would not be the last time he threatens to murder (kill) someone. John's behaviour and subsequent committal to St John's occurred only two years after his brother David's, incarceration for murder in 1864. What we'll never know is how much the events regarding David affected and influenced John, who would have only been ten years old when David committed the murder and only fourteen years old when David was sent to Broadmoor.

In trying to make sense of the circumstances surrounding John's committal, I found myself wondering whether, during a period when he was not in control of his senses, due to his epilepsy, John actually attacked his mother whilst she was trying to restrain or calm him; and, that she took to her bed to recover from some injuries sustained in the attack, and 'pneumonia' was the fateful outcome. If that was the actual case, would it be 'manslaughter' and, given all that had happened before with David, was there then an attempt by the family, supported by others, to cover up what really happened? Although this is conjecture, it does seem to be a plausible explanation. What is certain, family history repeated itself; at the age of 17 years, John Bloy was committed to the lunatic asylum.

According to the case records, although he was described as *'not improved'*, in July 1867, six months after he entered St John's, John was discharged into the care of the church. I could not find an explanation, other than what I have suggested as to why it was the Rector who had John committed in the first instance and why was he then discharged into the care of the church and not his father? John's condition clearly did not improve, quite the opposite; according to the census of 1871, when he was 22 years old, John was still registered as a lunatic in an asylum in Lincoln. He had been re-admitted to St John's not long after his earlier release. John's behaviour would continue to deteriorate and become more extreme.

Whilst searching for John's case history, it was possible to review the records of other patients committed to the asylum in the 1870s. The alleged causes of their lunacy made for interesting but very disconcerting reading. They did however provide an indication of the extent and limitations of society and the medical professions' understanding of mental illness in the 19th century. For example, an architect was committed to the asylum for having a *'masturbation history'*, another patient, described as a gentlewoman, had *'change of life'* diagnosed as the cause of her mania. Other causes listed were, *'shock to the system from the extraction of teeth'*, *'loss of an only child'*, *'stress of being unemployed'* and *'being frightened by a mad woman in Spilsby in 1881'.* The reasons for being committed were many and varied and most would probably not be allowed today, but that was then. As I read the records, it did seem that if you had anything at all wrong with you that wasn't the norm, or you were an inconvenience to your family, you could very easily 'be shut away'.

John, when he wasn't escaping and being on the run, would spend much of the next twenty years in and out of St John's in Lincoln. In the discussion regarding David, I pointed out that during one of his escapes, in 1886, John tried to get to David and also seriously alarmed his stepmother Sarah Bloy, who was in fear of him. While at large on another occasion, on 30th June 1890, he was arrested and tried for housebreaking and sent to Fair Mile Asylum in Berkshire. The asylum General Statement Book, July 1890 records:

A criminal patient has been admitted, named John Bloy, from Reading Prison, on a warrant signed by Her Majesty. The man, however, has shown no signs of insanity since admission. He is here 'during Her Majesty's Pleasure'. The Superintendent has therefore informed the Secretary of State of his present opinion of the case and has asked him either to sanction his being detained a few weeks longer to see whether he is a case of recurrent insanity, or to obtain a Royal warrant for his release.

This, I discovered, is the stage in John's life where the discussion between various authorities seeking his incarceration into Broadmoor began; surprisingly, with conflicting opinions as to his mental state and what to do with him. For example, the above statement from the Fair Mile Medical Superintendent that, *'he has shown no sign of insanity ……. or should he be kept for a few weeks longer'*. They kept him for a few more weeks. Whereas a short time later, the Superintendent at Broadmoor added:

...from what I know of this man, who has on several occasions, visited his brother here, he is naturally defective, incapable of earning his livelihood and unfit to take proper care of himself. He has repeatedly been an inmate of Lincoln Asylum at

Bracebridge. When he takes to drink he becomes epileptic…….. Would it not be possible to send him to the care of his father William Bloy?

The case file informs us, *'Father is 74 years of age and is sick… he states he is unable and unwilling to take care of his son'* and adds, *'the only place for John would be the Holbeach Union'*. He remained at Fair Mile from where in February 1891, he escaped:

A criminal patient, John Bloy, has escaped from the asylum on the 3rd instant somewhat mysteriously; he is a housebreaker, and seems as far as the Superintendent can discover to have picked the lock of his ward. Being aware that this patient has expressed a great wish to be sent to Broadmoor Criminal Asylum, where a brother of his already is, and thinking it very possible that he would commit a crime of sufficient gravity to ensure his confinement in Broadmoor, the Superintendent has taken special precautions to inform the police in Berkshire and Oxfordshire of his suspicions, and the authorities of Scotland Yard have also been supplied with his description, nothing has yet been heard of the patient.

What an ominous warning this superintendent has given, *'he would commit a crime of sufficient gravity to ensure his confinement in Broadmoor'*. John's freedom was short-lived as he was found on the 9th of March 1891, very ill by the roadside and was taken to the Amesbury Union in Wiltshire. He had a letter in his pocket from his brother David, which encouraged Richard Lyle, the Master of the Union to write to Broadmoor,

…will you kindly inform him (David) of his brother's illness, and ask him to give me any information he can concerning his brother, as to

*where he belongs, so that I may communicate with
his friends.*

The Fair Mile case file states, *'March 1891, the criminal
lunatic John Bloy, whose escape was reported at the last
meeting, has been brought back to the asylum'.* It was
considered pointless sending him back to prison. John
however, would make many more attempts to escape from the
Fair Mile asylum.

The discussion regarding John's welfare in the case files
reveals that some of the major questions about where he
should be incarcerated were: where should he be detained, the
County Asylum in Lincoln, The Holbeach Union Workhouse
or Broadmoor? And which authority, or who, was going to pay
for his upkeep? Within these records, I found another
submission arguing the case for his admittance into
Broadmoor, which added the most alarming and disturbing
dimension to his character and behaviour. This is an edited
extract from a letter that Dr Marsh of St John's Hospital in
Lincoln wrote in May 1891:

*This man's first admission here was on 17th January
1867. He was then 17 years of age.....and was
suffering from mania and epilepsy. Relieving officer
accompanying him said that on the day of death of
mother.... he had an epileptic fit followed by
excitement ... and threatened those around him....
His brother was an inmate here (Lincoln County
Asylum) and is now an inmate of Broadmoor. John
Bloy has made his escape from this asylum on no
less than 6 times. On three of these occasions he
took another patient with him. Thrice he affected his
escape by picking the lock of the ward. At lock
picking, he is adept. He used to tell some of the
inmates that he could pick any lock. On the last
three occasions, he was under special supervision
at the time, which he evaded by making an excuse to
go to the WC.*

On 31st July 1878 having been well for some time and of good behaviour he was allowed to go to the care of his brother who is a respectable man and in a good business in Grimsby as a marine store dealer. John Bloy committed theft on his brother and made a sexual assault on a little girl who visited the shop. He attempted to poison himself by drinking about a pint of Benzolene and was found adjusting a rope around his neck. On several occasions he was suspected of attempting sodomy on some of the inmates and I believe him to be capable of any villainy... He has since been an inmate of other Asylums and Unions. He did a great amount of mischief to many of the inmates.

As early as 1871 there were presentiments of John's wickedly evil nature, *I believe him to be capable of any villainy.* Despite these ominous warnings, there were still conflicting opinions regarding his mental state. I began to wonder whether John was actually manipulating the system and 'playing the game'. After all he was a crafty and devious man and, within certain activities, he could be very resourceful. Several medical examiners could not agree whether he was insane. For example in the Fair Mile report for the year ending December 1891, although it states that John was, *'Found to be insane on arraignment for housebreaking on 30th June 1890'*, it goes on to report on John's mental condition, *'... he is a man of rather low moral development, but as I have informed the Secretary of State in letters concerning him, I think it is difficult to certify that he is at the present time a lunatic'*. The report goes on to add, *'I think he might be sent to a Workhouse or to the care of his friends'*.

In May 1892, the Fair Mile case-file reports:

...the criminal lunatic John Bloy escaped during the night of April 30th about 10pm by picking first the lock of his single room and then that of the external door of the ward. The Superintendent accordingly

wrote a strongly worded letter to the Secretary of State in consequence of which the patient was removed, after his recapture by the police, to Broadmoor Asylum.

Enough was enough! In the early part of May 1892, the case being made for John's incarceration into Broadmoor took on a new urgency. On the 5th May, the Home Office instructed:

Sir, With reference to the case of John Bloy, a Criminal Lunatic who has escaped from the Moulsford (Fair Mile) Lunatic Asylum and is now at large, I am directed by the Secretary of State to say that if Bloy be captured in the neighbourhood of Broadmoor Asylum and brought directly there, he orders you to detain him pending the receipt of formal authority.
    I am sir
    Your obedient servant
    Godfrey Ludington
    Under Secretary of State

Moulsford (Fair Mile) Lunatic Asylum received the formal authority and John was captured the same day. On the 7th May 1892, he was sent to be detained in Broadmoor, where he would remain for the rest of his life. The case file entry for his admission into Broadmoor informs us that John, *'sometimes attempts to assault the officer in charge of him'*. No photographs of John could be found, but I now have a good idea what he looked like. Contained within the file, there is a brief sketch of his appearance; John was described thus: 43 years old, of fair complexion, fair coloured hair and having blue eyes. He was of medium build, 5ft -1inch tall and weighed 10st- 9lb. The description goes on to add: he had round shoulders, peculiar looking eyes, squints and a shuffling walk. He has burn marks above his right ankle and on left shin, in addition to a mark on the right side of his groin and a rash on his shoulders. Not what you would call a handsome man!

While in Broadmoor, John did not keep good health; there were several entries to this effect. For example in 1893, he was seriously ill with apoplexy, which his family in Grimsby were informed about. A further entry stated;

> *'...John Bloy when sitting by the day room fire smoking, commenced ranting and became unconscious and was immediately put to bed in the infirmary and seen by Dr Isaac at 3.45pm. Mustard poultices and leeches were applied at once. His temperature was one point below normal'.*

His father, William Bloy, who by then was 77 years old, was informed by letter of John's health on 9th December 1893. He recovered from that bout of illness, but he was never a well man from there on.

John never managed to escape again and was kept at Broadmoor in a deteriorating state of health until he died on the 3rd November 1904; he was 54 years old. Bright's disease was stated as the cause of death. Not surprisingly, his story didn't end with his death. Even from the grave he continued to torment his stepmother Sarah Bloy, who lived in fear of him. I have previously commented that John was not happy his father had remarried. Is it reasonable therefore, to assume John's unhappiness is intrinsically linked to the fact that he may have, albeit accidently, had something to do with his mother's death? And consequently, he really resented Sarah becoming part of his father's life. Nearly six years after John died, on the 4th February 1910 the minister of a Methodist Church in Croydon writes:

> *Dear Sir,*

> *Will you kindly inform me whether John Bloy is still in the Asylum or not. I write for his widowed mother [sic] who is associated with one of my churches and was startled a few days ago by the sudden appearance of a man who resembled her son. And*

inasmuch as she was threatened by this particular
son [sic] some years ago before he was put away,
the old lady has been in a state of agitation for some
days. An early reply will oblige, for which I enclose
a stamped envelope.
    Yours very truly
    Arthur Fawcett

When David Bloy died the following year in 1911, one of the darkest episodes in Walter's family history had finally ended.

Finding out the truth, however disturbing and deeply distressing it may be is what made the research I undertook so rewarding and fulfilling. Though I have to confess, because of the disquieting nature, there are aspects of David and John's story, which perhaps should have remained undiscovered!

Chapter Six

Making Their Way In The East Marsh Of Grimsby

During Queen Victoria's reign Great Britain became the richest and most and industrialised country on Earth. People were flocking into the towns and cities in search of employment. The population of the country as a whole was rising at an unprecedented rate and, due to the opportunities being provided through the industrial revolution, that of the towns and cities was increasing by leaps and bounds. In a very similar manner to that of the 'boom' towns of the 'California Gold Rush' during the period 1848 – 1855 in the United States, the growth of Grimsby was sudden and very rapid. Grimsby's population in 1800 was just over 1,500; by the end of the century, it had risen to nearly 70,000. Grimsby's 'gold rush' was fish-based. By a remarkable coincidence, the fortunes and precipitous growth of Grimsby occurred at the same time as the California Gold Rush, with the coming of the railway to the town in 1848 and the major development of the Grimsby Fish Docks in the 1850s. As the fishing industry developed, the Town expanded at an astonishing rate with many thousands of people arriving in the town. For some it was the call of the unknown and adventure. For others, it was the expectation of a better way of life, which is precisely why William and his younger brother Walter came to Grimsby.

By the last quarter of the 19th century, they were both living with their wives and families in the notorious East Marsh Area of Grimsby. And were building up their businesses: William was residing in Cressey Street, whilst running a 'Hawkers' business from East Street and Walter was listed as a 'Carter', living in Burgess Street. Walter, who arrived in Grimsby in the latter half of the 1870s, was probably encouraged to make the move by seeing how well his brother was faring. William, on whom I now briefly focus, had arrived in Grimsby much earlier. Records indicate that he established his business during the early part of the 1860s.

Grief and tragedy seem to be a regular lifestyle feature of this branch of the Bloy family tree. I was sorry to discover that, just like his brother Walter, William Bloy and his wife Harriett (nee Markham), who was born in 1847 in Wisbech, Cambridgeshire, also suffered appalling family misfortune. Three of William and Harriett's five children also died young. Their son William, died on the 11th April 1880 from measles and pneumonia, when only 17 months old. A second son, whom they had also called William, died on the 16th October 1883 from convulsions and bronchitis, when only three months old. And then, just a month later, their daughter Elizabeth also died when just three years old. The unhealthy living conditions and appalling overcrowding of the area of the East Marsh where they lived most certainly would have been contributory factors.

It is difficult to imagine how, but the census records show that in 1881, living with William, Harriett and their children, 13 year-old daughter Harriett and their seven year-old son George, in Spring Street, were seven lodgers: four of whom were described as 'Hawkers', plus a couple of sailors and a general labourer. Eleven people, including nine adults, living in one 'two up – two down' house must have been horrendous; especially when you consider that personal sanitation was provided through communal boxed privies that often had double or triple seats. I find it difficult to even contemplate being sat on the privy doing your 'business', with one or maybe two others sat alongside you, doing theirs. For obvious reasons, these privies were affectionately known as 'thunderboxes'. For me, being on the toilet is so personal; the thunderbox scenario doesn't bear thinking about!

Whether William and Harriett's lodgers saw Grimsby as a place for making their way in the world can only be assumed, as they had journeyed to Grimsby from as far afield as

Middlesex, Liverpool, Manchester, Nottingham and Sunderland. There are a wide variety of records, which indicate, due to the coming of the railway, the expansion of the docks and the growth of the fishing industry, that this was typical of the migration towards Grimsby in the second half of the 19th century.

William's family would suffer more appalling misfortune; within three years of their third child dying, his wife Harriett, when only 39 years old, died from broncho – pneumonia on the 28th March 1886. And, similar to the funeral arrangements that had been made for Walter's children, Harriett and her children were also buried in the Ainslie Street Cemetery. Sadly, during the 1880/90s and in just over ten years, the two brothers, William and Walter, who had both come to Grimsby with such high hopes and expectations for the future, had buried seven children and in William's case, his wife. How ironic is it, when people nowadays walk their dogs and children happily play in the park land that the Ainslie Street Cemetery became, they are doing so over the last mortal remains of many adults and their children who came to Grimsby and helped make it the town that it became.

During the early part of the 1880's, Walter and his wife Lucy looked after their niece Elizabeth (William's daughter) when she was a baby. Why they chose to do this may be explained by the fact that in 1881, they were childless; their son William had died in 1880 when only a month old and William and Harriett were living in a dreadful overcrowded situation with their two older children and the seven lodgers. Perhaps more relevantly, just before Elizabeth was born, William Bloy, at the 'General Quarter Sessions of the Peace', held in Grimsby on the 26th October 1880, was sentenced to six months' imprisonment with hard labour for larceny. During his time in prison, his wife Harriett may have struggled to cope and turned to her in-laws for help. Details of William's trial were published in an interesting manner by the local newspaper, 'The Grimsby News', on the 27th October 1880:

'STEALING AND RECEIVING'

Henry Bond (17), a fisher-lad, and William Bloy, on bail were charged – the former with stealing, and the latter with receiving well knowing it to have been stolen, a quantity of fat, value 7 shillings, the property of Charles Calvert, smack owner, Grimsby. Bond pleaded guilty, and Bloy not guilty. Mr Russell was for the prosecution. The former was directed to stand down, and the case against Bloy was taken. Prosecutor, who lives in King Edward Street, said that early in September last, he had a keg of fat standing in his back yard, and he missed it on the 24th of September, and acting on certain information, he went to see Bloy. He found him at Mr Brown's and said "You have purchased some fat from a boy belonging to me, haven't you?" He said "Yes I purchased it for 2 shillings."

Prosecutor then said "Didn't you know that boy was apprentice to me?" The reply was "That boy as you term him is as big as what you are." The Witness next charged prisoner with having purchased things before from the lad – a pair of boots – and to having then been warned not to purchase anything more from him or else law would be brought against him. Bloy said that if the prosecutor would pay him the 2 shillings he had given for the fat he might have it; but prosecutor declined the offer, and said if the fat were not given up within an hour information would be given to the police.

It was not given up, and complaint was made to the police. Police-constable Ellis deposed to visiting the premises occupied by Bloy, who was a marine store dealer, and kept a book of his dealings. His visit was on the 13th October and the last entry in the book was the transaction as to the fat, which was entered as weighing 1st - 7lb net. The real quantity of fat was 29lb. The Prisoner in defence, said the lad Bond came to him and said his master had 'broke' and told him he might make what he could of the fat. He weighed the fat, took off what he thought affair tare for the tub and paid Bond for it a fair trade price. He denied that he had ever been warned by the prosecutor about dealing with the lad, and on this point he called Bond, who, on being sworn, said he had never been to his shop before, and did not know him. Some time ago he had parted with a pair of boots, but not to Bloy, with whom he had had no transactions at any time. Jonathon Cox, a Cooper, New Market Place, also called by Bloy said he had bought fat from the prisoner. The price depended on the quality. He had examined the "grease" in court, and valued it at 17 shillings per cwt. at the most.

The jury, after a brief consultation, returned a verdict of guilty. Bond pleaded guilty likewise to a previous conviction for felony. The Chairman, in sentencing Bond to three months imprisonment, with one year's police supervision, said the sentence was lighter than it otherwise would have been in cases of this kind, but the court believed the prisoner to have been led away by Bloy. His receiving the fat from Bond, and giving so small a sum for it, showed he had been in the habit of leading boys in prisoner's position to commit depredations of this kind. The court considered Bloy to be much more guilty in this case than Bond, and therefore sentenced him to six months hard labour.

William was sent down to Lincoln Prison with hard labour, which in Victorian times was very hard indeed. As an element of segregation became part of a prison sentence, for both petty and serious crimes, hard labour was often carried out in a prisoner's cell or under guard in silence. Most prisons had a 'Treadmill' or tread-wheel installed, where the prisoner simply walked the wheel all day. In some prisons, the treadmill provided flour to make money for the gaol, from which the prisoners earned enough to pay for their keep. However, in later times, there was no end product and the treadmill was walked just for punishment. It became loathed by the prisoners. Another equally pointless device was the 'Crank'. This was a large handle, in their cell, that a prisoner would have to turn thousands of times a day. This could be tightened by the warders, making it harder to turn, which resulted in their nickname of 'screws'. It is hard to believe that these punishments were not abolished until 1898, which is just a couple of generations ago!

Ironically, a cousin of William and Walter's, the son of their uncle Allen Bloy, who was also called William (b.1846) and still lived in rural Lincolnshire, fared much better at the General Quarter Session that was held three years previously in Spilsby on the 23rd October 1877. He was acquitted of larceny. This particular William was the brother of Henry Bloy, who at the time was the Police Constable of Digby, a village situated just outside Spilsby. Henry must have been a very relieved policeman indeed to see his brother acquitted. How embarrassing it would have been had he not!

To develop an understanding of how William and Walter had fared business-wise in Grimsby, in addition to the reference library and national censuses, local trade directories were scrutinised. The following information, which has been taken from a range of Grimsby Trade Directories, provides important dates and business records for them both and is worthwhile to note.

Referring in the first instance to the business development of our Walter's grandfather, Walter Bloy was listed in the 1880 Grimsby Trade Directory, as being employed as a 'Carter', operating from Burgess Street. He must have somehow prospered and saved up or acquired some start-up capital. Because, fifteen years later in 1895, Walter was registered in the same Trade Directory, as a self-employed Coal Dealer and

'Wagonette Proprietor', meaning he had a horse and cart for hire; the Victorian equivalent of a 'White Van Man'. If you wanted something shifted, he had the means to do it. Six years later in 1901, Walter's Coal Merchant business appears to be still thriving because the family had moved addresses. With his wife Lucy, who would sadly die later that year, and his son Walter Sidney, now aged 16 and employed as a 'news office boy', he was then living at 115 Victoria Street. Also living with them at that time was a lodger Joseph Robinson, a labourer from the nearby village of Killingholme, and a servant Beth Crayston aged 36. As it appeared to have become a male household after Lucy died, i.e. Walter, his son and a lodger, I'm inclined to think that Beth Crayston may have been their servant, who looked after them. If this was not the case, she was just another lodger!

In 1903, two years after Lucy's death, Walter moved his Coal Merchant's business to Garden Street, where it remained until his death thirty two years later. Further relevant entries in the Grimsby Trade Directories indicate that his son, Walter Sidney, had left the newspaper business and joined his father's Coal Merchant business. At the time of his death in 1916, Walter Sidney Bloy was also described as a Coal Merchant. Walter Bloy senior would carry on trading as a Coal Merchant in Garden Street until he went into administration in 1923. And, after being released from administration in 1924, according to the trade directories he was still listed as a Coal Merchant in 1933. He died in 1935

When I examined the businesses of Walter's great-uncle William, it does appear that despite the setback of being imprisoned in 1880 for receiving stolen goods, William became a successful businessman; perhaps more so than his brother Walter. William Bloy first appears in the Grimsby Trade Directory in 1880 when he was registered as a Marine Store Dealer operating from East Street, whilst residing at Cressey Street. By the 1890s, William, was still trading as a self-employed Marine Store Dealer. According to the 1891 census document, William, then age 57 and living with his family at 86 King Edward Street was described as a self-employed 'hawker', which undoubtedly meant that he sold items, which he 'hawked' around to potential customers. He was, in modern parlance, a 'wheeler dealer' and as we have seen from his court case for 'receiving stolen goods', not adverse to a bit of dodgy dealing. His son George, my father's first cousin, who, some years later, would correspond with his Uncle David in Broadmoor, although only 16 years old at the time of the 1891 census, was also described as a hawker.

By 1906, William was operating as a Marine Store Dealer, from 184 King Edward Street, where the business became successful and remains to this day. George, now aged 32, was listed as a Bottle Dealer operating from 175 King Edward Street. During the early 1920s William Bloy and Sons were still dealing in Marine Stores from King Edward Street; George had moved his business to 180 Burgess Street. And then, sometime between 1923 and 1935, William and George's businesses must have merged together, because by 1935, William Bloy and Sons were listed as general dealers in all kinds of Scrap Metals and second-hand bottles operating from 184 King Edward Street. The advert William Bloy and Sons used within the trade directory of 1935 to promote their business claims that the business was originally established in 1865, may indeed be correct as William arrived in Grimsby shortly after the 1861 census. Curiously though, in Dawson's 1871 Directory of Grimsby there are no Bloy businesses listed at all! That does not mean William wasn't in Grimsby and already trading in some fashion at that time. He just wasn't listed in Dawson's directory. Walter of course, couldn't appear in any trade directory as early as that, as he didn't arrive in Grimsby until much later.

William and latterly, Walter, established their businesses in Grimsby during an exciting period in the 19th century when the town grew rapidly. The population increased eightfold; Grimsby became the world's biggest fishing port with new support businesses for the docks and fishing industry springing up. As it is close by the docks, much of this expansion and population growth took place in the East Marsh area of Grimsby, where William and Walter lived and worked. In

1876, the East Marsh was described by a Borough Councillor as *'such a vile place'*. Life in the East Marsh during the second half of the 19th and into the 20th century was certainly not a bed of roses! To provide a further historical context for this story I believe it is important to be aware of the fundamental differences of what life must have been like during the 1870s and 80s in the East Marsh of Grimsby, compared with village life in rural Lincolnshire. Developing a sense of awareness of the social circumstances, and the hardship and deprivation they, and others, must have faced as they made their way in the world, will help us appreciate all the more what they actually achieved.

The development of the East Marsh of Grimsby is not just a story of rapid industrial expansion, but also one of poverty and social injustice in Victorian England. A critical perspective of life in Grimsby in the 1800s, is provided by local historian, Dr Alan Dowling, in his book, 'Grimsby: Making the Town 1800 – 1914'. His seminal work, among others, has been extensively drawn from to provide context for this element of the story. The coming of the railway and the development of the new docks were commented upon in June 1847 in the Lincoln, Rutland and Stamford Mercury:

> ...*this place now presents a most animated appearance. The vast number of men employed at the Railway and Dock works, together with the great influx of strangers and new residents, has caused such a change in the aspect of trade as Grimsby has never witnessed.*

Although the second half of the 19th century saw Grimsby's rise to prominence as the world's premier fishing port, the Victorian period developed an almost draconian social code, exaggerating the class divisions, with the working class being deprived of opportunity and the ability to earn a wage above subsistence level. Many in Grimsby at that time were subjected to such hardships. Dowling points out that the Manchester, Sheffield and Lincolnshire Railway did not see as its concern the need to provide housing for this great influx of strangers and new residents. Fortunately, others such as the Freemen of Grimsby did and, were more than happy to turn agricultural land over for housing. Building plots were still vacant on the East Marsh Lots and East Fitty Lots. Moreover, they were in an ideal location to provide mass working class housing, being adjacent to railway line workings and handy for both the new Royal dock site and the new fish dock (Dowling, 2007: p 57-62).

Victoria Street, Grimsby - c. 1890

(Photograph reproduced courtesy of North East Lincolnshire Library Service)

With the development of the East Marsh of Grimsby during the period 1840 – 1870, the frontage area of Victoria Street North became commercial premises, or was generally occupied by middle class families. By contrast, the area of the East Marsh, which became Burgess Street, King Edward Street, Spring Street and Cressey Street, where William and Walter originally settled after arriving from Tydd St Mary, was developed with closely-packed working-class houses for letting, the consequence of which was intolerable overcrowding and appalling living conditions. This area very quickly acquired a reputation for containing some of the worst slums in Grimsby.

According to Dowling, in 1850 it was commented upon that many owners of small plots of land had *'knocked up a lot of small tenements not fit for dogs to live in'*. An inquiry for the General Board of Health in 1850 was particularly critical of the courts and back-to-back houses, which were crammed into the original lots of 360 square yards. The inquiry identified Ellis's buildings, off Lower Burgess Street, which was entered by a covered passage, often referred to, with some justification, as 'rat-runs', contained 12 two-storied houses with only a ten-foot width between opposing houses. The houses had no back doors; sixty people lived in, and shared toilets, in this court. Another block of 14 houses in King Edward Street were described as overcrowded, offensive and unhealthy, and were occupied by *'swarms of the vilest class'*. These houses were all back-to-back with the court's eight communal box privies facing the front of the houses close to the doors of the living rooms. The photograph below, which needs little explanation, shows Upper Spring Street that ran between Victoria Street and King Edward Street. Many people found that they could not afford the rents that were being charged and so they rented out space in their room to one or more lodgers who paid between twopence and fourpence a day. William, Harriett and their children, as we have already seen, at one stage shared their house in Spring Street with seven adult lodgers.

Upper Spring Street, Grimsby c. 1890s

(Photograph reproduced courtesy of North East Lincolnshire
Library Service)

Victorian England, among other things, was notable for a wide range of social contrasts. Great wealth and extreme poverty lived side by side because the slum housing, sometimes referred to by historians as rookeries, were often not much more than a stone's throw from the larger elegant houses of the rich. The name 'rookeries' was given to these dwellings because of the way people lived without separate living accommodation for each family. The analogy being whereas other birds appear to live in separate families, rooks do not. Neither did the very poor in the slum dwellings of the towns and cities.

Another example of the poor quality housing available on the East Marsh was Whitehall Yard, situated off King Edward Street, where seventy-seven people lived in only 18 houses. The house walls were only half a brick thick, which is only 4 inches, and the box privies, water closets a luxury still some way off in the future, were situated at the end of the court, *'the whole of which is a complete swamp'*. The stench, especially in the summer, must have been appalling. The smell, noise and general unpleasantness provide a dismal and depressing perspective of the 'two up – two down' living conditions for the not so well-off 'working classes' at that time. Within all this stench and squalor, to see children running around barefooted was a common sight during this period of history.

In addition to poverty, overcrowding and poor sanitation, the courtyards and alleyways became notorious as an area frequented by prostitutes and their clientele, who were often 'accommodated', day and night, standing up against the walls of the houses and passageways in full view of other residents. This became known in Victorian times as a *'tuppenny upright'*. An indication of the extent of this particular problem is revealed in the 1871 census, which documents that the residents of four of the houses in the Whitehall Yard included 10 prostitutes. It was therefore inevitable that, in areas such as these, associated anti-social behavioural problems such as muggings, drunkenness, disorderly conduct and violence would thrive and be commonplace. Extremes of antisocial behaviour would have been witnessed throughout the whole East Marsh of the 19th century.

Clearly, individuals or groups of people behaving badly in a deviant or a non-normative manner are nothing new. Throughout the centuries, many governments have tried to control, contain, or curb these forms of antisocial behaviour, often through the form of repressive legislation. In the mid-18th century, for example the *Gin Act* 1751 was voted, to reduce the type of binge-drinking so vividly portrayed by William Hogarth in his painting *Gin Lane* (1750). It doesn't take a great deal of imagination to think Hogarth could just as easily have been portraying the centre of any British town on a

Saturday night today. Ironically, begging and poverty were supposed to be swept away into workhouses during the Victorian era.

In the middle of the 19th century, Henry Mayhew, an investigative journalist, wrote a series of articles for the Morning Chronicle about the way the poor lived and worked. Though he was mainly writing about London, he could just as easily been talking about the slums or deprived areas of any industrialised town or city. Even today the world over, all slums have the same stench and feeling of social decay about them. Social deprivation and poverty stinks, both metaphorically and physically, wherever it is! In an article published on 24th September 1849, Mayhew described a street with a tidal ditch running through it, into which drains and sewers emptied. The ditch contained the only water the people in the street had to drink, and it was *'the colour of strong green tea'*, in fact it was *'more like watery mud than muddy water'*. This is an extract from one of his reports:

> *...as we gazed in horror at it, we saw drains and sewers emptying their filthy contents into it; we saw a whole tier of door-less privies in the open road, common to men and women built over it; we heard bucket after bucket of filth splash into it.*

He went on to say:

> *...the condition of a class of people whose misery, ignorance, and vice, amidst all the immense wealth and great knowledge of "the first city in the world", is, to say the very least, a national disgrace to us.*

Mayhew could easily have been referring to the East Marsh of Grimsby, where the Bloy brothers established their businesses. It is difficult to imagine how people could live, work and raise a family in such conditions. Little wonder then that infant mortality was so high among the 'working classes'.

In England during the second half of the 19th century, epidemics of Whooping Cough and Measles were frequent occurrences, and as we have already seen, two children, who would have been Walter's cousins had they survived, died through these diseases. In addition, Grimsby, and in particular the East Marsh, on several occasions had to contend with outbreaks of cholera. One particular cholera outbreak in 1893, which killed 246 people, was believed to have been caused by poor and *'unwholesome'* seafood products. The following is an extract from a bulletin 'Foul Fish and Filth Fevers' presented around that time in Seattle, United States of America, of all places, by J Lawrence-Hamilton from the Royal College of Surgeons:

Of all the food trades the fishing population are the most slovenly and dirty in their habits, overcrowded in their dwellings, and therefore more prone to endemic as well as epidemic infections; for, though apart from the manner in which inoculation occurs, cholera, jail-fever, virulent smallpox, typhoid, typhus, diphtheria, leprosy and the 'plague' etc., have all been associated with poverty and avoidable filth, of course unwholesome food and dirty surroundings diminish our resistance to these diseases, against which a healthier, stronger condition obtainable by sanitary conditions and good food become immune or free. When light is thrown upon the state of Grimsby, a fishing port of great importance, we find that their sanitation is imperfect and that the fish trade has remained in its old-fashion and unhygienic ways and that poverty is increasing.

Eventually, in 1861, the Grimsby Borough Council adopted building byelaws to prevent overcrowding and sub-standard building, but it was too late to affect the earlier development of the East Marsh. In 1876, shortly before Walter Bloy arrived from Tydd St Mary to live in this area of the East

Marsh, a local councillor drew attention to a tenement property in a yard off Lower Burgess Street. He complained that *'the houses were a disgrace to the owner and that if you travelled down the yard you were likely to either be suffocated by the stench, fall into a cesspool or be hung by a clothes line.'*

During the period 1840 - 1901 the population of Grimsby grew by approximately 65,000. Interestingly, according to census information of 1841 only 1.3% of all working males in Grimsby were listed as fishermen. But, by 1861 it had risen to 12% of a rapidly growing workforce. The reason was quite simple. After Grimsby was connected to the growing rail network and the rest of the country in 1848, it became possible to forward cargoes and fish landed at Grimsby onwards to the cities of Manchester, Sheffield and especially London. The 1850s in reality became the 'take off' years of Grimsby's modern fishing industry and support businesses. The first sailing smacks began operating from the town, and the now well-known Grimsby landmark, the Dock Tower, based on the design of the Palazzo Pubblico in Sienna, Italy, had become operational. In 1857, the first specialised fish dock opened and the port was growing and developing. William Bloy established and developed his Marine Stores dealer business in the 1860s to supply the local fishing and dockside businesses. Walter later established a Carter's business and then the Coal Merchant's business in the 1880s, to meet the needs of the growing population of the town.

The newly built railway lines and the speedy distribution opportunities created, meant that fish landed at Grimsby could be easily and rapidly transported by train inland; so everyone could have fresh fish. Inevitably the fishing industry grew; merchants from Spain, France and Germany as well as London became regular visitors to the town's fish market. Many fishermen, particularly those from the South Coast and the Thames region, were attracted by this new distribution system, and began initially to land their catch at this progressive port and then, ultimately to operate from Grimsby. The following figures illustrate the growth of Grimsby in terms of fish being despatched to the cities. In 1854, only 453 tons of fish were despatched that year by rail from Grimsby Docks Station. By 1900, this figure had increased to 133,791 tons of fish being despatched. Just ten years later, in 1911, 196,754 tons of fish were despatched by rail from Grimsby. These digressions are relevant to my metaphorical search for Walter as they provide an explanation why so many ancestors arrived in Grimsby.

It is not hard therefore, to imagine Grimsby as a 'boom' town with people arriving all the time thinking and hoping that they could make their fortunes. Local author Peter Chapman, in his book, 'Grimsby: The Story of the World's Greatest Fishing Port' (2002), points out that many did make their fortunes and became important 'movers and shakers' in the wider development of the Grimsby community. Although it is not the intention to discuss these people much further within this story, there is merit in citing some examples. Arthur Jeffs (1866-1945) for example, was one of the nine children of George Jeffs who, together with his brother Charles, came to Grimsby from Ramsgate in the growth years to found one of the best known of the many trawling firms. Another worthy of mention is Sir Alec Black (1873-1942), the trawling magnate, horse racing enthusiast and great philanthropist, one of Grimsby's foremost figures. Sir Alec came from a very modest family background, his mother sold cakes. He went to work on the docks and eventually owned the largest fleet of trawlers in the world (Chapman: 2002). Walter Bloy, the focus of this story, would actually work for Sir Alec Black for a short time during the 1930s.

To gain a meaningful and relevant perspective, the increasing population of Grimsby should really be considered in relation to the number of houses which were available. To do so would enable us to put some of the problems I have described in this section into context. When reviewing the relationship between the number of houses and the population, it needs to be borne in mind that the figures stated for the number of houses, represents Grimsby as a whole, and not just the East Marsh.

Year	Population	Houses
1801	1,524	265
1841	3,700	958

After the railway came to Grimsby in 1848 the population increased dramatically

1861	11, 067	2,364
1881	28,503	6,245
1901	63,138	13,841

Old Market Place, Grimsby c.1890s

(Photograph reproduced courtesy of North East Lincolnshire Library Service)

By the beginning of the 20th century, the town of Grimsby had developed into two distinct areas, the first being the idyllic small residential market town with churches, public houses and commercial buildings. As the photograph of the Old Market Place shows, it was clean, orderly and probably not a bad place to live and work. In contrast, the second area barely less than a mile away, spreading out from the East Marsh, a sprawling industrialised town, with an ever- increasing dependency on the docks and its main product, fish. It was into this environment of landlord exploitation, poverty, degradation, unhealthy living conditions and general hardship for some, that Walter's great-uncle William and grandfather Walter, had left the comparative tranquillity and much healthier, although impoverished, lifestyle of living in Tydd St Mary in Lincolnshire, to journey to Grimsby to pursue their dreams of a better life. As I now know that they were both relatively successful, this suggests to me that they must have worked hard to thrive in the cauldron of desperation and despair that was the Victorian East Marsh of Grimsby.

In contrast to Grimsby, Tydd St Mary is described in Whites Lincolnshire Directory (1872), as a pleasant village on the Wisbech Road in the most south-eastern angle of Lincolnshire, near the borders with Norfolk and Cambridgeshire. Its parish is bounded on the east by the River Nene, and has 974 inhabitants and 4772 acres mostly lying low, and formerly overflowed by the tides of Cross Keys Wash, but now by drainage converted into good land. It is in the Duchy of Lancaster, the manor Dunton is held by W. Goddard Jackson, Esq., and the Duke of Somerset and Trinity College, Cambridge among others, hold considerable portions of the land. The parish church (St Mary's) has a brick tower containing five bells, and surmounted by an elegant spire that is in the Decorated and Perpendicular styles. One of the south windows of the chancel has lately been filled with beautiful painted glass. At the east end of the northern aisle is an effigy of a knight in armour, probably a relic from the days of the De Roos family. The famous Nicholas Breakspeare, who later became Pope Adrian IV, was, according to Gough, at one time rector of this parish, but Archdeacon Trollope argues that this is in fact an error. The Mission house, in the Fen, is a handsome Gothic brick structure, erected in 1859 at a cost of £750. It is remarkable, as it is the first Church of England Mission house in the kingdom. The Wesleyans have a chapel, rebuilt in 1859 and with a pretty school building adjoining, which was attended by about 30 children. The free school was founded in 1740, by Dame Martha Trafford who left £185, which was laid out in the purchase of 15 acres of land, which was sold in 1811 for £600, with which, plus £100 borrowed, 12 acres of land at Tydd St Giles were bought. The school which was built in 1820 and rebuilt in1861 is attended by about 45 boys, of whom 35 are taught free. There is also an excellent national school for girls and infants.

This brief sketch of Tydd St Mary, with its good land, manor houses, handsome churches and schools, contrasts quite remarkably with the picture that I have presented of the East Marsh of Grimsby of the same period. When William and then Walter first arrived in Grimsby, it must have been a culture shock for them that took some getting used to. What is certain, living in Tydd St Mary they would have known, or been known, by nearly the whole of the village community. In Grimsby, until they became established and had made a name for themselves, they would have been just more faceless strangers, among the sea of many thousands that were arriving in Grimsby each year, as the population expanded. This was the choice they made in preference to living in a spartan family existence of trying to scrape a living as agricultural labourers in a rural village.

Before I finish discussing the Bloy family lineage and, move on to exploring other aspects of Walter's extended family, a brief summary of the history, fate and misfortunes of his immediate ancestors on his father's side is probably appropriate to recap at this stage. Walter's father Walter Sidney Bloy (b.1886) died in 1916, the result of a motorcycle crash; his grandfather Walter Bloy (b.1857) would live to the age of 78 before dying in 1935. However before he died, he would see all of his children, except Walter Sidney, die whilst still infants. The death of his daughter Grace Mabel was particularly harrowing. In addition to his children dying, his wife Lucy (Walter's grandmother) died when just 39 years old. Walter's grandfather also had to live with the knowledge and shame that two of his older brothers David (b.1844) and John (b.1850), were incarcerated in Broadmoor Criminal Lunatic Asylum, one of whom had stood trial for murder; and the other a deeply disturbed and deranged man, about whom there were some lingering concerns as to whether he was involved in the death of their mother Mary Ann (Walter's great-grandmother) who was only 48 when she died. In addition to which, Walter's grandfather would also experience the further shame of witnessing his eldest brother William (b.1840) being sent to jail with hard labour for larceny. As if that was not enough, Walter's grandfather also experienced, the public humiliation of his Coal Merchant's business going into administration. The consequence of that was his exclusion and being ostracised from the lives of Alice, his widowed daughter-in-law and. his grandchildren.

William, Walter's great-uncle, would see his wife Harriett die, like Lucy at the age of 39, and three of his children die whilst still infants. Walter's great-grandfather William Bloy (b.1816) and great-great-grandfather William Bloye (b.1780), were both impoverished agricultural labourers who had to live, struggle or thrive with whatever work they could obtain, under the 'hiring fair' system that was in operation in the late 18th and through the 19th century. There is no doubt whatsoever that, in financial terms, these ancestors were desperately poor and would have struggled to scrape a living. They were paupers.

To conclude this section; if I put aside for one moment any discomfort and unease I feel about my great-uncle David being a murderer and great-uncle John's lunacy, I confess I take some satisfaction in what my Bloy ancestors achieved. Knowing what I now know, and discovering how members of the family had strived to make a comfortable life, fills me with a sense of pride, as they succeeded against all the odds and in the face of adversity. My rationale is quite simple. It is, as I have previously said, from these humble, impoverished, agricultural labourer beginnings that all the Bloys in Grimsby and there are many, have been descended.

Chapter Seven

Being A Freeman And The Smith Family History

Through my father Walter I am a Freeman of the Borough of Grimsby by birth. I have always assumed that my Freeman status had been passed down through several generations of the paternal side of the Bloy family. However, when I researched the family history of Walter's mother, Alice Smith, I discovered that this was not the case at all. Before I explain this erroneous assumption and explore the ancestry of the Smith family in more detail, for purpose of clarity, I believe it is relevant to consider what being a Freeman actually means and how it shapes our story. Moreover, what does it tell us about the ancestors who were Freemen? Exploring the significance of the Freemen of Grimsby provided further contextualisation in respect of the history of the East Marsh of Grimsby. For example, it was Freeman land that was turned over to create housing in the East Marsh for the rising population during the early part of the 19th century. The more I understood of the history and role of the Freemen, it became abundantly clear that there was far greater importance attached to being a Freeman in the 19th and preceding centuries, than there is now in the 21st century. Discovering that several generations of Walter's extended family were enrolled Freemen of Grimsby, added an important social dimension to the history of the family.

The Freemen's Roll links the present to the past and, by understanding the history of Freemen and how one became a Freeman provides an indication of an individual's status and circumstances. Being a Freeman is a prestigious historical concept that, for Grimsby, started in the middle ages as the records of enrolled Freemen can be traced backwards several hundred years to the medieval times. Some would argue that the true origin of the concept of Freemen can be traced even further back to a legal system introduced by the Danes in around 900AD. During the early part of the 14th century, having secured the Charter giving the residents their freedom and the entitlement to two Burgesses (Freemen), Grimsby began to suffer a decline in trade. Primarily this was blamed on the silting up of the West Haven, (Grimsby's port area), with the consequence that an increasing number of ships started docking at Ravenserodd, a small village/port situated on the opposite side of the River Humber from Grimsby.

The convergence of the River Freshney, Grimsby's local river, into the West Haven to ease the silting up was considered essential and imperative. The Burgesses argued, because of the declining trade, they could not pay the fee-farm rent and, consequently, they petitioned to allow the King's waste places to facilitate that convergence, which was granted by 'Letters Patent' in 1341. Paradoxically, the medieval village of Ravenserodd was later destroyed during the latter part of the 14th Century by an 'Act of God'. As the sandbanks shifted the town swept away by the storms over the winter of 1356 – 1357, which led to its abandonment. With the subsequent increase in trade in the Haven and the movement of itinerant labour after the 'Black Death' plague, which was at its height during this time, the population of Grimsby began to grow again. A statistic which may be of interest to local historians is that, in 1360, the town of Grimsby supplied 11 ships and 171 mariners to King Edward III, as a contribution to the continuing war with France; this being half the number of ships and a quarter of the number of men provided by the port of London!

So, who are the Freemen of Grimsby and why are they relevant to this story? They currently number about 1060 and are descended from, or whose wives are descended from, Freemen of the old Borough of Grimsby, and who continue to reside within and pay rates to the Borough. As was typical of a male-dominated society, women could not become Freemen of the Borough in their own right. However, if they were the widow of a Freeman, their names could be entered onto the Freemen's Pastures Roll, enabling them to participate in the financial benefit that had been granted to the Freemen. The Pastures Roll lists the names and addresses of the Freemen of the Borough and the widows of Freemen who are currently entitled to benefit financially from the Freemen's estate, which is the land within the Borough, vested in the Freemen by the 'Letters Patent' granted by King Edward III in 1341.

Up until the Municipal Corporations Act of 1835, the life of a Freeman (Burgess) was one of public duty and responsibility. The Freemen were the only citizens permitted to vote in Parliamentary and Municipal elections and the only ones who could occupy positions of authority within the local government. Being a Freeman was a very serious business indeed. Each Freeman (Burgess), was required to swear an Oath of Allegiance, which I have reproduced here in *Middle English* with due reference made to *"The Rise of Grimsby, Volume 1, by Bob Lincoln"* published in 1913.

I must admit that, when I first read the Oath of Allegiance I initially struggled to make sense of it. However, that in itself does not matter. The nature and wording of the Oath indicates clearly enough how important the Freemen were.

The Burgess's Oath

This here, Ye Sir Mayor, Crowners, Bailiffs, and all the Court here present, that I shall trew faith bere, and trew Burgess be, to our Liege Lord the King, to his Heirs, to the Mayor here present, and his Successors and to the Commonalty of this the King's Burgh of Grymesby, for any Burage that I may claim or shall claim to hold of our Lord the King, and his Heirs, of the Mayor and Comalte of this the King's Burgh of Grymesby and their Successors. I shall be justifiable by the Mayor of this said Burgh for tyme being, to come to his summons what tyme that I shall be lawfully

*required by the officer thereto assigned. And not
absent myself without a cause reasonable to the
Mayor notified. Also I shall be justifiable by my
Mayor and his Burgesses to do and bere all the
Charges of Offices from the lowest to the highest
that belongs to the said burgh of Grymesby, at
any time that I shall by dew election chosen to
any of them. Also to the all franchises and
Freedoms by our Liege Lord the King and his
noble progenitors, graunted to the Mayor and
Burgesses of the said Burgh and all other
Ordinances, Freedoms and Customs, had and
used by the Mayor and his Burgesses for gud
gov'nance and mayntenying of this the King's
Burgh. I shall dewly sustene at my power.
Moreover, I shall not by reason of any Lordship,
or Mastership, nor ey'r means procure nor draw
no manner of Man to make profit agens the
Mayor or other Burg of Comen of this said Burgh
of Grymesby, theym to reprove or hurt whereby
any hev'ns or hurt may be to them, upon peyn of
forfitur of my freedom, if I thereof be lawfully
convicted. So help me God. And, by the contents
of the Book.*

In addition to benefitting financially from the Freeman
estate, there were many other advantages of being a Freeman.
Through the 'Letters Patent' granted to the Mayor and
Burgesses, certain waste and marsh lands, which were then
outside the Borough boundary, gave them the sole right to
pasture their sheep, cattle, horses, and the like, on this land.
This 'Freeman land' later became much more valuable as a
result of the development of the port and the building of the
new dock at Grimsby after 1796 and with the Manchester
Sheffield and Lincolnshire Railway Company line coming to
Grimsby in 1848. Land, which hitherto had been salt marsh,
became valuable building land; thus considerably increasing
the value of the Freemen's Estate through leases. Originally

the 'Letters Patent' referred to land in the area that became the East Marsh. In 1849, as a result of the Grimsby Pastures Acts, the Freeman estate was further expanded to include parcels of land in the Littlefield and Haycroft areas of Grimsby. The historical connection of the original granting of the land by the King was retained; when the East Marsh area was drained and developed during the 19th century, streets were named King Edward Street and Burgess Street; and were, as we now know, where for some time William and Walter Bloy would live and establish their businesses.

What is of particular importance and relevance to this story is, how did a man become 'free' and what does it tell us about those in Walter's family who were registered as 'Freemen'? After the granting of the 'Letters Patent', there were originally only two ways of obtaining freedom.

1. By being born the son of a Freeman; it being necessary for the father to be a residing Freeman at the time and for the birth to have taken place within the Borough.
2. Or servitude, by serving a seven-year indenture to a Freeman of the Borough.

These freedom criteria were later increased to include:

3. By marrying the daughter or widow of a Freeman
4. By purchase: in Grimsby it was necessary to be a Freeman of the Borough in order to trade within the Borough. Therefore, anyone who wished to trade within the borough bought their freedom to be able to do so. This practice became illegal in 1835.
5. By Gift: the recipient was expected to pay for the privilege. It was usually 'given' to potential Members of Parliament, the High Steward, the Recorder, and the like. This was also abolished by The Municipal Corporations Act of 1835.

In respect of our story, the purchase and gift options of becoming 'free' ceased to be in 1835, therefore any of Walter's ancestors who were made free and entered onto the Freemen's Roll after then, had to have done so by virtue of birth, marriage or the servitude of a seven-year indenture. I can immediately discount the servitude option, as none were indentured. It was a significant honour to be a Freeman, and it is worth noting that an individual's Freeman status could be permanently lost by: the receipt of parish poor relief in Grimsby or elsewhere, or by committing a felony. If, for example, Walter's great-uncle William had been a Freeman, he would have lost that status after his conviction for theft in 1880! Freeman status could also be temporarily lost if the Freeman went to live outside the borough, as Walter did. In these cases, a Freeman could be re-admitted onto the Pastures Roll, as Walter was, once they have returned to live within the borough for twelve months and, was again paying the rates to the borough. Freemen therefore, had to be law-abiding, upright and financially sound citizens who were contributing, through the payment of rates, to the upkeep of the community.

By understanding the tangible benefits, significance and responsibilities of being a Freeman of the Borough of Grimsby in the 19th century, I began to appreciate how influential the social status of my Freemen ancestors really was. In addition to the right to vote and the pasturing rights for their livestock, for the Freemen there were the added benefits of: freedom from the payment of tolls within and outside the borough, and the right of education for their children at the Corporation Grammar Schools for boys and girls, which opened in 1869 and closed in 1949. Through their involvement in the borough court, in practice, Freemen were running the town, as the Freemen's court provided all the local government Grimsby needed. Non-Freemen did not have the vote and therefore could not hold borough office. Until the reforms of the 1830s, all municipal duties were carried out by: Freemen, the Mayor, Common Councilmen, Aldermen, Constables and the Bailiff.

According to Dowling (2007: p.4), it was only the Freemen who were responsible for the day-to-day operation of the town's judicial and administrative systems. Unlike today, cases of assault, and drunkenness, being so commonplace then, were frequently settled with a fine, whereas theft would be dealt with much more harshly. For example, later in the story we shall see that, in 1830, an ancestor of Walter's wife, Grace Mary, was sentenced to be transported to Australia for seven years for the crime of stealing a coat. Although this particular sentence was given out in Spilsby and not Grimsby, it is appropriate to mention it now, because it conveys the prevalent attitude of the day. Theft was not tolerated! Dowling goes on to describe in explicit details how the courts would administer justice without fear or favour, *'in 1650, 'Ed. Wells, sen., being formally found guiltie of stealing 1 sheep...is adjudged to be stript from the wayst upward and whippt in the [Town] Hall till blood come'.* The spelling presumably is 17th century English and how it was recorded in the courts log. Dowling then goes on to show that there was no sexual discrimination in doling out this rough justice. *'In 1692, Bridget, wife of Henry Deane, found guilty of stealing a petticoat, and sentenced to be whipped at the whipping post, stripped to the waist, till her body be bloody'.* What very graphic and barbaric images these sentences provide!

My assumption that my Freeman status had descended to me through an unbroken line on the male side of the Bloy family was totally mistaken. A review of the Freeman Pastures Roll indicates that I had been made free 'by birth', at the Mayor's court in April 1971; and my father, Walter Bloy, had also been made free 'by birth' in October 1934 whilst residing in Fairmont Road, Grimsby; he was also re-admitted to the Pastures Roll in October 1944, when he returned to live in the borough after living from 1937-1944 in New Waltham, which was then outside the old Grimsby borough boundary. Whereas, Walter's father, my grandfather Walter Sidney Bloy, only became a Freeman by virtue of his marriage to my grandmother Alice Smith and was entered on to the Freeman Pastures Rolls in March 1910. Alice Smith was the daughter of George Henry Smith, a Freeman of the Borough. Prior to Walter Sidney Bloy being made 'Free', no other members of the Bloy family were listed as being Freemen of the Borough of Grimsby. Therefore, the Bloy family entitlement to Freeman status only started in the 20th century, in 1910. Although my entitlement for Freeman status, which came from my grandmother's family, had its origins in the early part of the 19th century, its source goes even further backwards into the 18th century, but not, as I discovered, through the Smiths' family lineage.

It is significant to note, in terms of potential status that the Smiths, Walter's maternal ancestors, were Freemen of the Borough of Grimsby during the 'boom' period of the 19th century when the town dramatically changed and expanded. Given the role of the Freemen, it is quite probable that they were involved in some of the crucial decision-making, which led to the Town developing in the manner it did. Consequently, it is not unrealistic to surmise that the Smiths may well have been active and important members of civic society in Grimsby during the 1850s and beyond. What a marked contrast this is to how Walter's paternal antecedents had lived; comfortable and respected, for one side of Walter's family, abject poverty and dire misfortune for the other!

George Henry Smith (b.1846), Walter's maternal grandfather, was enrolled as a Freeman by birth on 25th February 1878, and as he was granted Freeman status by birth, his father George Smith (b.1806), would have had to be a Freeman at the time George Henry Smith was born. At this point in my research, I found that the source of the family Freeman status changed yet again. George Smith was not a Freeman by birth; he had gained his Freeman status on the 30th July 1830, after his marriage in 1829 to Eleanor Jewitt, the daughter of John Jewitt, who had become a Freeman in 1802. John Jewitt was a Freeman by birth through his father Edward Jewitt (b.1748). Once I reached this juncture of the story, I took the search into my family's Freeman history no further. I must admit however, I found it a source of great delight and pride in knowing that my Freeman status, had I wished to do so, could be traced back on a continuous line, either through birth, marriage or even servitude, to the 14th century and the time of King Edward III. My family had played their part in shaping English history.

This has brought me to an appropriate position from which to explore, in more detail, who the Smiths and their antecedents were and, how they fit into and add to the story. The 'SMITH' Family tree shown below covers the period 1748 to the present and should be frequently referred to, to be able to make sense of my narrative.

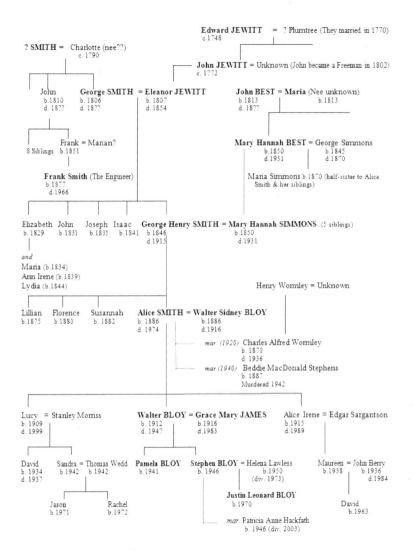

Edward JEWITT = ? Plumtree (They married in 1770)
c.1748

John JEWITT = Unknown (John became a Freeman in 1802)
c.1772

? SMITH = Charlotte (nee??)
c.1790

John   George SMITH = Eleanor JEWITT   John BEST = Maria (Nee unknown)
b.1810   b.1806   b.1807   b.1813   b.1813
d.18??   d.18??   d.1854   d.18??

Frank = Marian?   Mary Hannah BEST = George Simmons
8 Siblings b.1851   b.1850   b.1845
                                                                      d.1931   d.1870

Frank Smith (The Engineer)   Maria Simmons b.1870 (half-sister to Alice
b.1877   Smith & her siblings)
d.1966

Elizabeth John   Joseph Isaac   George Henry SMITH = Mary Hannah SIMMONS (5 siblings)
b.1829   b.1831 b.1835 b.1841 b.1846   b.1850
                                          d.1915   d.1931

and
Maria (b.1834)
Ann Irene (b.1839)
Lydia (b.1844)   Henry Wormley = Unknown

Lillian   Florence Susannah   Alice SMITH = Walter Sidney BLOY
b.1875   b.1880   b. 1882   b.1886   b.1886
                                      d. 1974   d.1916

                                        mar (1920) Charles Alfred Wormley
                                                        b.1870
                                                        d.1936
                                        mar (1940) Beddie MacDonald Stephens
                                                        b.1887
                                                        Murdered 1942

Lucy = Stanley Morriss   Walter BLOY = Grace Mary JAMES   Alice Irene = Edgar Sargantson
b.1909   b.1912   b.1916   b.1915
d.1999   d.1947   d.1983   d.1989

David   Sandra = Thomas Wedd Pamela BLOY Stephen BLOY = Helena Lawless   Maureen = John Berry
b.1934   b.1942   b.1942   b.1941   b.1946   b.1950   b.1938   b.1936
d.1937   (div. 1973)   d.1984

        Jason   Rachel   Justin Leonard BLOY   David
        b.1971   b.1972   b.1970   b.1963

                                                        mar. Patricia Anne Hackfath
                                                             b. 1946 (div. 2003)

Walter's mother, Alice Smith, to whom I have already made several references thus far in the narrative, was born in Grimsby in 1886, one of four daughters produced by George Henry Smith, a Freeman of the Borough of Grimsby and, his wife Mary Hannah Smith (nee Best, prev. Simmons), who had been left a widow at the age of 20. Curiously, Grandma Alice Smith was always referred to as being one of five daughters. However, all the census records relating to this part of the Smith family, between 1881 and 1901, appear to show that Alice was the youngest of four daughters born to George Henry Smith and his wife. They had never had a fifth daughter. This family mystery was finally cleared up when I discovered through additional research that Mary Hannah had been married twice. In 1870, with her first husband, George Simmons, a fisherman who was lost at sea during the first year of their marriage, she had a daughter Maria. Therefore, Alice and her siblings had an elder half-sister. When her husband died, Mary Hannah was still pregnant with Maria.

After Mary Hannah married George Henry Smith, the research appears to suggest that Maria adopted the Smith surname. If this was the case, it leads me to relate an unfortunate incident involving a thirteen-year-old girl called Hannah Maria Smith. Within the Grimsby Register of Still Births there is an entry which states that; Hannah Maria Smith, born 1870 and residing in Garden Street, was delivered of a stillborn child on the 6th June 1883. Is this her? The young girl's forenames, Hannah Maria and the surname Smith may just be coincidental, as too is the girl's date of birth, i.e.1870, and this girl is not Grandma Alice's half-sister. However, if it was indeed her, which I believe it to be, it would explain why Grandma's half-sister Maria, was sent away to live with relatives in Yorkshire, which I know for certain is an actual fact.

To be pregnant at thirteen years old was not a crime in the Victorian era. I was surprised to discover that in 1878, Parliament raised the age of sexual consent from 12 to 13. A subsequent newspaper campaign in 1885 led to it being raised to 16 where it remains to this day. The Grimsby Register of

Stillbirths had some very poignant and distressing entries, which reflects the dark and bleaker side of 'Dickensian' Victorian England: *'The body of a new born infant was found dead in a drain near Macaulay Street on 3rd November 1884'*. A further entry read *'Person unknown was delivered of a supposed still born child, found in the dock on 19th July 1886'*. There were several other entries similar to these. How heartbreaking and desperately sad to think that stillborn children had just been tossed away like a piece of any old rubbish.

At the time of Alice's birth, the family was living in Wellington Street, along with three lodgers, Joseph Dobbs, Richard Wordman and his wife Francis. Houses in Wellington Street were quite large, spacious and impressive in comparison to the 'back to back' houses of other parts of the East Marsh. They had small front gardens and reasonably sized rear gardens. Taking in lodgers to provide additional income was, as I previously learned with the Bloy family, common practice in those days. The Smith family started to prosper during the last decade of the 19th century. With the improving family fortunes, it is probable that Alice, being the baby of the family, may have been spoilt and indulged by her parents. If she had been, it may offer a plausible explanation why there was a not-too-nice, selfish and self-focused aspect to her character which I will discuss as the story unfolds. Although other family members disagreed, I considered it appropriate to critically examine Alice's character and nature; being Walter's mother, and as his father was dead, her behaviour, values and attitude would have been a major influence on him during his formative years. Consequently, I purposely extended the Smith family tree to include more recent generations to provide the framework for discussing Alice's character and what happened after Walter's accidental death in 1947.

As I have already stated, within the chronological review of Walter's maternal ancestors I discovered a family connection to medieval England through his great-great-great-grandfather Edward Jewitt (c.1748). This family name, which has a variety of spellings such as Jowet and Jouet can be traced back to 13th and 14th century and the time of King Edward III. This ancestral connection, which took the Smith family tree back into the mid-18th century, was established through the archived Freeman Rolls and has been included in the story just for historical interest. Tempting as it was to delve deeper it will not feature much further in this story. The focus will now be from George Smith (b.1806) onwards.

George Smith, Walter's maternal great-grandfather, who was born in Grainthorpe, a small village just outside Grimsby, had a brief association with the sea. He was, according to the census information of 1841, employed for a short time as a 'Mariner'. It was however, his later employment as a 'Well Borer', which proved to be more attention-grabbing, as it enabled a link to be established with the very successful and nationally renowned Grimsby engineer and businessman about whom I will talk shortly. George Smith's wife Eleanor (nee Jewitt), whom he married in about 1828, was born in Grimsby in 1807, the daughter of the Freeman John Jewitt. The Freeman's Pastures Roll indicates that George Smith became an enrolled Freeman by virtue of his marriage to Eleanor Jewitt, who therefore was the source of the Smith family's Freeman status in the 19th century and ultimately the Bloys' in the 20th century. I have previously commented that the role of the Freemen becomes of greater consequence the further back in time one goes. It could be safely presumed that the Jewitt family must have been important Freemen in 18th century Grimsby. As well as benefiting financially from the Freeman Estate, one of the most important aspects of being a Freeman was their entitlement to vote in the local and Parliamentary elections. The common man was not entitled to vote and therefore had no statutory role in influencing how the town would develop. This is clearly illustrated by the Grimsby Register of people who had the right to vote. The records of elections held in the 1850s and 60s indicate that George Smith, after becoming a Freeman, always exercised his right to vote. The electoral records made interesting reading, showing as they do how a person actually voted. Apparently there was no secret ballot then!

If we pause just for a moment to reflect on George and Eleanor's birth dates, i.e. 1806 and 1807, they provide an interesting historical timeline perspective for the story. When they were born, England, later to be Great Britain, had been fighting Napoleon's armies for nearly twenty years. In 1805, Admiral Lord Horatio Nelson had defeated Napoleon's navy at the Battle of Trafalgar and died whilst doing so, and the Battle of Waterloo, Napoleon's final defeat, was still about eight or nine years away. The population of Grimsby would have only been about 2000, with the town consisting of less than 300 houses. St James Church, the Bullring and Old Market Place would have been the heart of the town. And, although many ventures were being considered to boost the dock trade, (including whaling, which only lasted about 15 years and terminated with the loss of six whalers in 1821,) Grimsby, at the beginning of the 19th century, when George and Eleanor were born, would have had a close 'market town' type feel about it.

After their marriage in 1828, George and Eleanor's vigorous and, in a tiny home with only two bedrooms, clearly audible, sex life produced eight children, that neatly arrived in pairs: Elizabeth (b.1829), John (b.1831), Maria (b. 1834), Joseph (b.1835), Ann Irene (b.1839), Isaac (b.1841), Lydia (b.1844) and finally George Henry (b.1847), who would later become Walter's maternal grandfather. By the 1840s, George Smith had left the sea and found employment as a labourer before becoming a well borer, and lived with his family in King Edward Street, which after the migration of many thousands of people to the town, would become one of the most notorious areas of the East Marsh of Grimsby within a decade.

Returning for a moment to his Freeman status; George Smith had to have been made free and living with his family within the Borough by the time his children were born. Had he not been his sons would not have been entitled to claim their Freeman status by birth in later years. Subsequently three of George Smith's sons, all of whom had been born in Grimsby were enrolled as a Freeman by birth; Walter's maternal great-uncles, John Smith in 1865 and Joseph Smith in 1874 and then his grandfather George Henry Smith, in February 1878. There is no record of the fourth son, Isaac, also Walter's great-uncle ever being enrolled as a Freeman. Although he was entitled by birth, he had moved away from Grimsby and therefore would not qualify. According to the census information, Isaac, at the age of 36, was employed as a bricklayer and living with his wife Elizabeth, who originally came from Durham, in Barnsley. Walter's great-aunts, Elizabeth, Maria, and Lydia, being the daughters of a Freeman, would not become Freemen themselves, but could make their husband 'free', if and when they married and, if all the other criteria, which I have already outlined, were met. Becoming a Freeman by birth, because you are a financially sound, law- abiding citizen and contributing to the local community, contrasts quite manifestly with the circumstances and fortunes of Walter's paternal ancestors during this same period of the 19th century.

Similar to the Bloy family, the Smith ancestral heritage also forms part of the history of Grimsby's East Marsh. According to the census of 1851, George Smith had ceased to be a mariner and was employed as a well borer. At that time, he was living with his wife and just four of his children Joseph, Isaac, Lydia and George Henry, at King Edward Street North, which as I previously observed, was described in 1850 as, '*a lot of small tenements not fit for dogs to live in*'. Elizabeth, who would then have been aged 22 and John, aged 20, are not recorded on the census. It is therefore safe to assume they were no longer living with their parents. Where they had gone is difficult to tell. I know John survived and thrived, because fourteen years later in 1865, he became a Freeman. No further trace of Elizabeth could be found. Another daughter, Ann Irene, had she been alive, would have only been 12 years old when this census was taken. As she is not recorded and, given the frequency of infant mortality in this period of the 19th century, it wouldn't be unreasonable to presume that she may have died sometime between the consecutive censuses of 1841 and 1851.

Perhaps more germane to the story is that another of George Smith's daughters, Maria, had fared better. About 1855, she left home and later married George Russell with whom she had at least four children. When the next census was taken in 1861, two of her brothers, Isaac and George Henry [Walter's grandfather], were temporarily living with Maria and her husband at Holme Street, which is located in the southern part of the East Marsh. Isaac was then 20 years old and was employed as labourer and George Henry, only 15 years old, was described as a painter. During the 1860s, Isaac left Grimsby, met his wife-to-be Elizabeth, and then settled for some time in Barnsley. George Henry would also leave Grimsby and spend some time living in Leeds. Similar to her father, Maria's husband, George Russell was also employed as a well borer. There may well be a link here as to how she actually met her husband, but that is pure speculation and may be just coincidental. What is not conjecture however, is the family connection to the nationally renowned engineer and businessman, Frank Smith (1877-1966), described by Chapman (2002; p.142) as:

...an erudite artesian well expert, who invented 'expanded piling' which became a boon to construction work. The Globe Cinema in Victoria Street, Grimsby was the first building to be constructed on this principle. The Expanded Piling Company's rights were sold in 1991 for £21 million.

An examination of the family tree showed, that well boring was a profession several consecutive members of this part of the Smith family were engaged with. The famous engineer and businessman Frank Smith, who was born in 1877, obviously took a lead from his father, also called Frank Smith (b. 1851), and his grandfather, John Smith (b.1810), who were both employed as well borers before him. Frank Smith, (the engineer) was the first of several children produced by his father Frank Smith (b.1851) and his wife Marian. And Frank Smith senior was the youngest of nine children born over a fourteen year period to John Smith (b.1810) and his wife Harriett. It is through John Smith that the link to Walter's ancestors was established. John Smith is the younger brother of Walter's maternal great-grandfather, George Smith (b.1807) upon whom I have focussed this part of the story. Not surprisingly George Smith was also a well borer. Therefore the engineer and business man Frank Smith's great-uncle George was Walter's great-grandfather.

By 1871, another of George and Eleanor's children, son Joseph, had become a boot-maker, and was living in Barnsley as a widower with three young children all under 10 years old. Unfortunately, the census does not give the name of a deceased wife, so to track her down would be very difficult. Whilst I have no evidence to support this theory, having three children in quick succession, it is possible she may have died in childbirth. Joseph returned to Grimsby about 1873 and claimed his Freeman status in 1874.

My search for Walter now moves forward a generation and focuses on George Henry Smith, his maternal grandfather. During the latter part of the 1860s, George Henry left Grimsby and lived in South Yorkshire for a few years. By 1878 he had returned to Grimsby and, was living and paying rates within the borough; the Freeman Rolls indicate he became an enrolled Freeman of the Borough. So he must have been financially sound! There is however, some confusion and contradiction about where he lived and what he did during his time in South Yorkshire. I don't think he fared too well initially, as one set of records from 1871 shows a George Henry Smith, who was born in Grimsby in 1847, residing as a *pauper inmate* in a Workhouse in Leeds; whereas the census of the same year has a George Henry Smith, born in Grimsby then aged 23, living in Leeds and employed as a railway porter. Unfortunately, the census doesn't make it clear where this George Henry Smith was living at the time. I think that they are the same person. His 'stay' in the Leeds Union Workhouse may have been a temporary arrangement while he found work and accommodation. Further research of later census documents confirms a link to the railways.

Mary Hannah Smith (Walter's Grandmother) circa 1928 aged about 78

George Henry Smith's connection with South Yorkshire also includes time spent in Sheffield because, during the last quarter of 1873, this is where he married Mary Hannah Simmons (nee Best). Their first daughter Lillian was born there in 1875. If George Henry Smith was indeed employed by the Manchester, Sheffield and Lincolnshire Railway, which I believe he was, it would explain what he was doing in South Yorkshire. George Henry's wife, Mary Hannah Simmons (nee Best), was a widow, and the youngest daughter of John Best who originated from Halifax in Yorkshire. In financial terms, John Best and his family were reasonably comfortable as he had a prestigious well paid job; he earned his living as a Saw Mill Master. His wife, Maria, came from Louth in Lincolnshire and together they had six children. Three of them, Susan (b.1837), William (b.1841), James (b.1844), were born in Louth, Ann (b.1847) was born in Bradford and Mary Hannah (b.1850) and finally James (b.1853) were born in Grimsby. With the exception of Mary Hannah, for simplicity, all these other children are not shown on the family tree. When John Best eventually moved his family to Grimsby during the latter part of the 1840s, they lived in Spring Street on the East Marsh, a photo of which I included in a previous chapter. Within a few years, Spring Street would become one of the nastiest and vilest places to live on the East Marsh. But at that time in the 1840's, before the massive influx of migrants to the town and the subsequent overcrowding, it may not have been too bad a place to live.

Mary Hannah had experienced distressing heartbreak very early in her life. At the age of 19, on 28th February 1869, she married a fisherman, George Simmons. Unfortunately, it would be a very short-lived marriage; George Simmons was lost overboard in the North Sea during the early part of 1870. Through my research I found that being lost at sea, particularly from falling overboard from the deck of the fishing smacks that were pitching and rolling in heavy seas, was a very regular occurrence. For example, during one severe storm in February 1868, forty men and boys from Grimsby were lost and drowned in one day. Maritime records also show that in a two year period around the latter part of the 1870s nearly two hundred Grimsby fishermen were lost at sea, of which about a half were 21 years old or younger. George Simmons's death was yet another traumatic example of pure joy and extreme sadness coming together. At the time George Simmons was drowned, Mary Hannah was heavily pregnant. Maria, their only child about whom I have already written, and who was named after Mary Hannah's mother, was born in 1870 shortly after her father had died. Mary Hannah at the age of 20 became a widow with a child to support. George never saw his daughter!

After Mary Hannah remarried, Maria Simmons, who adopted the surname Smith, would later become the half-sister of Walter's mother, Alice Smith, and her three sibling sisters. Rather surprisingly though, I found, at the time of the 1881 census Maria, who would only be 11 years old, was not living in the family home with her mother, stepfather, and her half-sisters; she was living with her uncle William, Mary Hannah's brother. I could not initially establish why she was not living at home. Consequently I was left with several unanswered questions. Did she not get on with step-father and her half-sisters? I just don't know. Then I found the 1883 entry in the Grimsby Register of Stillbirths for a thirteen year old Hannah Maria Smith, whom I believe to be her and, was drawn to the conclusion she may well have been a precocious, sexually active, problem child and an embarrassment to the family! Sending her away to live elsewhere was how the family dealt with the problem – out of sight out of mind! As I have already said, I just don't know. What is absolutely clear however, from the subsequent census records of 1891 and 1901, is that Maria never lived with her mother and half-sisters ever again. She lived her life in Yorkshire.

Coincidentally, history would repeat itself later in the Smith-Bloy family story. After the death in the motorcycle accident of her first husband, Alice, (Walter's mother) sent her youngest daughter Irene to live with her sister Susannah. It was an unfortunate decision, which to this day, is still a source of rancour with Irene's daughter Maureen.

Prior to 1881 census, the Freeman register indicates that George Henry Smith had left Yorkshire and returned with his growing family to Grimsby, where he was earning his living as a painter and decorator. Although Lillian, the first child, was born in Sheffield, George and Mary Hannah's three other daughters were all born in Grimsby: Florence in 1880, Susannah, who was often referred to as Suey, in 1882 and finally Alice in 1886. Sometime during the 1880s, George Henry moved his family once more, this time to live in Albion Street, Grimsby, which is where they remained until after the census of 1891.

The Smith family fortunes continued to improve throughout the 1890s. By 1898, the family owned a tobacconist and confectioner's shop in Freeman Street. According to the Grimsby and Cleethorpes Trade Directory, George Henry Smith was trading as a tobacconist and confectioner at 203 Freeman Street. Grimsby. However, this entry in the Trade Directory, actually contradicts the information contained in the 1901 census, which described George Henry Smith as a painter and decorator. Whereas, his wife Mary Hannah Smith, was listed as a tobacconist *'on her own accord',* which means she was self-employed. This suggests, Mary essentially owned and ran the tobacconist and confectionary business. With what she would earn from the tobacconist shop and George Henry being employed as a painter and decorator, the family would have had the comfort and financial benefit of two separate sources of income.

In the 1890s, Freeman Street would have been an ideal location for a business of this nature; it was the main shopping area of Grimsby and remained so until the development of the old town centre some seventy years later. Being in the heart of the developing area of the town and the main thoroughfare leading to the docks it was absolutely perfect for passing trade. The majority of the male 'working class' population, and some women, still smoked a pipe in those days. So called 'tailor-made' cigarettes were just starting to grow in popularity. On entering the shop, the nostrils and senses must have been assailed by the various pungent aromas coming from the many containers of loose tobacco, which is how it was then bought. All the tobaccos would have had exotic sounding names that would conjure up images of the far distant places from where it had come. By 1906, Mary Hannah had sold the shop to a Gertrude Robinson and subsequently bought property which she then rented out. The shop, which I can recall going into and, ironically not knowing its history and link to my family, remained a tobacconist for many years until at least the 1990s. Whether it stayed in the family of Gertrude Robinson is of no consequence or further interest to Walter's story.

Chapter Eight

The Life And Times Of Alice Smith – Walter's Mother

In the subsequent chapters, I will be exploring the ancestral history of Walter's wife Grace Mary (nee James), before going on to talk about why I consider Walter, through his service as an officer in the Merchant Navy during World War 2, to be a hero. However, before I do that, as she was such a major influence on Walter's young life, it is appropriate to focus for a moment on the life and times of his mother Alice Smith. To do so will provide a framework for understanding Walter's early life and for me, address the cathartic element of this journey of discovery which I have undertaken.

Alice's father, George Henry Smith died in 1915 at the age of 68, when Walter was only three years old. Therefore he could not have really known his maternal grandfather. Alice, in the space of two consecutive years, lost her father and then a year later, in 1916, her husband Walter Sidney Bloy. Walter had lost both his maternal grandfather and then his father! On the other hand, his maternal grandmother, Mary Hannah Smith didn't die until 1931 and would have seen Walter growing up and starting out on his career in the Merchant Navy. As his paternal grandfather appears to have been excluded from the family, Walter wouldn't have had a male role model during his early formative years. Living with his mother, grandmother and sisters, Walter would, for several years until 1920, grow up in a female-dominated family, which was headed by a very strong determined lady.

Grandma Alice Stephen in 1940 (aged 54)

Alice was an attractive woman, not overly beautiful, but striking. Except for a short period in her life, after the death of Walter Sidney, she had the means to dress well in the latest styles. By all accounts, she enjoyed male company and having a good time, or so I was told. In later years, through her manner and dress, Alice adopted an almost regal appearance. Before that, at the age of 23, on the 15th September 1909, Alice married Walter Sidney Bloy, in the Grimsby Parish church of St James. Walter Sidney, who was also 23 years old, would be the first of Alice's three husbands. Alice's father, George Henry Smith, and Harriett Debnam (nee Bloy), Walter Sidney's cousin through his Uncle William Bloy, were the witnesses. Their marriage produced three children: the eldest, Lucy, was born in December 1909, Walter was born in June 1912 and (Alice) Irene, was born in 1915. Closer scrutiny of their wedding date and the date of birth of their first child surprisingly revealed that Alice was actually 6/7 months pregnant with her daughter Lucy when she married Walter Sidney.

Having to get married because you were pregnant was commonly referred to, in the past, as a 'shotgun' wedding. This metaphorical phrase, which suggests a reluctant groom being coerced to marry at the point of an irate father's shotgun, is seldom heard nowadays in these more 'liberated' times. Since the radical changes in social attitudes, heralded by the permissive age of the 1960s onwards, sex before marriage and children born out of wedlock are now far more socially acceptable and regrettably have almost become the norm. However, the societal moral attitude being what it was in 1909, if you became pregnant before marriage, it would have been an acute source of family shame. In late Victorian and Edwardian times:

> *...unmarried mothers and their infants were considered an affront to morality and they were spurned and ostracised often by public relief as well as charitable institutions. Children 'conceived in*

sin' were considered to have inherited their parents' lack of moral character and would contaminate the minds and morals of legitimate children.

I could not help thinking, was Walter Sidney forced to 'do the right thing' and marry Alice?

Alice's pregnancy would have been a source of scandal and embarrassment, which I'm sure both the Smith and Bloy families would have done their upmost to keep quiet. Especially as George Henry Smith was a Freeman and at that time the Bloys were a respectable family running a successful business. Most likely, both families would have been well known. It is difficult to picture how they actually managed to keep her pregnancy hidden. At 6/7 months pregnant, Alice would have been showing quite heavily when she walked down the aisle of St James Church. Perhaps they just brazened it out! After discovering this scandal, I find it difficult to understand why Alice reacted with such moral indignation after her son's widow, (my mother) remarried. Her behaviour was highly hypocritical. In my opinion, she had no right to take such a stance, given that she was heavily pregnant when she married Walter's father. But Alice was a strong woman, who had a forthright manner and was a mass of contradictions! The full reach of Alice's character in this regard will be related as the story unfolds.

After their marriage, Alice and Walter Sidney originally lived in Newmarket Street, in the East Marsh of Grimsby; which is where all their children were born. They followed the family tradition of naming children after their parents or grandparents; Lucy was named after Walter Sidney's mother, whilst Walter was named after his father and grandfather and (Alice) Irene was named after her mother. Shortly after Irene was born, the family moved to a better home in Clayton Street, which was part of 'old' Grimsby and had been named after one of Grimsby's foremost families of the 18th century. Moving to Clayton Street placed them nearer the centre of the old town market place and further away from the East Marsh. And it is where they were living at the time of the motorcycle accident. Until then, the family seemed to be doing well and prospering. Walter Sidney was working in the family coal merchant's business and, even though this was the time of the Great War, compared with many other families at that time, they appeared to live a relatively comfortable life. So much so that Walter Sidney could afford to buy the motorcycle, which would end up causing the family so much distress and heartbreak.

Out of curiosity, I searched through a range of records relating to the Great War to see whether Walter Sidney Bloy had seen any active service during this conflict before he died in the motorcycle accident. Try as I may I could not establish why he did not, or could not, answer Lord Kitchener's call, *'Your Country Needs You'* and join the Grimsby Chums. He was under 30 years old and would have been a fit and strong young man from his handling of the sacks of coal. He would have easily met the size and weight requirement. Perhaps because he was a family man with children, he may have thought his responsibilities were elsewhere and not with the Grimsby Chums at that stage of the War. Kitchener's campaign to recruit a new army was taken up with gusto throughout the country, no more so than in Grimsby. In the early days of the Great War, amid the jostle of events, the coming and going of troops and the organization of war workers and relief committees, the following Poster, from Alderman J. H. Tate, Mayor and Chairman of the Recruiting Committee, appeared on the walls of Grimsby:

To the men of GRIMSBY

Lord Kitchener has asked for 100,000 men for the Army, and a new Battalion of the famous Lincolnshire Regiment is to be raised as part of this number.

These men are wanted immediately to defend our country.

> **I am sure that the men of Grimsby who are so vitally interested in a quick and successful termination of the present struggle will not be appealed to in vain.**
>
> **Every able-bodied man has a duty to perform, and I ask every man in this town, able to bear arms, to come forward to help his country in the hour of its need.**

Consequently, the Grimsby Chums was a 'Pals battalion' of Kitchener's army raised in and around Grimsby and, after being taken over by the British Army, was officially named the 10th Battalion, The Lincolnshire Regiment. They were the only Pal's battalion to be called 'chums'. When the original call came from Lord Kitchener, the headmaster of the local Wintringham Grammar School in Grimsby decided to raise a 250-strong company of former pupils, which would be offered to one of the local territorial battalions. Many other non-Grammar School Grimsby men expressed a wish to join, so the process was handed over to the town council, which set about recruiting sufficient men to form an entire battalion. Alderman Tate's poster was a primary strategy for calling the town's stalwart men to arms. Many answered this bugle call!

When their training was completed, the Grimsby Chums joined the 101st Brigade of the British 34th Division and moved to France in January 1916 and first saw action in the Battle of the Somme. On the 1st July 1916, they were in the thick of the fighting as part of the first wave attacking the fortified village of La Boisselle. To aid their attack, a massive mine, known as the Lochnagar mine, was detonated beneath the German trenches at 7.28 am, two minutes before zero hour. At 7.30 am, the Grimsby Chums rushed forward to occupy the crater. Here many brave, young Grimsby men met their god that morning and would never see the Grimsby Dock Tower again. Trapped for the rest of the day, harassed by both German and British artillery, casualties were high. Throughout the day, just a small number of the Grimsby Chums made it all the way into the German trenches. The only officer to make it was 2nd

Lieutenant Harold P. Hendin who led five men to the German lines and, gathering stragglers as the day progressed, he held off a series of German counter-attacks for three more days before having to retire. In total the Grimsby Chums suffered 502 casualties on the 1st July 1916; 15 officers and 487 soldiers of other ranks. Of all the officers to go over the top, only two came back unwounded, and just about 100 men.

If Walter Sidney had joined the Grimsby Chums, he would not have been on his motorcycle with Alice on the evening of the 19th June 1916; he would not have crashed and died that night. He would have been in France preparing for the Battle of the Somme. Who is to say fate and providence wouldn't have been kinder to him and he would have been one of the 100 or so men who survived on that terrible first day? Although I have digressed again, I make no apology for doing so. Relating this brief snapshot of the Grimsby Chums, in addition to offering a historical perspective of the times, it provides an indication of the intense emotional pressure that young men such as Walter Sidney would have been under to answer Kitchener's call to join up. There is much documented and anecdotal evidence that in some quarters, fit young men who were not in uniform were considered, and in some cases actually accused of being, a coward. Many young men were maligned and publically shamed in this way and were sent white feathers. This was chiefly a malicious phenomenon in Britain. White feathers were typically handed over by young women to men out of uniform during wartime, the implication being that the man concerned was a 'shirker' or a coward.

The so-called 'Organisation of the White Feather' was initiated by Admiral Charles Fitzgerald at the beginning of the war in 1914 and was founded as a means of applying pressure to able-bodied men to enlist with the British Army. As the result of a growing perception of manpower shortages, the practice of handing out white feathers gathered pace during 1915 and continued, albeit sporadically, for the remainder of the war. It was far-reaching. Even soldiers home on leave and out of uniform found themselves the target of inevitably disgusted bearers of white feathers. And for those men who had to remain at home in key industries and businesses, the effect of being presented with white feathers was often one of acute public shame. Out of necessity, the government responded by approving the production of a badge bearing the legend "King and Country", thus marking out its wearer as someone effectively excluded from overt moral and emotional pressure to enlist.

Although I'll never know what Walter Sidney's motives were for not enlisting, perhaps being a coal merchant was considered a key business? I'd hate to think that my grandfather was a coward. Not an accusation, as we shall see, that could be levelled at his son Walter. What I can be certain of, Walter Sidney would have regularly seen the Chums in Grimsby as they were billeted for some time at Garden Street School and Doughty Road, which were just along the road from where the family coal merchant's business operated. At the time of Walter Sidney's death in June 1916, the Great War still had two more years to go before it ended and would see Grimsby lose more than 1100 men and 216 ships from the fishing fleet, a terrible ultimate sacrifice.

Returning the story to Alice, the primary focus of this chapter; according to what I have been told, family anecdotes and recollections, not all favourable, Alice was a lively person who certainly enjoyed a good time and having fun. Her pregnancy before marriage, and being on the back of the motorcycle when it crashed, bears witness to that, and suggests a liberated and risk-taking element of her character. There is no doubt that Alice liked male company. She married three times and after being widowed again when her third husband was murdered in Israel, Alice later moved a former childhood sweetheart, Elias (Pop) Fields, into her home as a 'lodger', when she was in her 60s. Without question, Alice was very driven, self-focussed, self-serving and had ambitions to be socially upwardly mobile. An ambition she ultimately achieved. When her grandchildren were born, Alice preferred to be referred to as grandma, not gran or granny, that was too common, but grandma. Truth be told, Alice was in reality an early 20th century version of a socially upward mobile 'yuppy'.

The division between the classes, in particular the middle and working class, had started to change in the aftermath of the Great War and continued with the rebuilding of the country after the Second World War. Despite these changing times, I believe that status, material wealth, possessions and image still mattered a great deal to my grandma.

After Walter Sidney died in 1916, at the age of 30 Alice was left a widow with three children to look after. Their daughter Lucy was seven years old, Walter was four years old and Irene was less than two years old; consequently, it must have been very difficult for Alice to manage. Her father-in-law, Walter senior, was 59 years old when the motorcycle accident happened. In addition to him being devastated at the loss of his last remaining child, he would have had to concentrate on running the family coal merchant's business without his son. Not a task, history shows us, he was too successful at. I concluded that he didn't appear to have been much assistance to Alice at all. Help for Alice was, however, forthcoming. One of her older sisters, Susannah, provided some support by 'temporarily' taking Alice's youngest daughter Irene to stay with her. Unfortunately, I was to discover that this sisterly help in the long run had life-long repercussions and recriminations.

When collecting the photographs, documents and certificates needed to build up the family story, I talked to the family members who could personally remember Alice, or could relate anecdotes told them by their parents. My cousin Sandra, Aunt Lucy's daughter, who probably spent more time with Grandma Alice than any of her other three grandchildren, including my sister and me, told me that to support the children in the period immediately after Walter Sidney died, Grandma Alice had worked as a cleaner, took in sewing and also worked as a barmaid. Basically, much to her credit, she did whatever she could to support the children. To bandy clichés, it was a Hobson's choice and needs must when the devil drives.

In hardship and material terms, this particular part of Alice's story is not too dissimilar to what Grace Mary's

(Walter's wife) mother had to do in similar circumstances. But, as the examination of Grace Mary's family will reveal, it is where the similarity ends. Through hard work and some good fortune, Alice would eventually succeed and prosper. Grace Mary's mother (my granny), although she worked just as hard, unfortunately would not fare so well. Within the context of my search for Walter, the full extent of these later material differences was brought home to me quite vividly through a photograph, circa 1930s, I found of Alice dressed in a full-length expensive fur coat standing next to a smart Wolseley car she owned. This photograph would have been taken at a time when my granny was living in poverty and, was really struggling to make ends meet and finding it hard to keep her family clothed and fed through subsistence living and the shame of public hand-outs.

After baby Irene went to stay with her sister Susannah, Alice took on a variety of work; she had to leave her eldest daughter Lucy at home to look after Walter. I am not disapproving of these actions, because I don't think Alice really had much choice at the time. To get someone to care for Irene for a short while after the accident, whilst grieving and trying to get organised, is perfectly understandable. I was, however, informed by Irene's daughter, my cousin Maureen, that her mother lived with her aunt for the whole of her young life until she married in 1939 and never ever returned home to live with Alice. Although I recognise I am making a value-laden judgement, I find it difficult to understand how anyone could permanently 'loan' out their baby, even if it was to one's own sister. Why wasn't Irene returned home after Alice married her second husband and had the financial security that this marriage brought her? What compelled Alice to leave the upbringing of her youngest daughter to her sister? Even now, I can see that it is still a source of rancour for Maureen.

Whilst I have no doubt that in her way, Alice loved her children, some of the comments she wrote on the back of old photographs, especially to Walter, appear to indicate this. Although I am given to understand she never displayed spontaneous acts of love and affection, such as a cuddle or hug. Alice was not an overly tactile person with her children or, as I later found out, her grandchildren. She was nearly 70 years old when I finally met her and truth be told, frightened me a little at first. When I was old enough to make sensible and perhaps more informed discriminations, I did find Grandma Alice's demeanour to be cold and impervious at times. Sadly I could never warm to her, however much I may have wanted to. Also, my personal experiences of heart-warming stories about my grandma are somewhat limited, unlike the wealth of childhood experiences I have of my granny. Granny's kitchen, with its black-leaded cast iron fire and oven and the smell of baking bread, as chaotic and noisy as it was at times, was like a welcoming second home to me where I always felt comfortable.

In 1920, less than four years after Walter Sidney's death, Alice and two of her children, Lucy and Walter, went to live with Charles Alfred Wormley, a 52 year-old widower, whose wife Eliza Ann had died three years previously at the age of 47. Where and how he and Alice had met is anyone's guess. It could easily have been whilst she was working as a barmaid. Charles Alfred Wormley had been born in 1870, at Greenwich in London, the son of Henry Wormley, who was a fisherman. When the Grimsby fishing industry rapidly grew in the second half of the 19th century, many fishing families migrated from the Thames (Greenwich) region to Grimsby, and this probably explains why the Wormleys had arrived in Grimsby. Regrettably, whilst still in his twenties, Henry Wormley, when sailing out of Grimsby, was lost overboard and drowned at sea.

Though he was always referred to, and styled himself as Charles Alfred Wormley, his two marriage registrations and his death certificate have him listed as Alfred Charles Wormley. For brevity throughout the remainder of this story, I will refer to him as Charles or Charles Wormley. Alice and Charles actually lived together 'in sin' in Holles Street for two years before they married on the 11th March 1922 at the Grimsby Registry Office: Alice was 36 years old and Charles was 52 years old. Becoming the husband of a Freeman's widow, Charles was entitled to be made free by virtue of his marriage to Alice. On the 2nd October 1922, the Mayor's court, which presided at the Town Hall, granted Charles Wormley his Freeman status. There were no children born to Alice and Charles, so the Freeman entitlement did not pass onto future generations of the Wormley family. In later years, both Lucy and Irene, being the daughters of a Freeman, would make their husbands free when they married and set up home in the Borough. Stanley Morris became a Freeman in October 1934, by virtue of his marriage to Lucy Bloy and Edgar Sargantson, became a Freeman in October 1939, after his marriage to Irene Bloy.

Why Alice had married Charles, who was 16 years her senior, is quite easy to understand. She was a young widow with three children, although one was not living at home. Alice was trying to do her best for her family, at what would have been a very grim time for all. The Great War had not long ended and for many, the years immediately after being widowed, would have been very testing. Although, I am sure Alice loved Charles, particularly if the evidence of old photographs is anything to go by; the marriage appears to have been very happy. And I say this without any cynicism intended: Charles would have been a way out of a difficult situation for her at a difficult time. The fact that Alice may have, for financial security, chosen to marry again, made it hard for me to understand why she would ostracise Grace Mary, her son Walter's widow, for doing exactly the same as she had done, by getting married again.

Even though I have previously referred to these actions of my grandma, I do so again at this point to illustrate her nature and characteristic within the perspective of how her story adds to the search for Walter. In 1949, two years after Walter's accidental death, Grace Mary, who had been widowed with two young children to care for, married my step-father Stanley Harold Shreeve who in due course would become one of Grimsby's top North Sea Trawler Skippers. Grace Mary subsequently gave birth to two children, my brother Stanley (b.1950) and my sister Gail (b.1952). Whether Grace Mary loved Stanley Shreeve or married him just for financial security, in relation to this story is not relevant or important. What is more pertinent is that this marriage led to so much bitterness. Grandma Alice's reaction to the marriage and the subsequent additional children, was to become estranged and isolate her son's widow for many years. This was the behaviour of a woman who was pregnant when she first married and very soon took a second husband when she was widowed!

Even now, I am at a loss to understand her reasoning for adopting this attitude, especially as by the time her son Walter died, Alice certainly had the financial resources to help Grace Mary, had she been inclined too. Having to struggle financially, which Alice did after Walter Sidney died in 1916, I would have expected her to be more empathetic and supportive for Grace Mary when she was struggling. Moreover, Alice's behaviour became even more difficult to comprehend when I discovered that, after Charles Wormley died in 1936 at the age of 66, within four years Alice actually married yet again. Captain Beddie Macdonald Stephen, a Merchant Navy ship's master, to whom her son Walter had introduced her, became her third husband. One rule for Alice and another for Grace Mary it seems!

Several times, especially when writing this particular chapter of the story, I have had to keep reminding myself that the original purpose of this story was to explore the life, the times and family of Walter Bloy and not just to provide a vehicle for closure on an episode of my childhood, no matter how tempting it was to do so. In practice though, this was not so easy to do. Consequently any critique or exposure of aspects of Alice Smith's character, while highly subjective, are intended and offered as an explanation of how people's lives, including Walter's and mine were influenced and shaped by her behaviour. I freely acknowledge, being able to write the story from my perspective did provide some closure and ended many years of hurt.

After Alice's marriage to Charles Wormley, who was employed as a foreman on the Grimsby Docks, the family financial fortunes improved considerably. By 1927, they could afford to sell their terraced home in Holles Street, where they had lived with Lucy and Walter since getting married, and buy from the builders and contractors, Howson and Bunn, a newly-built, semi-detached 'villa' in Fairmont Road. The house, which cost the princely sum of £615-0-0, though quaintly described as a villa, was in reality a standard three-bedroom, semi-detached house with a driveway and a garden, typical of what was being built in the 1920s and 30s. Within the context of the time, after years of living in a street of terraced houses with no front garden and very little at the back of the house except an outside toilet and a small yard, I suppose it would have seemed like a villa. Fairmont Road was also situated about a couple of miles away from the town centre, and in the 1920s, it would have been the suburbs of Grimsby until the town caught up. Then as now, the property ladder was the way to progress and Grandma Alice very quickly learned how to do that! Whatever her faults, she certainly had entrepreneurial flair, drive and business acumen.

Alice's fortune also improved after her mother, Mary Hannah Smith, at the age of 81, died in 1931. As George Henry Smith, her husband was already dead, Mary Hannah's estate was divided between three of her daughters, each receiving an equal third share of the amount available for distribution. The statement of receipts and beneficiaries of Mary Hannah's will indicate that Florence, who by then had married into the Cardwell family, received £198-0s-10d. Susannah, who had married into the Urquhart family and Alice both received £269-15s-3d, which is the equivalent, based on retail value, of about £13,000 today (2010). The average wage in 1931 was £3-5s-0d per week. Therefore, the amount Alice received from her mother's will represented about a year and a half's wages for some. Not an amount to be to be sniffed at! Interestingly, Mary Hannah Smith made no provision in her will for Maria, the daughter she had from the brief marriage to George Simmons, or to Lillian, the eldest of the four daughters she had with George Henry Smith. Maria we know was living in Yorkshire, it is not clear however, where Lillian had gone. I don't know whether she had actually died or, was estranged from her mother. What is certain, she was not a beneficiary in her mother's will.

In apportioning the cash distribution, Florence retained the family home in Newmarket Street, where Walter and his sisters had been born. Consequently, Susannah and Alice each received an equal sum of money that was the equivalent of the equity of the asset at 89 Newmarket Street. Hence the difference in the distribution! According to this financial statement, the actual cash available for distribution had come from the sale of another property that Mary Hannah Smith had owned in Hope Street, Grimsby. Just like her mother before her, Alice would also become relatively wealthy by becoming a property owner.

The 'villa' in Fairmont Road was home for Alice and her family from 1927 until 1933, and is where they were living when Walter was indentured as an apprentice into the Merchant Navy at the age of 15 in 1927; his step-father, Charles Wormley, provided the financial surety by signing Walter's Apprenticeship Indentures. Although Walter had left home and was training to be a Deck Officer in the Merchant Navy, which would ultimately lead to his service on the North Atlantic Convoys some 13 years later, this was the home he returned to when on 'shore leave'. In 1933, as they were clearly doing well, Alice moved the family again by going further out of town to the leafy suburban area of Scartho and New Waltham. Although they bought a house at 293, Louth Road, Grimsby, Alice did not sell the house in Fairmont Road; she let it out for rent. Her daughter Lucy after marrying Stanley Morris in January 1933 was living there when Stanley Morris was made 'free'.

Regrettably for Alice, her time with Charles at Louth Road would be short-lived. Just three years after they moved, on the 9th December 1936, Charles died leaving Alice, in financial terms, 'comfortably off'. So much so that in 1937 she could afford to move again, this time to a house named 'Sherwood' on Station Road, New Waltham. Alice lived here until she sold it twelve years later in 1949 for £2500 to Mr A. H. Gait, who is believed to have been a member of the printers and book shop family. Following the sale of 'Sherwood', Alice moved to 27 Southfield Road, Waltham, which is where my sister and I first met her. She really had itchy feet because within six years, she moved yet again to a house across the road at 6 Southfield Road, Waltham, which she bought for £2000 and later sold for £3100. Every time Alice moved home, she made significant profit on the house that she was selling. Whilst buying and selling a house does not seem to be remarkable event, it is worth taking a moment to briefly reflect upon Alice's house-moving activities within context and circumstances of the times. To do so provides a contrasting perspective to the fortunes of many others.

In 1927, when Alice and Charles bought the 'villa' in Fairmont Road, the country at large was still recovering from the Great War; many families were struggling and facing financial hardship due to rising unemployment and the aftermath of the General Strike of 1926. After the Wall Street stock market crashed in 1929, which led to the great depression and high unemployment, for many the 1930s were also very lean difficult years; Alice however was able to move home in 1933 and then again in 1937. Each time she moved, it was to a more expensive property. Most of the 1940s were shaped by Second World War and its aftermath. The late 1940s and the 1950s were by all considerations, due to the country rebuilding after the Second World War and the policies of the Attlee government and later Conservative governments, the austerity years. Nevertheless, Alice still managed to better herself financially by moving home in 1949 and then again in the middle 1950s. During these decades, which were so depressing for many, Alice actually prospered. In addition to the properties Alice lived in, she also built up a portfolio of terraced houses in the Wood Street area of Grimsby, which she rented out. Furthermore, during the 1930s, Alice also became a breeder of championship 'Pekinese' dogs, which were very fashionable at the time, for those that could afford them. When I thought about this in the context of the period, I found it strangely bizarre that the country was in depression, the ominous clouds of another war were gathering on the horizon and Alice was breeding expensive lapdogs.

Despite all her faults, it is evident that Alice always provided a prosperous and comfortable home for Walter to return to, when he was either on shore leave or studying for his officer's certificates. Even though I have been very critical and a little resentful of certain aspects of Alice's life and her self-serving, driven nature, I readily concede it is very much to her credit that she managed to continually advance herself. And while doing so, she buried three husbands along the way; Walter Sidney Bloy in 1916, Charles Wormley in 1936 and then Captain Beddie McDonald Stephen, who was allegedly murdered in Israel, in 1942. She even outlived her childhood sweetheart, Elias 'Pop' Fields, the lodger who moved into her home at Southfield Road when they were both in their 60s.

Alice met her third husband, Captain Beddie McDonald Stephen, through Walter joining the merchant ship SS Antigone, of which Captain Stephen was the Master. Walter's time on the SS Antigone and his service in the Merchant Navy will be comprehensively related in a separate chapter. Walter signed on to the ship on 1st March 1939 at Immingham, shortly before it embarked on a nine-month voyage for the Pacific Islands and New Zealand. The Second World War actually started while the SS Antigone was still in the South Seas and before it managed to return home safely to Britain. It would have been a hazardous journey for the ship as the Merchant Fleet were some of the earliest casualties of the war. Alice could have met Captain Stephen when Walter first joined the ship in March 1939, in which case their romance would have been by letter. Or, she may have met him when the ship returned to home waters in October 1939.

If this is when they actually met, the romance between Alice and Captain Stephen must have been very swift indeed; they married in Liverpool on 22nd January 1940, with her daughter Lucy and Alice's new daughter-in-law Grace Mary as the witnesses. Walter and Grace Mary had got married in Grimsby two days previously on the 20th January 1940. I was disappointed to find there was no photographic evidence available, to indicate that Alice actually attended the wedding of her only son.

Walter and Grace Mary James's wedding day

In the one group photograph I could find of Walter's wedding, Grace Mary's mother and father are there but, Walter's sister Lucy appears to be standing in for Alice. The contrasting fortunes of the two families can be seen quite markedly in the manner in which the ladies in this photograph are dressed. The bride's mother (my granny), is wearing a simple and plain dress, probably the best she could afford. And as there is snow on the ground, she most likely would be feeling the cold. Whereas, Lucy is wearing a very expensive luxurious fur coat and a hat! Further visual evidence of the differing circumstances between the two families can be seen in a photograph I found of Lucy's wedding to Stanley Morris, seven years previously in 1933. In this particular photograph, grandma and Walter's sister Irene are seated on the right. Walter is standing to the right of the groom, and Charles Wormley, Grandma's second husband, is standing behind the bride. This appears to have been a 'society' wedding with no expense spared, compared with the very simple wedding photo, taken in granny's back yard, of when Walter and Grace Mary married in 1940. Even allowing for the fact that the country was at war, the material differences in the two photographs illustrates a great financial and social divide between the two families.

Walter's sister Lucy's Wedding Day – 1933

Why wasn't Alice at the wedding of Walter and Grace Mary? All the evidence I found suggests she wasn't even in Grimsby. She was across the other side of the country, staying at the Washington Hotel in Liverpool, where the SS Antigone was docked, preparing to marry Captain Stephen. I'd prefer to think that she was at her son's wedding and, over the years, the photographs have been mislaid, but this is highly unlikely. How utterly selfish, that she could not bring herself to attend her only son's wedding, yet she insisted on her new daughter-in-law being a witness to her own wedding in Liverpool two days later. As an act of self-regard, that takes some believing.

This appears to be yet another example of Alice's nature that reflects an observation, not made by me I hasten to add, *'Alice thought only of herself'*? Moreover, does it offer a valuable further insight as to why she cut herself off from Grace Mary after Walter's death? What was her motivation? Did she think that Walter had married beneath him and she did not approve of the marriage in the first place? I regret to say that is the conclusion I am drawn towards. It may also explain why Alice never invited the newlyweds to stay with her after they married even though she had the room. Before they bought a home of their own, Walter and Grace Mary lived for a short while with Grace Mary's mother and her brothers and sisters in Victor Street.

Alice's marriage to Captain Stephen was very short-lived and because of the war, they wouldn't have spent a great deal of time together. In October 1942, while serving as the ship's master on the SS Antar, which was berthed at Haifa in Israel at the time, Captain Stephen was found dead in very mysterious circumstances; his body was discovered floating in the water of the dock. Although there was no actual sign of physical injury, both his wallet and papers were missing. Consequently, the local police treated the death as highly suspicious and possible murder. Captain Stephen was a powerfully-built man and reputedly a strong swimmer and would have been able to cope with accidentally falling in the water, unless he had injured himself whilst falling. But there were no signs of physical injury! The mystery is, what had happened to the wallet and his papers?

Despite all the police's investigations, no-one was ever apprehended and no motive other than a possible mugging established. It does seem likely that someone had literally got away with murder! But this was 1942 and there was a war on; very dangerous times indeed. Captain Stephen was buried at the Khayat Beach War Cemetery just outside Haifa, Israel. This is the inscription in the record of entry:

In Memory of Master BEDDIE MCDONALD STEPHEN
SS Antar (London), Merchant Navy
who died age 55 on 17 October 1942
Son of John Stephen and Maggie Stephen and husband of
Alice Stephen, of New Waltham, Lincolnshire.
Remembered with honour
KHAYAT BEACH WAR CEMETERY

The suspicious circumstances of Captain Stephen's death delayed any possible War Widows' pension that Alice may have been entitled to. Initially, the wartime Ministry of Pensions argued that Captain Stephen's death was not attributable as 'war risk' related and therefore Alice would not qualify for a pension. Alice counter-argued that Captain Stephen would not have been in Israel had it not been for the war. Fortunately, Alice had the tenacity, determination and independent financial means to support and sustain her during the six years she had to fight, for what she believed to be her rights. Not all war widows would have been so driven or so financially fortunate. Although Captain Stephen had died in 1942, it would be nearly four years later before the Minister of Pensions in July 1946, announced a change in Government policy that, ultimately allowed Alice's claim to be considered. The Ministry finally wrote to Alice almost a year later in April 1947. The letter is reproduced below:

Dear Madam [sic]

With reference to representations made on your behalf, I have to inform you that following the review of your case under the terms of the announcement by the Minister of Pensions on 25th July 1946, your claim has been admitted on the ground that the death of your husband was directly attributable to a war risk injury.

The question of an award of compensation to you under the War Pensions (Mercantile Marine) Scheme is under consideration and a further communication on the subject will be sent to you as soon as possible.

Yours faithfully,
L Hawkins
For Secretary

Mrs A. Stephens
"Sherwood"
Station Road, New Waltham, GRIMSBY, Lincs

This letter, written in 1947, provides an indication of the on-going battle Alice must have had with the Ministry of Pensions to get what she believed were her rights. Eventually, she won her case and received a War Widows' (Mercantile Marine) pension. However, after receiving the letter, it was nearly another year before Alice actually started to collect the war pension in 1948, six years after Captain Stephen had died.

If payment of the pension was backdated to when Captain Stephen died, which I don't know whether it was or not, the delay in making the payment would have presented Alice with a reasonable sum of money; a nice windfall gain. If it wasn't backdated, how much had she lost through red tape and bureaucracy delaying that which was rightfully hers?

Chapter Nine

Grace Mary's Famous Ancestor

In the opening chapter I commented that, once I began to research and write this story, it became something far more wide-reaching than just being able to claim Walter's war service medals. I had started out on a journey to discover my family's history. So far, my figurative search for Walter has, concentrated on discovering his paternal and maternal bloodline ancestry and what made him the person that he became. In addition to developing a reasonable understanding of two hundred years of his family heritage, I can now picture and appreciate the influence his home life and upbringing had on him before he married; more of which I will comprehensively discuss in the later chapter 'The Making of a War Hero'.

Before I go on to do that, my immediate focal point changes to his wife Grace Mary (nee James) and her rather surprising family heritage. Albeit, only for a few short years, Grace Mary was such an important part of Walter's life; she bore him two children, my sister Pamela and me. Therefore, in order to present the complete picture of the 'Search for Walter', this part of the story now focuses on discovering the lifestyle and times of Grace Mary and her extended family. To aid my understanding of her ancestral heritage, it was necessary to explore three separate family trees, the Nelsons and the Kiddles on her mother's side and, the Jameses on her father's side. A partial combined family tree is presented on the following page. And just as I discovered when researching Walter's roots through the Bloy and Smith families, many more revelations and surprises from all sides of Grace Mary's extended family were in store for me. As I peeled each layer of my 'metaphorical research onion', I was constantly amazed by what I found beneath, some of which really beggars belief.

Grace Mary was a very beautiful young woman. Although I am biased because she is my mother, it is easy to see why Walter, who was a bit of a ladies man, would have been smitten with her. Unfortunately though, two serious industrial accidents, providence and fate, would dictate that she was raised in very different social and financial circumstances to those of Walter. Although Walter lost his father at a very young age, Alice's remarriage meant, within reason, he never really had to go without, whereas for Grace Mary, most of her childhood would be a continuous struggle with dire poverty, ill health and outrageous family misfortune. However, as destitute as her family was at times, it was always a very loving family home.

Grace Mary James – Walter's wife as a young woman

GRACE MARY JAMES'S Partial Combined Family Tree from 1776 - 1947

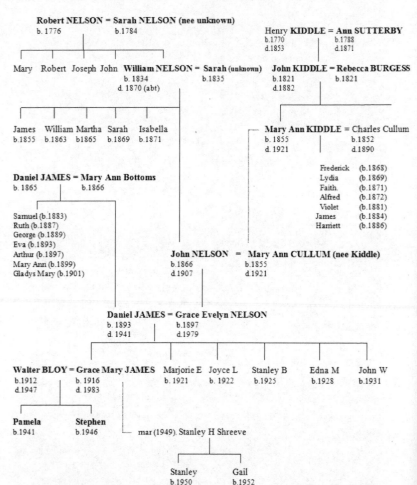

Robert NELSON = Sarah NELSON (nee unknown)
b.1776   b.1784

Henry KIDDLE = Ann SUTTERBY
b.1770   b.1788
d.1853   d.1871

Mary Robert Joseph John William NELSON = Sarah (unknown)
                              b.1834   b.1835
                              d.1870 (abt)

John KIDDLE = Rebecca BURGESS
b.1821   b.1821
d.1882

James   William Martha Sarah Isabella
b.1855 b.1863 b.1865 b.1869 b.1871

Mary Ann KIDDLE = Charles Cullum
b.1855   b.1852
d.1921   d.1890

Frederick   (b.1868)
Lydia   (b.1869)
Faith.   (b.1871)
Alfred   (b.1872)
Violet   (b.1881)
James   (b.1884)
Harriett   (b.1886)

Daniel JAMES = Mary Ann Bottoms
b.1865   b.1866

Samuel (b.1883)
Ruth (b.1887)
George (b.1889)
Eva (b.1893)
Arthur (b.1897)
Mary Ann (b.1899)
Gladys Mary (b.1901)

John NELSON = Mary Ann CULLUM (nee Kiddle)
b.1866   b.1855
d.1907   d.1921

Daniel JAMES = Grace Evelyn NELSON
b.1893   b.1897
d.1941   d.1979

Walter BLOY = Grace Mary JAMES   Marjorie E   Joyce L   Stanley B   Edna M   John W
b.1912   b.1916   b.1921   b.1922   b.1925   b.1928   b.1931
d.1947   d.1983

Pamela   Stephen
b.1941   b.1946

mar (1949). Stanley H Shreeve

Stanley   Gail
b.1950   b.1952

This partial combined family tree has been drawn and presented at this stage to frame an understanding of Grace Mary's heritage through the three families. As I explore each family in turn, more details, especially with the Nelson element of her family tree, will be revealed.

Grace Mary's maternal ancestral lineage stems from the Nelson family(s) who lived and worked in the Norfolk and Suffolk areas of England and the Kiddles, who came from the Louth area of Lincolnshire. Through her Nelson family heritage, there is a family connection that some may argue is too tenuous to be true, to one of our country's greatest heroes, Admiral Lord Horatio Nelson, which I will be discussing later in this chapter. For purposes of this early part of Grace Mary's story, my interest in her ancestral line starts with her maternal great-great-grandfather Robert Nelson who was born in rural Suffolk in 1776 and his wife Sarah (nee unknown), who was born in 1784.

Historical context for this period is provided by the significance of the great events that were happening in and around our country about the time that Robert Nelson was born. In 1776, the American Colonies declared independence from England. Thus began the War of Independence, which England lost to the Colonial Army; George Washington would become President of what eventually became the United States of America. King George III, who 'lost' the American Colonies and would reign for 60 years, had only been on the throne for 16 years. Captain Cook departed with his ship Resolution for the Pacific Ocean and Australia. James Watt had recently patented his steam engine. And the Industrial Revolution, 1760s -1830s, that would lead to England (Great Britain) becoming the most powerful industrialised nation on earth, was irrevocably changing life for the working man. My purpose in linking the families in this story to these little vignettes of history, as I have done throughout, is to demonstrate that not too many generations separate us today from some of the most defining episodes of our country's history. Events like these may have been some of the hot topics of conversation of their day!

Robert and Sarah Nelson had five children: Mary, Robert, Joseph, John and William. According to the census of 1841, Robert, like many others of that time, not surprisingly was employed as an agricultural labourer. Through his efforts and enterprise Robert appeared to thrive, as by 1851, at the age of 76, he had become a Market Gardener with seven acres of land. For the moment, from this point forward my interest in the family is with their youngest son, William Nelson, who was born in 1834. To explain the reason for this, I have to temporarily jump forward one generation.

Grace Evelyn Nelson, Grace Mary's mother and Walter's future mother-in-law, was born on the 6th Jan 1898, originally believed to be 28th December 1897, the only child of John Nelson and his wife Mary Ann (nee Cullum). When I researched this part of the family ancestry, I was astonished to discover a well-kept secret about this marriage, which I am sure Grace Evelyn knew nothing about. My review of the census documents and other records all appear to indicate that John Nelson may have already been married when he wed Mary Ann Cullum. As I could not find any evidence to suggest his wife had died and he was actually a widower, I can only conclude that Grace Mary's (my mother) grandfather had committed bigamy!

John Nelson arrived in Grimsby in 1895 at the age 29, as a steward on a merchant ship that docked on the River Humber. He took up lodgings with Mary Ann Cullum (nee Kiddle), a widow with seven children from her marriage to Charles Cullum. Mary Ann Cullum who ran a boarding house at 120 Orwell Street, which was in the heart of the Grimsby dockland area, appears to have spent most of her married life pregnant. In addition to the seven children she delivered that survived, according to the Grimsby Register of Stillbirths, Mary Ann Cullum also had stillborn children in 1887 and 1889. Considering the gap of nine years between Alfred (b.1872) and James (b.1881), I am inclined to think she may have also had other stillborn children in this period, which are not recorded in any records. Throughout, all the research I undertook confirmed what I was already disposed to believe. In Victorian times, women were literally baby-making machines. Large families were not just the norm, they were expected. It was the women's duty (fate) to provide them. Queen Victoria with her husband Prince Albert led by example, they had nine children, four boys and five girls.

Close scrutiny of the available records show that John Nelson had been born in Liverpool in 1866, the fourth of six children produced by William and Sarah Nelson. This is contrary to what his daughter, Grace Evelyn Nelson, had always been led to believe. Her understanding, now mistakenly so, was that John Nelson's father, her grandfather, was also called John Nelson and worked as a publican in Liverpool, because this is what her father had told her and is what she told me. Unfortunately, this is most likely another family myth, as no records could be found of a John Nelson being a publican in Liverpool that confirmed this belief. A plausible explanation for this 'misunderstanding' will be offered as this part of the story progresses. My research produced fairly strong evidence to suggest that, in all probability, John Nelson's father was actually a William Nelson who was born in Suffolk in 1834.

The census of 1861, some four years before John Nelson was born, records William Nelson as an agricultural labourer then living at 11 Slater Street, which was near to the docks in the Toxteth region of Liverpool. Slater Street then, would have been at the heart of the hustle and bustle of a very busy working dockside area. Today with its pubs and clubs, it is a popular part of the Liverpool nightlife scene. William's wife Sarah (nee unknown), originally came from County Down in Northern Ireland. Sarah was living in Liverpool when she met and married William Nelson in about 1855. I was not really surprised to discover an Irish family connection. It is a reasonably safe assumption to say many families in England will have some connection with Ireland, which can be traced back to the mass migration that happened during this period of the 19th century. History informs us that by the mid-1800s millions of working class people in Ireland were suffering intolerable hardship, starvation and abject poverty because of, among other reasons, the Great Potato famine of the 1840s and the oppressive nature of the English landowners. In Ireland, these were very desperate times indeed and are still remembered with much bitterness today, some 160 years later. Consequently there was mass migration out of Ireland 'to a better life' in England (Great Britain), or for some, even better still, the United States of America. Between 1845 and 1848 approximately one million people died in Ireland and a similar number of people emigrated.

As a result of this mass immigration, from the middle of the 19th century onwards, nearly all of the great civil engineering works and development in England, such as the railways, canals, tunnels, viaducts, docks and roads were completed through the sweat and toil of what became known as 'Irish Navvies'. By the 1850s a quarter of a million navvies, a force greater than the number of the Army and Royal Navy put together, were constructing the network of railways that were criss-crossing the country. Tramping from job to job, the navvies and their families worked in appalling conditions and often lived for many years on end in rough timber and turf huts, which they built for themselves alongside the railways, bridges, tunnels and cuttings they were constructing. In the 1840/50s, there was no compensation for death and injuries. Famous railway engineers like Isambard Kingdom Brunel resisted all efforts to provide their workers with adequate housing and sanitation and safe working conditions.

There were very few mechanical aids such as earth-movers or JCB diggers in those days. Consequently, millions of tons of rock and earth would have been excavated through hand tools, gunpowder and pure hard graft. Sadly, in these working conditions, not surprisingly there were many fatalities. In one particular case, the Woodhead Railway Tunnel, built between 1839 and 1852, the death rate among the navvies was higher than that of the soldiers who fought with Wellington at the Battle of Waterloo. The navvies and their families developed a reputation for fighting, hard living and hard drinking. Respectable Victorians viewed them as degenerate and a threat to social order. Much of this criticism however, was unjustified. Despite terrible exploitation, deprivation and backbreaking work, the navvies achieved great feats of civil engineering, which to this day remain as visible testimony and monuments to their efforts.

The situation was not really much better for some of the Irish immigrants that made it across the Atlantic Ocean to the United States. During the four-year period that the American Civil War was raging (1861 - 65), thousands of Irish immigrants were drafted almost immediately they disembarked from the ships, into either the Confederate or Union armies; which army they joined depended on whether they had landed in the North (Union states) or the South (Confederate states) of the United States. They were then required to fight for a cause they knew little about and in a country they had only just arrived in. The reality of this intolerable set of circumstances is that young Irish men, who may have originated from the same part of Ireland, could end up on opposite sides of a war they didn't understand and would be killing the opposing soldiers, who not long before may well have been their neighbours back home. Again many thousands died. The story of this tragedy is a common theme among Irish folk songs and, can be regularly heard today in the bars and pubs of Dublin and other Irish cities.

Yet again for good reason, I have digressed. I believe it essential to keep doing so, to provide the contextual canvas over which I can paint in the texture and colour, in relation to my family's history, of what happened and why. Then as now, there was regular sailing between Ireland and Liverpool. Given the prevailing circumstances in Ireland, it is not too difficult to understand why Sarah had left County Down and arrived in Liverpool. An examination and analysis of the pre-famine 1841 census revealed that Irish-born people accounted for over 17 per cent of the population in Liverpool and by 1851 this figure had risen to over 22 per cent. Although many Irish settled in the city, the census of 1871 shows that the Irish population of Liverpool had started to decline; a large percentage had re-emigrated to the USA or moved to the industrial centres of Lancashire, Yorkshire and the Midlands of England.

On the other hand, why William Nelson arrived in Liverpool from Suffolk is not so clear and is anyone's guess. Even though this is conjecture, it is credible to believe. William may have seen the City of Liverpool as a place where he could make his fortune and have a better life. Especially as we now know that agricultural labourers would have been very poorly paid and would have very little opportunity for advancement in rural England. The rapid development and industrialisation of Victorian England encouraged many people to move around the country to seek work. We have already seen that both William and Walter Bloy left rural Lincolnshire in the 1860/70s and went to Grimsby to try to better their lot. William Nelson was probably no different to them; he had moved to Liverpool to better his circumstances.

William and Sarah had at least five children together before William, when just 36 years old, died of suspected typhoid in 1870. Because of the nature of the disease, it is safe to presume that William and his family, not unlike the Bloy family of the same period, initially lived in very unsanitary conditions. Typhoid was not uncommon among the poorer working class. Sarah was pregnant with their fifth child (Isabella) when she became a widow at only 30 years of age. The census returns of 1871 make no mention of daughter Isabella; but she does appear on the following census in 1881 when aged 9, which implies she was born just after the previous census, and confirms Sarah would have been pregnant when William died. Although originally employed as an agricultural labourer, William, before he died, established a 'carrier' business that Sarah, now the head of the family, took over and developed on her *'own accord'* even further. By the 1881 census, Sarah was listed as a 'cart owner', her elder son William was a 'wheelwright', the eldest daughter Martha was a housekeeper and the youngest daughters, Sarah and Isabella were schoolchildren. Her other son, John Nelson, Grace Mary's grandfather, in whom we are now interested, was then aged 15 and employed as a 'carter'. The family appeared to be flourishing as they had moved to Pembroke Street, which in the late 19th century was a nice location in the Mount Pleasant area of Liverpool.

I am aware from first-hand knowledge, told to me by my granny, that John Nelson was a merchant seaman when he arrived in Grimsby in 1895. This is where his story starts to become both confusing and interesting. Between the censuses taken in 1881 and 1891, John had ceased being a 'carter' and had become a sailor. Moreover by 1891, he appeared to have acquired a wife, Jane, who was born in Denbigh, North Wales in about 1864. What is not clear is, when in the 1880s did John Nelson marry Jane and what happened to her? Trying to track this union down was like looking for the proverbial *needle in a haystack*. Other than the census information, I could find no information that would help me locate where and when they had married, whether there were any children or had Jane died. Perhaps more importantly, was he still married to her when he arrived in Grimsby?

I also find it hard to explain, why did John Nelson choose to leave the ship he was serving on when it reached the River Humber? Jumping ship, as it was often called, was not uncommon in days gone by. Many a seaman did it and settled in whatever port they had landed in. I wondered if this is what John did. I was also curious that, if he was a serving seaman and would have had a berth on a ship, why did he need to go into lodgings with Mary Ann Cullum? It is possible that he had signed off the ship and was actually looking for a new berth on another ship and the lodgings were only temporary. This is pure supposition but worth considering; had he met Mary Ann in one of the many pubs found in the dockland area where she lived and, deciding he liked what he saw, chosen to stay in Grimsby? My granny told me her father never returned to Liverpool or perhaps more tellingly, never ever contacted his family again during her lifetime. Although I found this hard to understand, it encouraged me to think that he may have been running away from something or someone!

Admittedly, I may have posed more questions than answers, but that's the nature of genealogical research. I think he was still married when he arrived in Grimsby. Bigamy, particularly with sailors, was not uncommon in those days, if the oft-used expression *'a girl in every port'* is anything to go by. If John Nelson had 'jumped ship' and left his responsibilities behind in Liverpool, how could his true wife Jane, who may have been illiterate, and, assuming she was still alive, have begun to track him down? Would she have had the ability and wherewithal to do so? Moreover does it explain why, when giving his family details for the marriage certificate at his wedding to Mary Ann Cullum, he named his father as John Nelson a Publican in Liverpool, of whom, try as I may no trace could be found. Interestingly enough, when you receive copies of marriage certificates from Government Records Office, there is a disclaimer that states *'this certificate is not proof of identity'*. John Nelson could have told the Registrar anything he wanted too. When and by whom are family details checked? Sir Walter Scott sums it up nicely. *"O, what a tangled web we weave, when first we practise to deceive".*

Though I was fairly sure that the father (William) and grandfather (Robert) I had found for John Nelson were correct, proving the next claim, which I originally thought was totally preposterous, convinced me that I had tracked down the right family tree. For John to say his father was also called John and a publican in Liverpool, would mean that it was virtually impossible for him to claim to be a descendant of Admiral Lord Horatio Nelson, which he always maintained that he was. However, if his father was indeed William Nelson from Suffolk, then John's claim has more validity. According to my granny, (his daughter), John Nelson always had a picture of Admiral Lord Horatio Nelson hanging in his home and was unwavering in his conviction that there was a family connection to the great man. In fact, he would get quite irritated with those who dismissed it as a fanciful idea and wishful thinking on his part.

My first reaction when my granny told me this story was to be dismissive; what a load of old nonsense! On reflection, it would have been too easy for me to reject the idea out of hand, particularly as John Nelson may have been economical with the actualité in respect of who his father was and whether he was free to marry Mary Ann Cullum. However, as I had concluded that his father was William Nelson, whose family came from the Suffolk area and not Liverpool, I decided to research this possible connection further; I already knew from my interest in English history that Lord Nelson had family links with this part of England. Moreover, if a connection to Lord Nelson's family could be found through the Nelsons of the Norfolk - Suffolk area, it would re-affirm the notion that John Nelson's father could not have been from Liverpool as he had stated.

Once I started on this phase of my journey of discovery, to my complete surprise and I must add, joy, I found John Nelson's claim to be very plausible, a word I use deliberately. I became quite enthusiastic at the prospect of being able to establish an undisputable link. Because Lord Nelson's ancestral lineage has been frequently researched and documented, a proven link for John's claim would then take Grace Mary's (my mother's) ancestry back, not just to the 18th century, but at least two hundred years earlier to the 16th century and the time of Henry VIII and his daughter Elizabeth I. What an exciting thought!

John Nelson was born in 1866, just 61 years after Lord Nelson's death, which in terms of family history is really not so long ago. John's memory of what he had been told about family affairs and history would be reasonably fresh in his mind. He would have been able to relate his knowledge to others with some degree of accuracy, just as I am doing with this story based around the death of my father Walter Bloy, which was 65 years ago. I must stress however, that I make no ardent claim at all as to the legitimacy of John Nelson's assertion and will leave the readers to make up their own mind; I know what I think. To that end, I am presenting what I have found to be facts and have redrawn the extended Nelson family tree, which encourages an argument to be made that supports John Nelson's, perhaps not so outrageous, claim. There is no chance though, that he was as closely related as he would have liked to believe. All the male lines descended from Nelson, or even Lord Nelson's brothers, are known very well to have died out. However, there is a real chance of an earlier connection, because both John Nelson's and Lord Nelson's family were from the same Norfolk area. Looking for this earlier association is where I chose to focus my research.

William Nelson (b.1834), whom I believe to be John Nelson's father, came from Thingoe Rougham, which is a small village of just over 1000 people, situated near the ancient town of Bury St Edmunds in the county of Suffolk. William was the last-born child of Robert Nelson (b.1776), who was himself one of nine children. The fact that Robert Nelson is my great-great-great-grandfather on my mother's side of the family, I believe is not in dispute, but understanding his lineage should help establish whether the connection to Lord Nelson is reality or fantasy. Robert Nelson's father was not one of Lord Nelson's brothers, that much is absolutely certain because the history of Lord Nelson's siblings is well documented. Although the Rev. Edmund Nelson, Lord Nelson's father, also had eight siblings who lived in the Norfolk-Suffolk area, looking at birth dates, it is not possible that Robert Nelson could have been the offspring of one of the Reverend's brothers. I needed to find another link to Lord Nelson's family tree.

Further research established that Robert was actually the sixth child of nine produced by William Nelson, (b.1730) and his wife Sarah (nee Bass), whom he married in 1763 at the Thomas a Beckett church in Westley, Suffolk. Robert also lived and worked in the Hawstead / Thingoe Rougham area of Suffolk for the whole of his life and eventually became a market gardener. His father, William, was a husbandman and would normally have been a wealthier person than a common agricultural labourer. William was the fourth of ten children born to Edward Nelson (b.1700) and his wife Jane (nee Parker), the daughter of Nicholas Parker and Ursula Twiddy. Edward and Jane, who had married in 1723, lived in the Norfolk village of Colkirk, which is very significant in relation to my search for a link to Lord Nelson's family tree.

Connecting GRACE MARY'S Family Tree to Admiral Lord Horatio Nelson

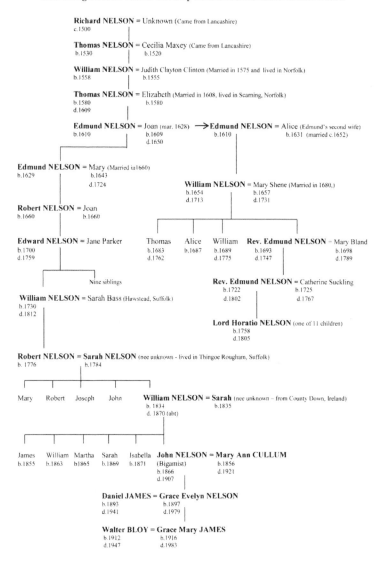

Richard NELSON = Unknown (Came from Lancashire)
c.1500

Thomas NELSON = Cecilia Maxey (Came from Lancashire)
b.1530   b.1520

William NELSON = Judith Clayton Clinton (Married in 1575 and lived in Norfolk)
b.1558   b.1555

Thomas NELSON = Elizabeth (Married in 1608, lived in Scarning, Norfolk)
b.1580   b.1580
d.1609

Edmund NELSON = Joan (mar. 1628) →**Edmund NELSON** = Alice (Edmund's second wife)
b.1610   b.1609   b.1610   b.1631 (married c.1652)
d.1650

Edmund NELSON = Mary (Married in 1660)
b.1629   b.1643
d.1724

William NELSON = Mary Shene (Married in 1680,)
b.1654   b.1657
d.1713   d.1731

Robert NELSON = Joan
b.1660   b.1660

Edward NELSON = Jane Parker   Thomas   Alice   William   **Rev. Edmund NELSON** = Mary Bland
b.1700   b.1683   b.1687   b.1689   b.1693   b.1698
d.1759   d.1762   d.1775   d.1747   d.1789

Nine siblings

William NELSON = Sarah Bass (Hawstead, Suffolk)
b.1730
d.1812

Rev. Edmund NELSON = Catherine Suckling
b.1722   b.1725
d.1802   d.1767

Lord Horatio NELSON (one of 11 children)
b.1758
d.1805

Robert NELSON = **Sarah NELSON** (nee unknown - lived in Thingoe Rougham, Suffolk)
b. 1776   b.1784

Mary   Robert   Joseph   John   **William NELSON** = **Sarah** (nee unknown – from County Down, Ireland)
b. 1834   b.1835
d. 1870 (abt)

James   William   Martha   Sarah   Isabella   **John NELSON** = **Mary Ann CULLUM**
b.1855   b.1863   b1865   b.1869   b.1871   (Bigamist)   b.1856
b.1866   d.1921
d.1907

Daniel JAMES = **Grace Evelyn NELSON**
b.1893   b.1897
d.1941   d.1979

Walter BLOY = **Grace Mary JAMES**
b.1912   b.1916
d.1947   d.1983

William and Sarah Bass were the first of this branch of the Nelson family tree I discovered who were living in the Thingoe Rougham area of Suffolk. All earlier ancestors on this family line from Edward Nelson backwards and those of Lord Nelson to whom I will be referring, came from a small cluster of Norfolk villages that are within an eight mile radius of each other, with the village of Colkirk at the centre. Other Norfolk villages such as Wendling, Sporle Fransham, Swaffham and Burnham Thorpe, which are frequently named and documented in the genealogy of Lord Nelson also feature regularly in the family tree of John Nelson and are key locations in terms of geographical importance. Not surprisingly, much of this part of the East Anglia region claims some connection to Lord Nelson, which may be a strategic marketing 'hook' to attract potential tourists.

As I found three consecutive generations of John Nelson's ancestors that took my search back to the 17th century and who lived in Colkirk, I felt cautiously optimistic that I was getting ever closer to proving the link. Edward Nelson, to whom I have already referred, was the son of Robert Nelson (b.1660) and his wife Joan. And encouragingly, this Robert was the son of an Edmund Nelson (b.1629) and his wife Mary, who was born in 1643 and died in 1724; all of whom lived in Colkirk. My optimism was further justified when I discovered this Edmund Nelson had a father also called Edmund Nelson, who was born in 1610 and lived in Scarning just a few miles from Colkirk, as too did Lord Nelson. At this juncture, it may be useful to refer back to the family tree, because I decided to re-examine the documented ancestry of Lord Nelson to see whether the two ancestral paths would come together.

Lord Nelson's parents were the Reverend Edmund Nelson (b.1722) and Catherine Suckling (b.1725), whose great- uncle was Sir Robert Walpole. For a time, they lived at the Rectory in Burnham Thorpe, just a few miles from Colkirk and where Lord Nelson was born. His paternal grandparents were the Reverend Edmund Nelson (b.1693) who came from Sporle - Fransham and Mary Bland (b.1698) from Hilborough, the daughter of John Bland (b.1672) and his wife Thomasine (b.1676). Again, both of their original home villages are within the eight mile catchment area of Colkirk; Lord Nelson's great-grandparents were William Nelson (b.1654) and Mary Shene (b.1657), the daughter of Thomas Shene (b.1621) and Alice (b.1625) who also came from the same area of Norfolk. And then to my immense delight, I discovered that Lord Nelson's great-great-grandfather was called Edmund Nelson and had been born in 1610.

My delight was temporarily subdued when I discovered that this Edmund Nelson was married to Alice (b.1631) who was 21 years younger than him and from whom Lord Nelson's ancestry were descended; whereas the Edmund Nelson on John Nelson's family line, had married Joan (b.1609) in 1628 and it was from this marriage John Nelson's ancestry can be traced. Fortunately, my investigation revealed that they are the same Edmund Nelson. Joan was his first wife, who had died about 1650, and Alice his second wife. Consequently, I concluded that Lord Nelson's great-great-grandfather and John Nelson's great-great-great-great-great-grandfather is indeed, the same person. I offer no more and leave you to make up your own mind. Of course, I may be totally wrong in my original assertion that John's father was William Nelson from Suffolk and not John Nelson, a publican from Liverpool. As I don't think I am, Grace Mary (Walter's wife), is a distant relative of Admiral Lord Horatio Nelson.

Chapter Ten

Scoundrels, Deportation and War Heroes

Returning to the main theme of this part of the story: who was Mary Ann Cullum (nee Kiddle) whom John Nelson married and how relevant is she to my search for Walter?

Mary Ann Cullum (nee Kiddle), hereafter referred to as Mary Ann, who could neither read nor write, was Grace Mary's (Walter's wife to be) grandmother. She was born in 1855 at Eastgate, Louth, Lincolnshire, just one year after the infamous 'Charge of the Light Brigade', immortalised in the poem by Lord Alfred Tennyson, himself a son of Lincolnshire. This was the time of the Crimean War and Florence Nightingale, the lady with the lamp. George Hamilton-Gordon, the 4th Earl of Aberdeen was Prime Minister, and William Ewart Gladstone, who would later become Britain's oldest Prime Minister, was the Chancellor of the Exchequer when she was born. Mary Ann would be 13 years old, and would have given birth to her first child before Gladstone became Prime Minister for the first of the four occasions he held that office. Charles Dickens was producing much of his work at this time.

Census records show that Mary Ann was the sixth of eight children produced by John Kiddle and his wife Rebecca (nee Burgess), whom he married in 1840. There are some contradictions about what her father, John Kiddle, did for a living. According to some records, he was a 'journeyman'. The word *journeyman* comes from the French word *journee*, which means the period of one day. The title refers to the journeyman's right to charge a fee for each day's work. Journeymen would normally be employed by a master craftsman, but would live apart and might have a family of their own. Whereas, consecutive census records of 1851 and

Mary Ann Cullum c.1910

1861 describe him as a 'Poultry-man'. As I delved a little deeper, I noticed that John Kiddle's occupation appears to have changed again. On both Mary Ann's birth certificate and the marriage certificate for when she married John Nelson in Grimsby in 1896, her father was described as a Hackster or Huckster. Not knowing what a Hackster or Huckster was, I checked and, to my surprise, discovered that it was a derogatory term for a scoundrel, bully or a ruffian! Initially I could offer no explanation or meaning other than that. However further research later revealed that John Kiddle was, to use the expression of the day, a bit of a rapscallion who had a criminal record.

To aid understand my narrative, the family tree shown below highlights ten generations of the KIDDLE ancestry from the late 16th century up to the latter part of the 20th century.

During this stage of my research, the accuracy of census records was called into question because, in the 1861 census, the family surname had been spelled as it sounded – Kiddall. Furthermore, Mary Ann was referred to as Margery Ann and, as it had not been corrected, it suggested to me that the whole family may have been illiterate or had limited reading ability. The incorrect name reflects what I discussed earlier about how names could get changed, by being spelled as they sounded. Although, by the census of 1871 the names had reverted back to Kiddle and Mary Ann, alternative spellings of Kiddell and even Riddle, when someone had interpreted the K as an R, were also seen.

William **KIDDLE**
c.1590s

William **KIDDLE** = Sarah ?? (married before 1680; lived in Stoke Trister, Somerset)
c. 1660

William **KIDDLE** = Elizabeth ?? (married before 1704; lived in Stoke Trister, Somerset)
b.1680
d.1756

Five siblings ———— Henry **KIDDLE** = Mary ?? (married before 1730; lived in Stoke Trister, Somerset)
b.1704
d.1760

Thirteen siblings ———— Henry **KIDDLE** = Jane COX (married in 1762; lived in Shaftesbury, Dorset)
b.1739

Eight siblings ———— Henry **KIDDLE** = Ann SUTTERBY (married in 1806; Henry was a soldier from Dorset, in the
2nd, or Queens Bays Regiment of Dragoon's guards.)
b.1770   b.1773
d.1853   d.1871

Jane	Edward	Henry	Catherine	Charles	John	Matilda	Harriet	Elizabeth	Edward
b.1807	b.1811	b.1813	b.1813	Frederick	b.1820	b.1821	b.1824	b.1829	b.1829
	d.1816			b.1817					
				d.1861					

John KIDDLE = Rebecca BURGESS (married about 1840)
b.1820   b.1821
d.1882

Emma	Betsey	Henry	James	Alfred	**Margery**	John	Joseph	George	Fanny
b.1842	b.1846	John	b.1851	b.1853	**Ann**	Valantine	b.1860	b.1861	b.1864
		b.1849			b.1855	b.1858			

(Note: Margery Ann is actually Mary Ann)

Mary Ann KIDDLE = Charles Cullum (married in 1873)
b.1855   b.1853
d.1921   d.1890

Frederick	Lydia	Faith	Alfred	Violet	James	Harriett
b.1868	b.1869	b.1871	b1872	b.1881	b.1884	b.1886

(…………Grace Evelyn Nelson's half-brothers and sisters………)

John NELSON = Mary Ann CULLUM
b.1866   b.1855
d.1907   d.1921

Grace Evelyn NELSON = Daniel JAMES
b.1897   b.1893
d.1979   d.1941

Grace Mary JAMES = Walter BLOY
b.1916   b.1912
d.1983   d.1947

With genealogical research, there are occasions when we will never know for certain where our distant ancestry came from, and at best, can only make an educated guess. Some of the earliest references to what became the family name Kiddle, were as a form of fish trap made of willow wood; the name for these fishermen was kiddlers. Evidence of these traps has been uncovered in parts of the south-east coastline, including Dorset and Somerset, where my exploration of the Kiddle family line will take us. A few references to the name Kiddle appear as early as the 14th century at Barking, where the most important industry until the middle of the 19th century was fishing. The earliest mention of salt-water fishing by men from Barking was in 1320, when several were prosecuted by the authorities of the City of London, conservators of the Thames, for the illegal use of kiddle nets, with too fine a mesh. How ironic that as far back as seven hundred years ago people were being prosecuted for taking undersized fish. It seems that nothing changes!

The earliest references to Kiddle as a surname appeared during the 16th century. My interest, in relation to this story, starts with the birth in 1680 at Stoke Trister in Somerset, of William Kiddle, whom I believe to be the son of another William Kiddle (c.1660) and his wife Sarah (nee unknown). After examining other family trees on genealogy and family tracing web-sites, I concluded that this William Kiddle was the common ancestor of the Kiddle family in Louth, Lincolnshire, from whom Mary Ann is descended. In about 1700, William married Elizabeth (nee unknown), with whom he had at least six children before he died on the 28th April 1756 in Bourton, Dorset. Records indicate that the parish registers of Stoke Trister were destroyed by fire and new registers were started in c.1750. Bishops' transcripts for this period are un-reliable; therefore, one can only guess at the whereabouts of births, deaths and parentage. It is believed the occupations of the Kiddle family at this point in history were linen weavers; linen was in demand as it was used in the making of ships' sails at this time.

The family ancestry of the Kiddles of Louth can be traced back directly to William and Elizabeth's second child, Henry Kiddle, who was born in 1704 and baptized on the 12th December 1704, in Stoke Trister, Somerset. This Henry married Mary (nee unknown) sometime before 1739, and together they had 14 children, before he died at the age of 56 in 1760 at Silton in Dorset. Nothing else of interest at this stage could be discovered about Henry and Mary. However, it was their first-born child, also called Henry (b.1739) and baptised in Penselwood, Somerset, who provides the link to the later Lincolnshire Kiddle family and Mary Ann Cullum's (nee Kiddle) ancestry. Henry married Jane Cox on the 14th April 1762, at St Peter's church, Shaftsbury, Dorset and together they had at least nine children. In respect of Mary Ann's lineage my concentration now is on Henry and Jane's second child, who was also called Henry (b.1770). This particular Henry Kiddle is Mary Ann's grandfather and on whom I now focus.

In 1790, at the age of 20, Henry Kiddle, who was a fairly tall man about 5ft 10 inches in height, had fair hair, grey eyes and a fair complexion, enlisted into the 2nd Regiment of Dragoon (Queen's Bays) Guards, at the time of the French Revolutionary Wars, 1793-1802. He gave his place of birth as Bourton in Dorset and his occupation as a breeches maker, which appears to tie in with the discovery about the Kiddle family as linen weavers.

The regiment, which has an illustrious history, was first raised from the neighbourhood of London as the Earl of Peterborough's Regiment of Horse in 1682, by the regimenting of various independent troops, and ranked as the 3rd Regiment of Horse. In 1767, the regiment was ordered to switch to riding bay horses (those with white or dappled-white hair) and renamed the '2nd Dragoon Guards (Queen's Bays)'. This is accentuated in the regimental badge which is simply the word 'BAYS' within a laurel wreath surmounted by a crown. The regimental motto is *"Pro Rege et Patria"*, which is Latin for "For King and Country". With over 300 years of service to the Crown, The Queen's Bays (2nd Dragoon Guards) has a regimental history second to none, having participated in every major conflict and campaign undertaken by England (United Kingdom) since its formation in 1682 to the present day.

The regiment fought in Germany, the Low Countries and northern France during the first three years of the French Revolutionary Wars, where they often provided the only British contingent in a largely Austrian, Prussian and Hanoverian force. On one occasion in the battles against Napoleon's forces, one squadron of the Bays, under the command of Major Craufurd, attacked a picket of French, consisting of six officers and about a hundred and fifty men, and took no less than a hundred and four prisoners, the remainder being killed in the attack; and till the close of the campaign the Queen's took their share in the privations, the reverses and conquests that ended with the winter retreat of 1794. They also fought as infantry at the siege of Dunkirk in 1793, since the ground there was too marshy to operate as cavalry, before arriving back at South Shields at the end of 1795.

Although I cannot say for certain whether Henry Kiddle took part in these actions against the French, I suspect he may well have done, because he was a serving Dragoon Guardsman, having enlisted three years before. However, I do know that he must have seen violent action, where he had to fight for his life, because he was injured and invalided out of the regiment on the 24th November 1809. When he was discharged from the army, Henry received 14 days' pay *'to carry me to Chelsea.'* Further scrutiny of his army records indicate he had enlisted at the age of 20 and served as a private for 12 years and 223 days, and then as a corporal for 4 years and 163 days, for a total of, including time on leave, 18 years and 21 days service. He was discharged and rendered unfit for further service, after having lost the sight of his left eye and the sight and vision of his other eye being *'much impaired'*.

Henry first appears in Louth in 1806 whilst still serving as a soldier, by marrying Ann Sutterby in St James church of Louth, which would host many Kiddle baptisms, burials and weddings over the next fifty years or so. For the next part of my journey of discovery, I am indebted to a Paul Kiddle of Basingstoke who, in 2001, posted his research into the Kiddle family history on the internet. According to his research, Henrys origins would have remained a mystery if it were not for two chances. Firstly: in 1884 Ann Kiddle (nee Sutterby) was clearly experiencing some trouble over the absence of a baptismal record for her eldest son, also called Henry. Accordingly, she made a declaration that this Henry junior had indeed been baptised at home in 1813. In the course of a diatribe against the inefficiency of the then rector of Louth, she gave the details of her husband, that he was an *'out pensioner of Chelsea hospital'* from the 2nd Regiment of Dragoons (or Queen's Bays), which has now been confirmed, from his army discharge papers. Secondly, Henry Kiddle lived long enough to appear on the census of 1851, which was the first census to name his place of birth as Dorset! From this and other records it was possible to establish that he was indeed from Bourton in Dorset, and that his parents were Henry Kiddle (b.1739) and Jane Cox, who had married on the 13th April 1762 at St Peter's church, Shaftesbury, Dorset.

Despite extensive research, I can't fully explain how or why Henry Kiddle settled down in Louth or why he was even there. Henry would have left Bourton, Dorset, after joining the army as a young man. At that time, the regiments were fighting under the Duke of York and quite possibly would have embarked from ports on the east coast of England for Germany and the Low Countries to carry the war to Napoleon's forces. This is of course pure conjecture. I'll never know for certain. It is possible that Henry may have stayed in Louth on route to Lincoln, which may have been a 'temporary' garrison town, or, the army could have been using the Louth navigational canal, which opened in 1770, to ferry troops back to Lincoln from the east coast. For sure, Henry Kiddle's battalion were certainly in the area and it is certain that he married Ann Sutterby in Louth in 1806 while still serving in the army. Furthermore, as he was discharged in 1809, some three years after his marriage, his injuries were sustained whilst living in Louth or nearby and still in the army.

After being discharged from the army, Henry was employed as a labourer in Louth from 1815-29 and later in 1851 as a groom; he died in 1853 and was buried in Louth aged 83 years. It seems that Henry and Ann remained in Louth for most, if not all of their married life, as all the baptisms of Henry and Ann's children, recorded between 1813 and 1832, were in Louth. Together Henry and Ann had ten children, all of whom, with the exception of their first child, were born in Louth. John Kiddle (Mary Ann's father) was their sixth child and quite remarkably, all his siblings, four sisters and five brothers, bar one, survived to adulthood. John's brother Edward, who was born in 1811, died when only five years old, four years before John was born. Two other siblings, Henry and Catherine (b.1813), were twins.

Throughout, the records indicate that the Kiddles certainly believed in having a large family: Henry and Ann's daughter Jane (b.1807) married William Stokes in 1824 and produced seven children. Henry (b.1813), a basket-maker, married Elizabeth Green in 1831 and had four children. Henry's twin, Catherine, married Henry Moses in 1834 and produced nine children. Charles Frederick, who became a shoemaker, married Sarah Arliss in 1837; they had 13 children. John (Mary Ann's father) with Rebecca Burgess had eight children. Harriett (b.1824) married Thomas Wilson in 1841 and also had eight children. And finally, Edward (b.1829), the youngest of the siblings, married Mary Ann Paddison in 1854, with whom he had at least five children. Not including the sisters, Matilda (b.1821) and Elizabeth (b.1829), for whom I could find no record of whether they had any children or not; seven of Henry and Ann's children produced fifty-four grandchildren between them for Henry and Ann to enjoy.

Mary Ann, as I previously discussed, would follow the family trend, not that she had much choice, and have seven children plus at least two stillborn children with her first husband Charles Cullum. The Kiddle family, all of whom lived in the Louth and Hogsthorpe area were undoubtedly a hardy and virile lot. Until starting this metaphorical search for Walter, I didn't know that, from these fifty-four grandchildren of Henry Kiddle and Ann (nee Sutterby), I must have what will probably be by now, hundreds of distant relations living in this part of Lincolnshire, just sixteen miles away. My journey really has been one of discovery after discovery!

Patriarch Henry, the old soldier, would live until the ripe old age of 83 before he died in 1853. Rather curiously though in the census of 1851, when he was 80 years old, Henry was actually 'residing' in the Eastgate House of Correction in Louth. I could not establish though what misdemeanour he had done to warrant being there, when he was admitted, or for how long he 'stayed' there. Was he a bit of a rapscallion too? His wife Ann, who did not die until 1871 when she was a notable 98 years of age, was recorded in the census as living in Northgate, Louth with her youngest son Edward. On this census, she was described as a Chelsea Pensioner's wife. I now know why.

Having a direct ancestor, my great-great-great-grandfather who fought in the Napoleonic Wars as a Queen's Dragoon Guardsman, I have to admit was not only a surprising revelation but a source of immense pride. In the National Collection there are many paintings of officers and men of the 2nd Regiment of Dragoon (Queen's Bays) Guards, at the time of the French Revolutionary Wars. Particularly stirring are the paintings of the Bays; mounted on their distinctive horses, wearing their blue and gold tunics, with sabres drawn charging at full tilt into the enemy lines. I am so proud that my great-great-great-grandfather would have been one of them. What an exciting thought.

Just as we saw with both the Bloy and Smith family history, Henry's son, John and his wife Rebecca also experienced the tragic heartbreak of infant mortality. During the 1850s, Mary Ann's two elder sisters died: Emma when she was about 12 years old and Betsey when she was only five years old. Though I have no further knowledge of the fate of the youngest sister Fanny, the census records appears to indicate that all Mary Ann's brothers thrived, married and had families of their own. When her brother Henry married, his wife was also called Mary Ann, and together they had at least five children. My interest here is how frequently the Henry and Mary Ann combination of names has occurred throughout all the family trees within this story.

John Kiddle and his family continued to live in Louth, whilst he looked for work as an agricultural labourer or poultry-man. Life would not have been too easy for them. This was still the time of the hiring fairs. If agricultural labouring work dried up, or was seasonal, men could be unemployed for several weeks on end; and because they had hardly enough to live on when they were working, would most likely have little or no resources to sustain them during the lean months. For many the shame of the Workhouses (Unions) would have been inevitable.

Perhaps this potential for regular hardship explains why in April 1866, at the General Quarter Sessions of the Peace held at Louth, John Kiddall [Kiddle] was sentenced to 12 months imprisonment with hard labour for larceny? The comments of the court's Chairman, added further explanation as to why her father John Kiddall [sic] was described as a 'Huckster' in Mary Ann's marriage and birth documents. From what was said about him in court, there is no doubt that he was a character! The court proceedings were reported in the Louth News on 14th April 1866. I quote:

'DUCK STEALING AT WEST ASHBY'

JOHN KIDDALL, 47, poulterer and ROBERT TOWNEND, 26, poulterer, were charged with stealing a duck the property of John Simons, of West Ashby, on 31ˢᵗ March. Mr Mellor prosecuted; Mr Yeatman defended. Mr Simons had seen his three ducks and a drake early on the morning in question, and on returning home, between three and four o'clock in the afternoon found one duck had gone, a second with its leg broken and a third injured on the back. Witnesses stated in evidence that they saw the prisoners coming from Horncastle towards Louth; when near Simon's house they saw them skulking by the side of the hedge, one with a stick and the other with a whip in his hand. Kiddall was seen with something about the size of a duck under his coat tails, and a lot of feathers were found near the spot where the accused were suspected of striking the ducks. Edward Stebbings saw the cart coming into Louth and Kiddall behind it with a duck in his hand. Mrs Musson said she called at Turner's the poultryman, and enquired for a couple of ducks; they had none, but Kiddall, who was there, said he could sell her one which he produced. Mr Yeatman made an ingenious defence, but the jury returned the verdict of guilty. The Chairman in passing sentence, said the bench had felt it necessary to make a distinction in the sentence to be awarded, as upon enquiry, they found Kiddall's character was a notoriously bad one, whilst there was no previous complaint against Townend. The sentence of the court against Kiddall would be twelve months' hard labour at Spilsby, and against Townend three months' hard labour at Louth.

After being sentenced to 12 months' hard labour at the Spilsby House of Correction, initially I could find no further trace or census records for John Kiddall (Kiddle). Mistakenly I was drawn to the conclusion that he may have died while he was in prison. History, records and anecdotal evidence indicates that in 1866, a 12 month prison sentence to be served with hard labour would have been very difficult, both physically and mentally, to endure. Many prisoners actually died while incarcerated and were often buried in unmarked graves. This however, would not be John Kiddle's fate. I 'rediscovered' him in the census of 1881. He had moved from Louth to Alford and was again employed as a Poulterer. I allowed myself a wry smile; thinking, I hope the poultry he sold this time had been legally obtained!

An uncle of John Kiddle, who was also called John Kiddall (Kiddle), whom I believe to be the seventh child of the nine born to Henry Kiddle (b.1739) and Jane Cox, did not fare too well at the hand of the law. In 1829, this particular John Kiddle was sentenced to two months' imprisonment and to be whipped for larceny. Not a lot of good that did him! He was clearly a serial offender, because one year later on the 13th July 1830, he was sentenced to seven years' transportation to the colonies, arriving in New South Wales, Australia after a voyage lasting eight months on the vessel Lady Harewood. He served his sentence and was presented with his 'Certificate of Freedom' on the 24th July 1837, the year that Queen Victoria came to the throne. Whether he remained in Australia is not known. The crime for which he was deported away from his family - he stole a coat! He was lucky that he hadn't been hanged for this theft as many would have been not many years before.

Only a few years previously, Sir Robert Peel, who had become the Home Secretary in 1822 in Wellington's government, introduced far-ranging criminal law and prison reform as well as creating the Metropolitan Police; the terms 'bobbies' and 'peelers' originated from his name. The number of crimes for which the death penalty was mandatory, were considerably reduced. For example, until 1827, defendants found guilty of stealing goods worth 40 shillings or more (£2.00 in today's money, more than a week's wages for some back then) from a dwelling house were subject, without favour, to the mandatory sentence of death. In 1827, as part of the series of Acts repealing the death penalty for various types of larceny, the minimum value of goods stolen from a dwelling house in order for the death penalty to be invoked was raised from 40 shillings to 100 shillings (£2.00 to £5.00). By revaluing the goods stolen to a level below this threshold, juries could avoid imposing the death penalty. The last time this verdict was used was in 1834.

Louth in the early to mid-19th century, where Mary Ann Kiddle grew up, was a small market town with a population of 8000, still more than twice that of Grimsby. Whilst it would have been a struggle for working class families, it is reasonable to assume, as Louth was a market town with the main work being agricultural, that actual living conditions were not too dissimilar to those in Tydd St Mary; unlike the social circumstances to be found in Grimsby at that time, where in the 1830s a 'House of Industry'(workhouse) was opened for 100 paupers, which included a treadmill for grinding corn and crushing bones.

At the age of 15, Mary Ann (allowing for her pregnancies, which I will discuss shortly) was working as a domestic servant girl for the family of Wright Simons, a Publican, at the Tavern at 66 Eastgate, Louth. Working in domestic service was not at all uncommon; by the 1850/60s, one in nine (11%) of all women were employed in domestic service. In August 1873, at the age of 18, Mary Ann married Charles Cullum in the parish church of Alford, Lincolnshire. Charles Cullum was the son of Jeremiah Cullum, a labourer, who had moved to Lincolnshire from Suffolk and was employed as a 'bondsman'. Bondsman is an alternative word for what was known in the middle ages as 'Serfdom' and was the enforced labour of serfs on the fields of landowners, in return for protection and the right to work on their leased fields. Jeremiah Cullum worked the land.

According to later census documents, Mary Ann and Charles had several children in quick succession, seven of which survived, these being: Frederick (b.1868), Lydia (b.1869), Faith (b.1871), Alfred (b.1872), Violet (b.1881), James (b.1884), and Harriett (b.1886). This I know to be correct, because my granny told me; they were her half-brothers and sisters. However, close scrutiny of the census records regarding the birthdates of some of the children creates an intriguing dilemma and perhaps questions how accurate the census records of this time actually were.

If they are accurate, and, as Mary Ann was born in 1855, she would have had to give birth to Frederick (b.1868) when she was only 13 and Lydia (b.1869) when she was 14. And as the age of sexual consent at that time was still 12, the law wasn't being broken. From the copy of the marriage certificate I obtained, I know she and Charles Cullum didn't marry until 1873, which led me to the conclusion that she was already the mother of two other children, Faith (1871) and Alfred (1872), when they married? Though I have no evidence to confirm it, there is the distinct possibility they were living together as husband and wife, *'over the brush'*, as it was known as for unmarried couple to cohabitate. And they were already the parents of four children before they actually got wed. What can be said for certain is that Mary Ann became the mother of those four children before she was eighteen years old; whether Charles was the father of all four, or of any, may be questionable.

In addition, when the frequency with which Mary Ann gave birth to all her children was closely examined as a timeline, some gaps needed further research. I discovered, after the birth of Harriett in 1886, Mary Ann had stillborn children in 1887 and 1889, which were recorded in the Grimsby Register of Stillbirths. And, within a year of marrying her second husband John Nelson, she gave birth to Grace Evelyn, my granny. Taking into consideration that her first four children were all born within the period 1868-72, why she would not fall pregnant again for nine years (until 1881), I think this is highly unlikely. Undoubtedly Mary Ann had no difficulty in conceiving. I am inclined to think that the gap of nine years between the births of Alfred (b.1872) and Violet (b.1881) can be explained by assuming Mary Ann may have had other stillborn children that were not recorded, because records were not kept at that time. If my assumption is correct, Mary Ann would have spent most of the period between 1868 and 1889 pregnant and as we now know, had seven surviving children and possibly at least four stillbirths before Charles Cullum died in 1890.

By 1881, Mary Ann Cullum's life changed, she and Charles had left Louth and the agricultural life behind and were then living in Bath Street in Grimsby. Most probably Charles had been lured to Grimsby in the hope of finding work as the town expanded. The records suggest they never returned to Louth; Grimsby is where they remained and is where Charles died, just nine years after arriving, when he was only 38 years old.

As I searched through my granny's family documents to develop this part of the story, I found two very poignant black-edged *'In Memoriam'* cards. During the Great War, the Cullums, like many other families, suffered casualties. Harriett's husband, James Johnson (Mary Ann's son in law), when just 32 years old was lost at sea as a result of enemy action on December 21st 1915. His *'In Memoriam'* card from his loving wife and children read:

"HE ANSWERED HIS COUNTRY'S CALL"

We little thought when leaving home
He'd never more return,
That he so soon in death would sleep,
And leave us here to mourn.
We cannot bend beside his grave,
For he sleeps in a silent sea,
Our Father knoweth where he lies'
And angels guard the spot

Less than a year later in the conflict, Mary Ann's youngest son, James also just 32 years old, was killed in action on the Somme with the Grimsby Chums on the 18th October 1916. His *'In Memoriam'* card from his youngest sister Harriett, to whom he was very close, read:

FROM HIS LOVING SISTER HARRIETT

He has gone to the home of the blest,
His sickness and sorrows are o'er;
He has gone to the land of the rest,
Where trials shall meet him no more.
Mourn not for him whom God has blest,
And taken to his heavenly rest,
Freed from all sorrow, grief and pain,
Our loss is his eternal gain.

These two *'In Memoriam'* cards, which are now nearly 100 years old, are part of our country's social history and, remind us of the terrible waste of young lives lost in the Great War. Although typing these few comments, not surprisingly, saddened me and caused me to reflect on the heartbreaking messages they contained. I was also proud that some of my granny's immediate family, in addition to her husband Daniel James (my maternal grandfather), whom I shall be discussing shortly, had *'done their bit'* for King and Country; even though two paid the ultimate sacrifice. Unfortunately, from another point of view, this episode encouraged me to question again why Walter Sidney Bloy (my paternal grandfather), had not answered his country's call. Though I'll never know, I would hate to think that he had been given a white feather!

After the death of her husband Charles in 1890, to make ends meet and to support her children, Mary Ann Cullum started to run the boarding house in Orwell Street. She was a striking looking woman and a notable character in her own right. Well liked, well known, and respected in the neighbourhood, and was often called upon to act as the midwife. Home births and the local 'midwife' were in the main, how things were done in those days. I suppose having had at least seven children of her own she would know what she was doing. Mary Ann was also regularly called upon to 'lay people out' and prepare them for the funeral when they had died. How ironic, that Mary Ann had the skills to bring babies into the world and then again at the end of their life preparing people for departure to the next.

She was also a generous person by nature and often helped out those in need by feeding them and giving the occasional free lodgings. Shortly after arriving from Liverpool, John Nelson lodged with Mary Ann, who was nearly 10 years his senior, for just over a year. Clearly age and the small matter of seven children didn't deter them because Mary Ann, when aged 40, married John Nelson at St Andrew's Church on Freeman Street, Grimsby on 1st November 1896. Perhaps it was to be expected, due to the age difference between Mary Ann and John Nelson, not all of her seven children welcomed the marriage. John Nelson was only two years older than Frederick, Mary Ann's eldest child! Soon after they married, John and Mary Ann's only child, my granny, Grace Evelyn Nelson (Walter's future mother-in-law), was born in 1897. However, by 1900, Mary Ann's five eldest children had all left home.

At the time of the 1901 census, eleven people were living at the boarding house in Orwell Street. John and Mary Ann, their daughter Grace Evelyn, who was three years old, and John Nelson's step-children, James (age 17) and Harriett (age 15), to whom I have just referred in respect of the *'In Memoriam'* notices. In addition there were six boarders, which included a husband and wife and their child, plus another man and his daughter. Yet again, another example of overcrowding, especially as the houses in Orwell Street were not particularly large, mainly two up and two down, though Mary Ann's boarding house did have three bedrooms. John and Mary Ann, together with the children Violet and Harriett Cullum and Grace Evelyn later moved to a much larger house in Victor Street, Grimsby.

John Nelson, who had left the Merchant Navy before getting married to Mary Ann Cullum, found employment as a cook on the Grimsby trawlers. Like Mary Ann, he too was very popular with the neighbourhood and with the local children, in particular because of his generosity. When he died in 1908 at the young age of 42 from pneumonia, it was a tragic loss to Mary Ann and their daughter Grace Evelyn, who was only 10 years old at the time. Nevertheless, Mary Ann had fortitude if nothing else; she carried on renting the house in Victor Street, from a Jewish Minister Mr A. Castle, and continued to take in boarders to earn a living and provide for her family. In later years, her daughter Grace Evelyn would remain at home, even after marrying herself, to look after her mother until she died at the age of 67, in May 1922.

To continue the story and before I focus totally on Walter and his war service, it is appropriate to review the James's (Grace Mary's paternal) family history. After all, they became Walter's in-laws.

Chapter Eleven

Curses, Poverty And The Means Test

Grace Evelyn Nelson, (Walter's future mother-in-law), hereafter referred to as Grace Evelyn, followed the tradition of the time by marrying young. At the age of 19, on the 8th January 1916, she married Daniel James at St Andrew's Church in Freeman Street, Grimsby. Coincidently, this was the same church where her mother and father had married twenty years before. Daniel James, who was often referred to as Bert, was an athletically built, handsome fair-haired man who came from Hitchin in Hertfordshire. He was serving in the Royal Navy as an able seaman on HMS Forth when he met and subsequently married Grace Evelyn.

Daniel James had joined the Royal Navy in 1910 as a volunteer boy sailor and saw active service throughout the First World War (1914 –1918) and beyond. He was first registered as Boy '2nd class' on HMS Impregnable, which was a training establishment that had started at Devonport in 1862, and was active until 1929. As training ships were replaced or added to the establishment, each was renamed *Impregnable* when they took on the role. When Daniel joined the service, HMS Black Prince was HMS *Impregnable III* between 1910 and 1922. He remained in the service for eleven years achieving the rating of able seaman before he was invalided out on the 6th July 1921. I have been unable to determine why he was invalided out of the service only a few months before completing the twelve years he had sign on for.

Daniel's Certificate of Service indicates that he served with distinction in at least 16 of His Majesty's vessels, some of which were shore-based training ships. He was awarded Chevrons in five consecutive years, 1914 - 1918 and also earned a good conduct badge in 1916 and then again in 1920. Daniel clearly had some ability; he was passed to be a leading seaman on 29th January 1918 and then passed an Education Test Part 1 in April 1920. For his service he was awarded the British War Medal on 11th December 1923. I was intrigued to also discover Daniel received two payments (1920 and 1922), which was his share of the Naval Prize fund.

Frequently during his time in the Royal Navy, Daniel would return to HMS Vivid, the Navy barracks at Devonport, which was commissioned in 1890, and operated as a training unit. The base was renamed HMS *Drake* in 1934. Several ships were renamed HMS *Vivid* whilst serving as depot ships for the base: HMS Vivid was the original depot ship between 1892 and 1912, and HMS Cuckoo was HMS *Vivid* between 1912 and 1920, which covers the periods that Daniel spent time there on some aspect of his training.

During the early part of his sea service, Daniel served on HMS Albermarle, a pre-Dreadnought, Duncan-Class battleship that had been named after George Monck, 1st Duke of Albermarle. When commissioned, she was amongst the fastest battleships of her time, but eventually became superseded by the new 'Dreadnoughts' which began entering service from 1906. Daniel also served on board HMS Cornwallis, another pre-Dreadnought, Duncan-Class battleship that, after being commissioned in 1904, spent most of her pre-war service with the Mediterranean Fleet. At the outbreak of World War 1 (the Great War), HMS Cornwallis was part of the 6th Battle Squadron, which was composed of pre-Dreadnought battleships and based at Portland. Rather fortunately, Daniel had left this vessel and was serving elsewhere when the ship met its doom in the second year of the war. From January 1915, HMS Cornwallis served in the Dardanelles campaign bombarding Ottoman Turkish forts and providing support for Allied forces landing on the Gallipoli Peninsula. Apart from a short period of service in the Indian Ocean, HMS Cornwallis remained in the Mediterranean and it was here that she was lost to a torpedo from a German submarine. The vessel stayed afloat long enough for most of her crew to abandon ship, although fifteen men of her complement of 720 died as a result of the explosion of the torpedo.

When he was not undergoing training at HMS Vivid, Daniel served for most of World War 1 as an able seaman on board HMS Forth, which was a submarine depot ship that spent some time in the North Sea theatre of war, operating as a support vessel for the submarines that were on station to protect the River Humber from German Battleships. The first Tenth Submarine Flotilla, as it was then called, had been created at the beginning of the war in December 1914. Based on HMS Forth at Immingham on the River Humber, the flotilla comprised five C- Class submarines and was commanded by Rear Admiral G.A. Bullard. Later the flotilla's base was moved to HMS Lucia on the River Tees.

While Daniel was based at Immingham, which in the early part of the 20th century was a very small town centred on the dock area, it is reasonable to assume that he may have spent some of his 'shore leave' in Grimsby. As it is only ten miles down the road and being so much larger than Immingham, it would have been a more attractive proposition for a young man looking to enjoy his time ashore. It is not too big an assumption therefore to think that this is how he met Grace Evelyn. Where he met her, I have no idea!

Daniel James's family came from the Hitchin area of Hertfordshire. His father, who was also called Daniel, was born in Baldock in 1865 and earned his living as a bricklayer/ contractor. With his wife Mary Ann (nee Bottoms), who was born in 1866, he had eight children. Not surprisingly, they too had married when very young. Daniel was only 18 years old and Mary Ann just 17 years when their first child Samuel was born in 1883. Samuel was soon followed by: Ruth (1887), George (1889), Daniel (1893), Eva (1894), Arthur (1897), Mary Ann (1899) and Gladys Mary (1901). Marrying young and having large families, despite the poverty and hardship, I frequently discovered, was commonplace during the eighteenth and nineteenth century. Unfortunately, the records appear to indicate that, by today's standards, a great many women died relatively young, having been literally *'bred to death'.*

Daniel James and Grace Evelyn Nelson's Wedding Day

For Daniel and Grace Evelyn, married life started out so well. On her wedding day, Grace Evelyn was conveyed to the church in a horse-drawn carriage pulled by a pair of matching white horses. For that period, and due to the expense, this was most unusual and must have been quite a show. It is easy to picture all the neighbours being out on the streets, cheering and shouting good luck and best wishes as the horse-drawn carriage passed by. This was typical of Daniel James, who was given to flamboyant gestures, as we shall see later with the purchase of the piano, to organise the carriage and white horses for his bride to be. Grace Emily Smith, whom I came to know as little Aunt Grace, (she was only just over 5ft tall), was a bridesmaid and Fred Robert Newton was best man at the wedding. I've not a clue as to who Fred Newton was! Looking at the wedding photo, I'm fairly sure that he must have borrowed the suit. The jacket seems to be burying him and the trouser bottoms have been turned up more than is normal. No matter, but it did make me smile!

Grace Evelyn and her husband returned home to live with her mother, Mary Ann Nelson (nee Kiddle), in Victor Street, Grimsby. Their first child, Grace Mary (my mother), who would become Walter Bloy's wife, was born later that year on 3rd December 1916. As Daniel was still on active service, he was sent to Hong Kong in 1916. I'm not sure why or how, but according to my granny, she had the opportunity to go too. I am somewhat sceptical about this; the country was at war. Maybe, with the passage of time, my granny's recollection was not quite as it was. However, because she had a baby on the way and with her mother's advancing years and failing health, she declined to go. Daniel was still away in Hong Kong when his daughter Grace Mary was born. He did not see her until he returned home in 1920, by which time she would be nearly four years old. For the final part of his sea service, April 1919 – March 1921, Daniel was an able seaman on HMS Ambrose, which was also a submarine depot supply ship, which prior to the war had been a merchant ship.

**Baby Grace Mary, mother Grace Evelyn and great aunt
Grace**

With Daniel, particularly in the early years of their marriage, it was to be feast or famine. It must have been a very difficult time for Grace Evelyn, having both a young baby and an elderly mother to look after at a time when the country was fighting the First World War. When Daniel was away from home on active service, Grace Evelyn received only £0-19-0d per week (£0.95 in new money) or 19 shillings (19 bob) as we used to call it, from the Royal Navy. To make ends meet, she needed to work. Just as Alice had done after Walter Sidney Bloy had died, Grace Evelyn worked hard to support her family, taking several jobs, including serving on the stalls on Freeman Street market and working in a range of shops. For a while she found employment in Dewhurst's the butcher's shop and had to take baby Grace Mary with her so that she could be breastfed at the back of the shop. By this time, her mother was not capable of looking after the child or even herself. The working hours in the shop were long, from 8.00am until 6.00pm. After finishing work, Grace Evelyn then had to return home each night to clean and cook at home. This I discovered was a foretaste of things to come. Grace Evelyn's lot would not improve; from the 1920s onward the majority of her life would be one of drudgery.

In those early years of her married life, all the cooking would have been done on a cast-iron range and oven that was built into the fireplace and had to be cleaned and blackleaded regularly. Town gas would be installed sometime later. The house in Victor Street was very large and her mother was getting weaker. All the while, Daniel James was away at sea serving in the Far East. Letters and the occasional postcard were few and far between. Worrying about what Daniel may have been facing on his wartime service with the Royal Navy and having to look after her baby and an elderly and increasingly infirm parent could not have been easy for Grace Evelyn; especially as she was barely out of her teens herself.

How often must she have thought 'it's a long road that has no turning and better days must surely lie ahead'?

While he was away at sea, Daniel regularly sent home several large sums of money. Where this money came from is anyone's guess. Gambling and playing cards is a likely source. On one occasion he sent £100 to Grace Evelyn, with instructions to buy a piano. This was not an inconsiderable sum of money, bearing in mind that his wife was only receiving only £0 19s 0d per week in wages from the Royal Navy. I have already suggested with Daniel it was feast or famine. Being the dutiful wife, the piano was duly purchased for the princely sum of £68–5s-0d from Holder Brothers Ltd based on Cleethorpe Road, Grimsby. Grace Evelyn negotiated the deal, which she did very well. The receipt dated 12th January 1920 shows that she managed to get a free piano stool and free tuning for up to six months and the option to return the piano within six months if it did not meet expectations. That walnut piano with its inlaid mother of pearl decorations and brass candlestick holders had pride of place in the front room of 177 Victor Street and then later, after they had moved to the house next door, the front room of 179 Victor Street, until Grace Evelyn died in 1979.

Many are the grandchildren, myself included, who tried to play a tune on that piano. Among the so-called working class, if you could afford it, having a posh front room, which was probably only used on special occasions and Sundays, was considered sophisticated during the early part of the 20th century. Having a piano was a status symbol. I suppose the really important factor was that people walking past Daniel and Grace Evelyn's house could see the piano through the window in the 'posh' front room.

On another occasion, Daniel sent a further £100 home to Grace Evelyn to be deposited in Farrow's Bank, where it remained for only ten days before the bank went into liquidation. The Great War had been over for two years and, there was hope of a peaceful and prosperous future for all. Unfortunately, for the many shareholders and depositors of Farrow's Bank, Christmas 1920 would be a far cry from this hope. Five days before Christmas, on the morning of 20th December 1920, on the doors of the bank's seventy-three branches, there was posted a notice headed "Payments Suspended". Thousands of ordinary people found that they had lost every penny they had. Public outcry was loud. The then Chancellor of the Exchequer, Mr Neville Chamberlain, was asked in the House of Commons if the Government was aware of the disaster? *"Yes"*, was his reply; *"they had been aware of its imminence for some little time"*. This is the same ineffective and dithering Neville Chamberlain who later, in 1938 would return from his meeting in Munich with Adolf Hitler, *'declaring peace in our time'*. Thomas Farrow and William Walter Crotch, who would both stand trial for 'conspiracy to defraud', were held responsible for the Farrow Bank disaster. Grace Evelyn eventually received a payment of £10 from the liquidators. Small compensation, as £100 was a large sum of money to lose.

Curiously, the £100 for the piano and then the £100 to be put on deposit in Farrows Bank were both sent home in 1920, not too long before Daniel returned home with a much larger sum of money. Where was all this money coming from? Grace Evelyn, through her husband's actions, experienced having a fortune and also the misfortune of being 'cursed'. While in Hong Kong, Daniel became a Freemason, which was to prove very helpful to his wife in the 1930s when their luck and family fortunes dramatically changed for the worst. Grace Evelyn's mother, Mary Ann Nelson, died in 1922, but not before she had seen Daniel return to England with £1000 in cash in his suitcase. Even now I still find it hard to imagine. This was an absolutely phenomenal sum of money for those times; it is the equivalent of about £41,000 in today's money. But, better still in terms of spending power, when related to the average earnings index, it was comparable to approximately £220,000 in today's retail terms.

Daniel James – the Sportsman

How Daniel had acquired the money and where it had come from is shrouded in mystery and has never been properly or convincingly explained. It is difficult to comprehend, how an able seaman on low wages could amass such a large sum(s) of money in a short space of time. The only explanation ever offered by my granny, which could be another family myth, is that Daniel had 'won' the money in Hong Kong, by cheating a Chinese businessman at cards and as a result he had been 'cursed'. Curse or no curse, these allegedly ill-gotten gains did not serve them well.

When reflecting in her later life and thinking about all the bad luck they had had from the moment Daniel returned home from the Far East, Grace Evelyn often referred to the story of the 'curse'. She was convinced that all the misfortune and misery that the family experienced was connected to the 'curse' and the £1000.

Whilst it will never be truly known where the £1000, or the other money, actually came from, what I do know for certain is that Daniel wanted to use it to set up as a publican in his home town of Hitchin, where his brothers and sisters lived.

Unfortunately for Daniel, the publican dream was over when Grace Evelyn decided that she did not want to go. Had they gone to Hitchin, the family fortunes may well have been completely different – but that's fate and life is full of 'if only' and 'buts'. What is not really clear is what actually happened to the money, particularly as within a few years it was all gone and the family would be suffering financial hardship and struggling to keep the proverbial 'wolf from the door'. Allegedly, one of Daniel's relatives borrowed £200 from him that was never repaid. Even so, what happened to the other £800, the equivalent of many years' wages? A brief hand-written thank you note, which my granny had kept, indicated he had sent some money to a 'friend in need' who lived in Belle Vue, Manchester. The tone of the note intimates that this sum was probably never returned. By all anecdotal accounts, this would have been typical of Daniel. As he was a very generous man by nature, I wonder, is this where the money went; with people telling him their sob story and taking advantage of him? I think we know the answer to that.

After he had been honourably discharged from the Royal Navy and returned from China, Daniel consequently took employment initially as a transport worker for John Sutcliffe and Sons and later as a coal heaver, a job he always hated and which brought him nothing but bad luck and misfortune. Nevertheless, despite not having much, Daniel and Grace Evelyn enjoyed a very happy loving marriage and had five more children: Marjorie Evelyn (b.1921), Joyce Lillian (b.1922), Stanley Bert (b.1925), Edna May (b.1928) and John William (b.1931). And, as happy as it was, the marriage appeared to follow a typical working class pattern. Mother would be tied to the house looking after the home and the children and the father working all the hours god sent; and spending very little time at home when not at work. Daniel's routine seemed to be work, pub and sleep. As hard as this would have been for Grace Evelyn, for me it evoked the nostalgic images we often see in old sepia photographs: noisy, smoky pubs, illuminated by flickering gas lamps or early electric lights, men in flat cloth caps with pints in their fists and pipes in their mouths and someone, somewhere in the background, knocking out a tune on an old piano. Ah, nostalgia's not what it used to be I hear you say! By all accounts, Daniel liked his music and developed a reputation for singing in the local pubs, *Jingle of Gold* being one of his favourite songs.

Daniel's wage whilst at Sutcliffe's was only £3-2s-3d per week and £3-10s-0d per week when he worked as the coal heaver. These low wages put the £1000 he had brought back from Hong Kong into real perspective. Because of the low wages, for Grace Evelyn it was a desperate daily struggle to make ends meet and raise the six children. To maintain the family home she was a tower of strength and took whatever work she could and regularly baked her own bread to feed her children. Despite all the desperate financial difficulties the family experienced, they were happy together until a sequence of atrocious bad luck irrevocably changed the family's fortunes forever.

In January 1927, whilst working for Sutcliffe's at the Immingham Dock, Daniel had an accident at work and lost a finger. The accident report describes the injury as 'Traumatic Neurasthenia'. Having to take time off work to recover, the consequential loss of wages meant, yet again, even more deprivation. Eventually, through the Workmen's Compensation Act 1925, Daniel was awarded compensation of £300. Strikes, hardship and subsistence living were common enough for most 'working class people' at that time without the added burden of 'industrial accidents'. The General Strike of 1926 contributed to more poverty, destitution and hardship for many families. It is little wonder then, that my mother Grace Mary, their eldest daughter, was sickly with rheumatic fever during her childhood.

To aid her recovery, she was sent to stay for a while with her Aunt Eva (Daniel's sister), in Hitchin, Hertfordshire. Coincidently, this is similar to what had happened when Walter's sister Irene was sent to stay with Aunt Suey (Susannah). Aunt Eva wanted to keep Grace Mary and raise her as her own daughter. However in this case, unlike the situation with Walter's sister Irene, this was not to be. Grace Mary was returned home to her mother and siblings in Grimsby after she had recovered. Sadly for Daniel, Grace Evelyn and their family, the fickle finger of fate would soon intervene again; this time with far more severe and critical consequences.

In April 1933, Daniel was the victim of a far more serious accident at work. He was accidentally buried under several hundredweight of coal, which was 'shot' down into the hold of the steam trawler, he was working on. The official report recorded: *'when the contents of a basket of coal fell on his head whilst he was down in the fish room of the steam trawler Jeria'.* This was indeed an unfortunate and unlucky accident. He shouldn't have even been there. As was Daniel's nature, he was doing an old friend a good turn and covering a shift for him. Regrettably, this accident was to shape and shorten the remainder of his life. Daniel suffered a fractured skull and coal dust, which was difficult to remove, entered the open wound and the fractured bones; he was permanently incapacitated by the injury and would never work again. Daniel became a shadow of the person that he once was. His personality changed from being a happy-go-lucky man always ready to burst into song, into a sullen, morose and brooding man given to unbearable headaches and raging tempers. It must have been hard to live with him, never knowing when or how his mood may suddenly change. What I find extremely sad about this part of his life is that his youngest children, my Aunt Edna May and my Uncle John, because of the age they were at the time of Daniel's accident, would only have known the nature of their father as the man he became and not the kind hearted and generous man he originally was.

To support the family financially, Daniel received compensation of £1-10s-0d per week (£1.50 in new money), which was about a third of his weekly wage, until a settlement agreement of £825 was finally reached in May 1938, some five years after the accident occurred. These were desperately hard times for Grace Evelyn and youngest of her six children. The local Lodge of the Freemasons initially helped out financially, but that was only in the short term. The meagre financial compensation Daniel finally received for a life-changing industrial accident puts further into perspective just how much the £1000 was that he had had in his possession, some 17 years earlier.

Unfortunately, the family's run of bad luck did not end with the financial settlement. Out of the compensation they had received, they were required to pay back to the Public Assistance the equivalent sum of money that had been advanced to the family during the previous five years. Consequently the repayment of this rather draconian form of support left them with very little of the compensation. The family was no better off. And, as we know, unlike today, there was no all-embracing supportive welfare state in the 1930s. These were the days when families had to suffer the shame of being 'Means Tested'; which was an investigative process undertaken to determine whether or not an individual or family was eligible to qualify for help from the government. You had to prove, in intimate domestic detail, just how poor you were. It imposed form-filling, impertinent questions, and regular highly visible and shaming visits from investigators, who were licensed to peer into your cooking-pots, rule that one chair per person was enough, and could order you to sell your spare blankets and other goods and chattels you possessed.

The accident ultimately led to a reversal of roles. Daniel took over the home duties and Grace Evelyn became the main wage earner, taking work wherever she could find it, such as being a charwomen, scrubbing out offices, or taking in washing. The family now knew the shame of real deprivation and financial hardship, with the children having to wear donated old police boots and hand-me-down clothes. My granny used to tell the story of how Daniel stayed up one night, trying to burn the numbers off these police boots, to avoid any further shame on his children when they went to school wearing them the next day. Being a proud man who loved his family, it must have been heartbreaking for him to realise how desperate the family fortunes had become. Despite his incapacity, he was still a loving father who wanted to do whatever he could for his children. Sadly, only eight years after the accident, Daniel died from broncho-pneumonia on the 8th December 1941, when aged only 47, just six months after the birth of his first grandchild, Pamela Diane, my sister.

It is worth just reminding ourselves that during this period of great continuous distress and deprivation for my granny and her family, Walter's mother and his sisters were walking around in full length fur coats, driving a Wolsey car and investing in property. In financial terms, the fortunes of Walter's family and Grace Mary's family couldn't have been more poles apart.

It wasn't all bad luck; for once fate intervened favourably. Grace Evelyn James's life was certainly hard and frequently shaped by more than her fair share of misfortune. However, on one occasion, she was very lucky. It seemed that, for once fate or God had intervened in her favour. During World War II, on the 13th July 1943, the Germans launched a bombing raid on Grimsby. Grace Evelyn and some other family members, she could not recall who, went into their Anderson air raid shelter when the air-raid sirens had sounded. For several hours, as they sat huddled together, all they could hear was the 'thudding' of the bombs as they fell and exploded. Sometimes the explosions were so loud it was almost as though the bombs were falling on top of them. After the all-clear was sounded, and they emerged from the shelters, Grace Evelyn discovered she'd had a narrow escape; some bombs had nearly fallen directly on top of them. The consequence of which would have been catastrophic, Anderson shelters were no match for a direct hit.

Grace Evelyn's house in Victor Street backed onto a row of terraced housing in Guildford Street. A 'stick' of bombs had hit and totally obliterated a block of six houses that were situated immediately behind her home. As the war records and newspaper reports are contradictory, I don't know for certain what the exact casualty count for this act of bombing was. Many people had died and more than one hundred were made homeless. One stubborn old lady, despite repeated requests, refused to enter the air raid shelters when the sirens sounded; a stubbornness she expressed with a few choice expletives about 'Germans of uncertain parentage'. For this act of defiance she lost her life - she was literally blown to pieces. All they ever found of her was a remnant of a coat hanging off a nearby lamppost. The only structural damage to Grace Evelyn's home was that part of the roof was missing and all the garden walls had been blown down. These were eventually replaced when she was awarded £19-17s-2d from the War Damage Commission, *'in settlement of your claim under Part I of the War Damage Act'*.

Within all this calamity and casualties, there was however an amusing ending to the story. An occupant of one of the Guildford Street houses, whom everyone had assumed to be blind, an assumption he actively encouraged, because he always wore dark glasses, carried a white stick and never worked, was witnessed directing salvage operations at his home, pointing to whatever was salvageable, saying *'that's mine, that's mine'*! Grace Evelyn, justifiably it seems, had always been suspicious of the gentleman's alleged blindness, because of the manner in which he 'looked' at the young women as they walked past his house, whilst he sat outside.

I have to say, my granny, Grace Evelyn, was a lovely woman given to malapropisms and misuse of the English language. I sat with her in the 1970s and asked her to talk to me about her life, which fortunately I wrote down in an old notebook and then stored away in a drawer in a bureau. Why I did that, I don't really know. Now, nearly 40 years later, it was rediscovered and is the source for much of the information contained in this part of the story. During that conversation, when pointing out how hard she had had to work all her life, she uttered the line that has stayed with me ever since, *'Stephen, I've been a scrubber all my life'.* For the benefit of those that don't know, 'scrubber' is a derogatory term used to describe women of easy virtue. Obviously, I know that my granny was referring to all the jobs she took as a charwoman and an office cleaner. It still makes me smile when I think about it. She would have been horrified had she known what scrubber actually meant.

I am able to conclude this chapter with a happy postscript by fast-forwarding to 1958. Grace Evelyn won £1,322 with the 'Treble Chance' on the football pools. Even this stroke of good fortune has a slight tinge of 'what may have been'. She had done the football pools with Cope's, which was a much smaller company compared with the main football pool companies of the time, Littlewoods or Vernons. Had she done the 'pools' with either of these, her pay-out for the Treble Chance, as it was called, could have been as much as £75,000. But when you have very little, £1,322 is not an inconsiderable sum to win; especially as it brings to mind again just how valuable £1000 was, thirty-seven years before in 1921. The Grimsby Evening Telegraph reported Grace Evelyn's good fortune as:

GRIMSBY WOMAN WINS £1,322

A Grimsby woman, Mrs Grace James, who says she knows nothing about football, and who has only started to do the football pools this season, has won £1,322 – 2s – 0d for a total outlay on the coupon of 1 shilling. Mrs James, whose husband died in 1941, said, 'her first buy will be a new bath'.

This was the family that Walter Bloy had married into. Given the vast social differences between his family, upper middle class and that of his wife (Grace Mary), poor working class, confirms for me that he had married against his mother Alice's wishes!

Chapter Twelve

Walter – The Making Of A War Hero

My journey of discovery has now come round the full circle as I return to the primary focus of the story: Walter, a boy sailor becoming a war hero. In the opening chapter, I explained how the television documentary about the North Atlantic convoys of the Merchant Navy during World War 2 and the images of sinking ships and drowning sailors had prompted me to research and write Walter's story. I also suggested that the officers and crew of the merchant ships were all heroes, not for any single act of heroism, but for the fact that in every crossing of the Atlantic they were, without questioning their safety, putting their lives on the line against an enemy they could not see. Death and destruction could, without warning, come silently out of the darkness and there was very little they could do about it. In fact, one of the themes of the documentary was that the Merchant Navy officers and sailors were the 'unsung' heroes of that terrible conflict.

By May 1940, Great Britain had its back to the wall and for a time, stood alone against the might of the German military machine, as all of Western Europe had fallen. The resumption of the land war in Western Europe didn't effectively happen until after D-Day on the 6th June 1944, although by the end of 1941, the United States and especially the Soviet Union (USSR), in land war terms in Eastern Europe, were certainly supporting the war against Germany in a combat sense. Great Britain standing alone is usually taken as May 1940 until late 1941, by when the USA and the USSR became fully involved. After the fall of France, until the American and other allies started to arrive in the country in the build-up to the invasion of France on 'D-Day', Great Britain had to be kept supplied to sustain the war effort against the German forces. If it had not been possible to do so and Great Britain had fallen and had become an occupied country, D-Day, code-named operation 'Overlord', could not have happened and the defeat of Nazi Germany in Western Europe may have taken much longer, or perhaps not happened at all.

The only way these vital provisions, goods and armaments could get to Great Britain was by being shipped across the Atlantic Ocean on the ships of the Merchant Navy. Without the unwavering commitment and frequent sacrifices of the sailors and ships of the Merchant Navy, it would have been difficult for the country to keep going; they were literally in the front firing line. No matter how much protection the Royal Navy, the Royal Air Force and the Royal Canadian Air force, could provide to the North Atlantic convoys, it was reluctantly acknowledged when each convoy set sail, that not all the ships would make it. The German strategy of U-Boats 'hunting' in wolf packs out of their base ports on the west coast of France would see them sinking merchant ships faster than they could be replaced. Thousands of ships were sunk, with the loss of millions of tons of valuable cargo.

Cargo could be replaced; replacing the ships was not so easy, everything that could sail was taken into service: tramp steamers, old coastal vessels that were not designed for ocean-going voyages, and old 'tubs' that were long overdue in going to the breaker's yard. In what became known as the 'Battle of the Atlantic', in total, about 30,000 Merchant Navy sailors lost their lives. I found myself wondering whether the veterans of the North Atlantic convoys questioned what fate may have in store for them with each sailing; were their names on one of the torpedoes this time and it would be their last sailing. I suspect not; with the minimum of fuss, they just quietly got on with it and did what they had to do.

How does a naïve, innocent, 'wet behind the ears', young man such as Walter, become a war hero? It is quite simple: by being there and doing their duty. They may not always be there by choice, but that's irrelevant – there they are and they do what they have to do. Admiral Lord Horatio Nelson prior to the Battle of Trafalgar in 1805 famously signalled to the British fleet *'England expects that every man will do his duty'*. It wasn't necessary to send that signal to the officers and sailors of the Merchant Navy during the Battle of the Atlantic. Just like the men and women of all the other services who were fighting the War against Nazi Germany, the merchant sailors got on with their job and did their duty. And, as I have already said, so many of them paid the ultimate sacrifice.

I have now reached the stage where the focus for the remainder of the story will be an examination and reflection of the life and fortunes of Walter Bloy; his time in the Merchant Navy and how he served his country with honour and will conclude with his death, in 1947, the details of which we are now familiar with. To arrive at this point, the previous chapters have taken us on a long and meandering journey through more than two hundred years' history of his extended family. This brief recollection is offered to revert back to the specific centre of attention, Walter and his life. And, as I have done throughout, it will be kept within an historical contextual framework. Walter Bloy was born in 1912, less than three months after two of the most important historical incidences in the early part of the 20th century. Undoubtedly these would have been some of the major talking points of the day. Even now, one hundred years later, they are still frequently discussed and analysed. One in particular, the sinking in April 1912 of the R.M.S. Titanic on its maiden voyage to New York, has generated a whole new industry of collecting memorabilia, both real and reproduced and has been the subject of many feature films. The other incident was the deaths in March 1912, of Captain Robert Falcon Scott and his intrepid colleagues, as they were returning across the Antarctic ice from their ill-fated attempt to be the first people to reach the South Pole. They had been beaten in this adventure by just one month, by the Norwegian explorer Roald Amundsen. This too is still the subject of much debate and many feature films, but unlike the Titanic, has not had quite the same impact on today's memorabilia market.

Walter's very early childhood would be shaped by the death of his grandfather George Henry Smith in 1915 and then the death of his father (Walter Sidney) in the motorcycle accident in the following year. Walter was born at home in Newmarket Street, Grimsby, where he lived for a few years with his parents and his sisters Lucy and Irene. At the time of his birth, Walter Sidney was working in the family coal merchant's business, and though the family certainly didn't live in an ivory tower, they would have been financially comfortable and were starting to prosper. So much so that, in 1915, when Walter was three years old, the family moved to a better and much larger home in Clayton Street in Grimsby and Walter Sidney could afford to buy the motorcycle, which would change the family fortunes forever.

After the tragic death of his father in 1916, the family continued to live at Clayton Street for another four years, although as we now know, Walter's sister Irene had gone to live with her aunt. Alice, being a widow, with no other means of financial support, took on all manner of work to support the children Lucy and Walter. Although I could not find any anecdotal evidence to indicate whether Alice's mother, Mary Hannah Smith, who had money, offered any financial support, I'm inclined to think she did. After all, Alice would later be a beneficiary in her will. On the contrary I am certain, from the evidence of subsequent events, that Walter Sidney's father didn't offer much help at all. Alice and her children had hit a bad patch during this time. Financially, even with help from her mother, it would have been much harder for them until Alice met and moved her family, in about 1920, to live with Charles Wormley, at his home in Holles Street, Grimsby. Walter was then eight years old. When they married in 1922, Charles became Alice's second husband and Walter's step-father. From the moment, at the beginning of the 1920s, that Charles entered the life of Alice and her children, the family never looked back again; unlike Grace Mary (Walter's wife-to-be), whose family hardship, misfortune and destitution started round about this same time.

By all accounts Charles was a good stepfather to Alice's children, and provided a happy home. Anecdotes that were related to me demonstrate that 'stepfather Wormley' is remembered with great affection. I also found many photographs taken during the 1920s of Charles with Alice, and if the cliché that every picture tells a story is anything to go by, the photographs appear to suggest, although he was 16 years her senior, they were in love and very happy together. Although many of the pictures that were taken as a family group photo contain Walter's sister Lucy, there are none that I could find that showed Irene with her stepfather during this period because, as we now know, she never came back home to live.

Charles Wormley, who was not short of money, provided security for Alice, Lucy and Walter; they never again faced the desperation of financial hardship. How well the family was doing, is evidenced by what they did and how they dressed. Alice and Lucy dressed in very fashionable 'flapper' girl clothes. Then as now, to dress in the height of fashion would not have been cheap. Alice would soon be wearing her fur coat! For them life in the 1920s was comfortable compared with so many around them. Although he would not have been over-indulged, in moderation Walter would not have really wanted for anything; he had an easy and secure childhood. I have already related within Alice's story, in 1927, as the family fortunes continued to improve they moved to the extravagantly named 'Semi-Detached Villa' in Fairmont Road, Grimsby, which was bought for cash and became the family home until 1933. This was the home that Walter returned to during his Merchant Navy apprenticeship days.

All I managed to find out about Walter's schooling is that he attended the Corporation Grammar School for the children of Freemen in Grimsby. I also have reason to believe that he spent some time at Trinity College in Hull, which was a preparatory school for potential Merchant Navy Officers, because the photograph of Walter as a boy in the Merchant Navy uniform is typical of a Trinity schoolboy of that time. I cannot confirm whether he was a good and studious scholar or not. I have to assume he must have had some abilities for him to be accepted as an apprentice officer in the Merchant Navy. During his childhood, Walter regularly attended the 'Sunday School' at the United Methodist Church in Freeman Street, Grimsby. Shortly before his fifteenth birthday, in June 1927, he was presented with a bible for good attendance. This proved to be a most fortunate gift for him to receive; approximately sixteen years later, during one of his voyages in the North Atlantic convoys, the bible would actually save his life.

By all accounts, Walter was a happy and healthy child. On the 28th February 1928, at the age of 15, he left home and joined the Merchant Navy as an indentured apprentice officer. Walter was registered as apprentice with the Shipping Federation to the company Sir R. Ropner and Co, Steamship Owners of West Hartlepool. Co. Durham, which is where he would be based for nearly four years. The indenture document was signed by William Ropner, who was referred to as the master; one of Walter's schoolteachers J. Ridsdale, who lived in Cleethorpes, was the witness to Walter's signature. Stepfather Charles Wormley signed as surety for the indenture and, also provided the financial means for all the clothes, kit and equipment Walter would need as an apprentice. The indenture document, which is printed on linen, forms a legally binding contract that today, makes fascinating reading as it is a piece of social history and of a practice, sadly now long gone. I quote an extract:

> *The said Walter Bloy hereby voluntarily binds himself Apprentice unto the said Master and his assigns, for the term of four years from the date hereof; And the said Apprentice hereby covenants that, during such time the said Apprentice will faithfully serve the said Master and his Assigns, and obey the lawful commands, both of the said Master and his assigns and of all officers of any vessel on board of which he may be serving under this Indenture, and that the said Apprentice will not absent himself from their service without leave; In*

consideration whereof, the said Master hereby
covenants with the said Apprentice, that during the
said term he will and shall use all proper means to
teach the said Apprentice or cause him to be taught
the business of a Seaman as practised in
steamships, and provide the said Apprentice with
sufficient Meat, Drink, Lodging and, except in Great
Britain with Medicine and Medical and Surgical
Assistance, and pay the said Apprentice the sum of
£60 in manner following; that is to say in the first
year of service TEN POUNDS, for the second year
of service TWELVE POUNDS, for the third year of
service EIGHTEEN POUNDS, and for the fourth
year of service TWENTY POUNDS, together with a
further sum of FIVE POUNDS payable after
satisfactory service for the term of this Indenture,
and twelve shillings yearly in lieu of washing, the
said Apprentice providing for himself all sea-
bedding, wearing apparel, and necessaries except
such as are hereinbefore specially agreed to be
provided by the said Master.

The document goes on to describe a range of do's and
don'ts, for which the 'said Apprentice' will be punished and or
fined. As I studied the document further, it became clear that,
unless the apprentice had considerable financial support from
the family, i.e. ability to provide *sea- bedding, wearing*
apparel and necessaries etc, and with the low wages that the
apprentices actually received, it would have been almost
impossible, or at least very difficult, for some young men to
enter into the Merchant Navy as an apprentice officer. For
many children, male and female, as soon as they were old
enough, or in some cases looked old enough, they had to go
out to find work to help supplement the family income. These
were very hard times indeed. With the dire financial straits
Grace Mary's (Walter's wife to be) family had to contend with
the 1920s, it is evident that neither of her two brothers could

have afforded to enter the Merchant Navy as an apprentice officer if they had wanted too.

So began Walter's Merchant Navy career that would see him, not that many years later, doing his duty and playing a vital role during the dark years of the war. Walter signed his indentures on the 28th February and on the 1st March 1928 he said good-bye to his family in Grimsby and, I suspect, rather nervously and apprehensively joined his first ship, the SS Gullpool. He was only 15 years old and had left the comfort, security and safety of his family behind. Walter would learn his 'trade' at the hands of others, mainly through 'guided' experience on board ships sailing, initially around the coastal waters of Great Britain and after receiving his Continuous Certificate of Discharge Book, some foreign trips. Walter remained on the SS Gullpool until the 16th February 1929, serving a total of 326 days on this vessel. Under the watchful eye of the ship's officers and other experienced able seamen such as the bo'sun, he would have started to learn the craft and skills of seamanship such as: practical navigation, docking, steering and manoeuvring the ship, the loading and discharging of cargo, how the ship needed to be kept in trim and many other Board of Trade regulations.

This would be the basic pattern of his apprenticeship. Perhaps more importantly, Walter would have learned the vital factor of how to be part of a hierarchical team that has a clearly defined 'pecking order', which a ship's complement is and has to be. What is certain, being a young apprentice he would have been the butt of practical jokes, something I too experienced, as my working life also started out as a Merchant Navy apprentice. A typical example of a practical joke I faced was being sent by one officer to another officer to ask for a 'long stand', which I assumed to be a piece of equipment. Not getting a response, and after what seemed an age, I said to the officer *'what about the long stand sir'*, to which he replied *'well isn't thirty minutes long enough or do you want to wait longer?'* The penny dropped! I'm sure Walter would have experienced similar jokes. Being asked to fetch a 'left-handed teacup', a 'tin of striped paint' or falling for the tale of the

'Golden Rivet', i.e. the last rivet used when the ship was being built, are three others I recall. There is nothing malicious intended in these jokes, they taught you important social skills that remain with you all your life.

Walter as an apprentice – vessel unknown

Walter's sea service record shows that the SS Gullpool was sailing from Blyth on Tyneside to Liverpool and Cardiff before returning to the Tyne. Walter then joined the SS Heronspool on 30th April 1929 and completed 624 days' sea service until he left this vessel on 29th March 1931. Walter's continuous training would be much the same as he experienced on the SS Gullpool. The voyages of the SS Heronspool were also mainly in coastal waters from the River Tyne to the ports of Cardiff, Barry, Newport and Swansea in South Wales and occasionally to the ports of Northern Europe. Most likely the cargoes of these ships would have been steel, coal, timber and perhaps grain. The final year of his apprenticeship from the age of 18 to 19, was spent on the SS Yearby, which he joined on 12th April 1931 and remained with until the 31st March 1932, completing 345 days of sea service on this vessel.

As an apprentice Walter completed 1295 days in total of actual sea service, which equated to 3 years 7 months 5 days. With his apprenticeship completed, his indenture document was then 'signed off' with this endorsement:

> *'I hereby certify that the term of service under this Indenture has now been completed by the said Walter Bloy to my entire satisfaction.'*

Signed By ....signature indistinguishable, (Master)
West Hartlepool - 12th April 1932

Walter received his Merchant Navy discharge book, number R103858, on the 11th April 1932, three months before his 20th birthday, from the Mercantile Marine Office in North Shields. He immediately re-joined the SS Yearby, as an Able Seaman. The boy was becoming a man.

What was Walter like? He was a handsome man of average build, with auburn (ginger) hair and blue eyes; he was not overly tall, just 5ft 9in and had a gentle nature and disposition. He was very popular with his friends and colleagues alike, a quality he appears to have retained throughout his life. After his tragic death, two aunts on my mother's side, often said of him, *'one of the nicest people you could meet who would do anything for anyone'*. He was also a keen sportsman, especially tennis and football. I found several photographs of him and his teammates of the football team of the SS Yearby.

Unlike all his previous berths, although the SS Yearby was also sailing from the River Tyne, it was not just to the home ports on the coastal waters I have already listed. The ship made several voyages to Argentina and Africa. According to immigration records, whilst serving on the SS Yearby, Walter visited Argentina on at least four occasions. Walter remained on this vessel until 24th October 1932, before leaving with the following reference from the Ship's Master.

SS Yearby

Dear Sirs,

This is to certify that the bearer, Mr W. Bloy served as an apprentice on board the above vessel from 29th March 1931 to 27th February 1932, also as an Able Seaman from February 28th.1932 to 24th October 1932. From the 1st June to the above date, he has seen bridge service on Watch with the Chief Officer. Throughout his service on this vessel, I have always found him to be strictly sober, and a willing and efficient worker, and in my opinion should make a good officer.

Signed Capt. P.M. Hill   (Master)

With such a glowing reference, things appeared to be going well for Walter; sadly all that was to change. After discharging from the SS Yearby, Walter would not return to sea for four more years. I am absolutely certain this was not his original plan. Walter, as I discovered, was about to experience, perhaps for the first time in his young life, failure and real disappointment.

Walter was 20 years old when he took extended shore leave from October 1932 until April 1933 and returned home to Grimsby to live with his mother and stepfather, who supported him financially, so that he could study for his 'Certificate of Competency as Second Mate of a Foreign-going Steamship'. This was Walter's first attempt at the Second Mate's Examinations and one which he was about to fail spectacularly. He was examined in Newcastle on 3rd April 1933. The results, which were published on 8th April 1933, by the Examiners of Masters and Mates, indicated that he had failed all elements; Written – failed, Orals – failed and Signals – failed. Walter was offered the opportunity to retake the examinations ten days later. An offer he declined. Being only 20 years old, it must have been very difficult for him to accept that not only had he failed, he had failed all elements. His disappointment is evidenced by the fact that he would not re-sit and successfully achieve the Second Mate's 'ticket' until 1941, eight years later, by which time the country would have been at war for two years.

Abject failure and not achieving what he wanted to, was probably a new experience for him. All the evidence appears to suggest that he struggled to deal with the disappointment. Consequently, he left the Merchant Navy and returned home to Grimsby to live with his mother and stepfather for a short time. Whether he was encouraged to do so by Alice or others, is anybody's guess.

Walter quickly found alternative shore-based employment. From April 1933 until June 1936, he was employed by Sir Alec Black, a Steamship owner based at Hutton Road on the Grimsby Docks, as a member of the company's shore staff. Although he stuck at the job for three years, following events indicate that Walter's heart was not really into shore-based work. The Merchant Navy is where he really wanted to be. So, in October 1936, when he was 24 years old, Walter returned to sea once again, signing on as an able seaman on the SS Hawnby, which was owned by Sir R. Ropner and Company, with whom he had happily served his apprenticeship. After a voyage which lasted nine months, including revisiting

Argentina, Walter was discharged from this vessel on 11th June 1937. Again, he left with glowing references from both the Ship's Master and the Chief Officer. I quote:

SS Hawnby, dd. 27th July 1937

Dear Sirs,

This is to certify the Mr Walter Bloy, has served on the above named vessel from 30th October 1936 to the 11th June 1937 in the capacity of Able Seaman under my command. During the whole of this period I have found him at all times to be a very keen and willing and hard-working man.

At all times he was honest, strictly sober and attentive to his various duties and I can recommend him to anyone requiring the services of a trustworthy man.

He now leaves the vessel in the hope of obtaining a berth ashore and in this respect I wish him the very best of success.

> *Yours truly*
> *J. Kenny (Master)*

Reading the above reference and in particular the line, *'He leaves the vessel in the hope of obtaining a berth ashore'*, I came to the conclusion that at this stage of his life, Walter was confused and really unsure about what he wanted to do. And moreover, he had also discovered girlfriends, the allure of which can deter a young man from being away from home for months on end. Within the boxes of 'treasures', my mother had kept hidden all the years of my childhood, among other important certificates, documents and letters I found many photographs of Walter with very 'fashionably dressed' attractive young women. The personal messages and terms of endearment, written on the reverse of these photographs certainly showed that he was popular with the ladies.

As much as his girlfriends would bring him joy, in contrast, there seemed to be some real uncertainty about his life and what he wanted to do career-wise. This I found rather surprising, as the manner in which he had recorded, saved and documented papers, references and other documents from which I have drawn extensively to produce this story, indicates that Walter was a man who liked things to be orderly. From a personal perspective having worked for many years in education and seen at first-hand how students react and respond to failure, I wondered whether the absolute and total failure of his first attempt at the Second Mate's ticket had affected Walter more than was acknowledged by him, his family or those around him at the time. Especially, as I would later discover, when he took and passed his St John's Ambulance First Aid Examination in December 1938, in reference to his employment, he had styled himself as a Second Mate. A position he wouldn't actually have until 1941!

From 1937 until 1939, whilst living at home with his mother, who became a widow for the second time in 1936, Walter had three different jobs; he was a driver-salesman for The Lincolnshire Farmeries Co Ltd from June to September 1937, a steelwork erector for Richards (Leicester) Ltd, Phoenix Iron Works from September 1937 until September 1938. And then from September 1938 for six months until February 1939, he was employed as a ship's rigger at the Humber Graving Dock and Engineering Co. Ltd, Immingham. Though he was a hard worker and received excellent references from all three companies it is noticeable how he kept changing his job, never really staying in one job for very long.

Walter was now 26 years old, and courting, or stepping out, as they used to call it then, with Grace Mary James, who would become his wife less than a year later. He had also made up his mind to return to his first love - the sea. On the 1st March 1939, just as World War 2 was looming ominously on the horizon, Walter signed on as an able seaman on the SS Antigone, which was owned by the New Egypt and Levant Shipping Company Ltd, and was docked at the Port of Immingham where he was working as a ship's rigger at the time. The Master of the SS Antigone was Captain Beddie McDonald Stephen, who would become Alice Wormley's (nee Bloy) third husband. I found several photographs of Grace Mary,(my mother) and Walter's mother on this ship while it was berthed at Immingham. There is no doubt that this is when and where Alice and Captain Stephen met.

Coincidently, when Walter signed onto the SS Antigone, it was exactly eleven years to the day since he had signed onto his first ship, the SS Gullpool.

Chapter Thirteen

The War Years And The Death Of My Father

On the 1st March 1939, with the war in Europe now just months away, Walter and the SS Antigone set sail for the Pacific Ocean and the South Sea Islands. Quite surprisingly, after our mother died in 1983, my sister and I found among the box of 'treasures' she had held on to, a handwritten diary-type log complete with many photographs, which Walter had kept of this voyage of the SS Antigone. I appreciate that, without the benefit of the photographs contained in the diary and being able to see the captions Walter has written, some of which are amusing, that this verbatim narrative that I am about to relate may seem bland. But it is Walter's voice speaking to us from all those years ago. The additional comments contained in parenthesis are my additions.

The Voyage of the SS Antigone 1939 - 1940

The voyage commenced on the 1ˢᵗ March 1939, we sailed from Immingham in Lincolnshire, England. After 21 days of stormy weather and a rough Atlantic crossing, we arrived at Baltimore, USA. The distance sailed was 4910 miles. Then after loading cargo, which took 14 days, the ship sailed on April 2ⁿᵈ for Japan, via the Panama Canal, which we reached on 11ᵗʰ April. Continuing on the 12ᵗʰ April, we entered the Pacific Ocean and after 50 days of hot weather arrived at Moji on 21ˢᵗ May, the distance from Baltimore to Panama 1777 miles and from Panama to Moji, 8748 miles.

[50 days at sea without sight of land - the SS Antigone had a top speed of about 12 knots.]

We discharged part of the cargo then sailed onwards to Yawata, Japan arriving on 30th May where we stayed for 10 days before sailing onwards from Japan on the 10th June for the South Sea Islands, arriving at Ocean Island on 25th June. The distance from Japan to Ocean Island is 3357 miles. After finally loading, we then sailed away on 3rd July 1939 for New Plymouth in New Zealand. The journey took 11 days, after the first five days we then entered the Southern Winter, and experienced very cold stormy weather. The distance steamed was 2326 miles and we arrived at our destination on 13th July.

[At this point, the diary has many photographs taken in and around New Plymouth, Mt. Egmont, the Lakes and the Pukekura Park in New Zealand.]

We left New Plymouth on July 25th and sailed to Wanganui a distance of 80 miles to finish our unloading. As we were laying off Wanganui for two days through the heavy sea, we witnessed on 26th July 1939, the stranding on the beach of the steamer SS Port Bowen. We entered the port on 27th July. Walter includes some photographs: *of the SS Antigone unloading and cargo being salvaged from the stranded SS Port Bowen. There is an attempt to re-float the SS Port Bowen by lightening her of cargo and using salvage tugs to re-float her. This was to no avail as heavy seas drove the ship further on the beach – condition now serious.*

The next photographs, some with Walter's captions show:

...the SS Port Bowen listing to starboard, with the lifeboat lowered, and getting a water line to the ship for the crew. The ship was nearly high and dry. The ultimate fate of the SS Port Bowen is unknown as we finally loaded and left Wanganui on 1st August 1939 and, steamed to Westport on the South Island of New Zealand arriving on 2nd August having sailed a distance of 220 miles. After staying overnight, we steamed away for Ocean Island once more, where we arrived after a very nice voyage on 12th August 1939. The distance sailed was 2491 miles and we were pleased to get back into the warm weather again.

Maritime records indicate that the SS Port Bowen was classified as wrecked in July 1939. Although war in Europe was now less than a month away, Walter's photographs show him and colleagues fishing, sunbathing and having fun, seemingly without a care in the world.

The ship sailed away from Ocean Island on August 16th and headed for Australia, the country I like best of all. We had a splendid trip finally arriving at Port Kembla, a small town near Sidney, East Australia, well known for its largest single span bridge in the world. We could see it as we passed the port on arriving on August 27th after a distance of 2300 miles. After unloading part of the cargo, we then sailed away on 31st August for Bunbury. We had a very bad voyage. Gales raged the whole trip and the ship made very little headway against the strong winds of the Southern Ocean. After being tossed about for 10 days, we finally reached the West side of Australia and once we got round the Cape, we run into fine weather once more. We finally arrived at Bunbury on September 14th after steaming a distance of 2057 miles.

The Second World War in Europe had now started, but no comments were made in Walter's diary/log. Walter does go on to describe how the second officer was accidentally killed in Freemantle on 27th September 1939:

After finally unloading at Bunbury, we then sailed away on 25th September for Freemantle a little further up the West coast. Here we anchored outside the port to prepare our ship for fresh cargo. On 27th September, while all the crew were busy cleaning the holds, it was on this ill-fated day, that the Second Office fell down the number 5 hold and was killed almost instantly. The Second officer was interred in Freemantle on 30th September 1939.

(Photographs show the funeral with most of the officers and some of the crew attending).

We proceeded into port on 6th October and commenced loading our cargo. The weather was glorious and we had some splendid times there. I had several half days off duty and spent the most of them at Perth, the capital of Western Australia, a lovely modern city and lovely surroundings. It is about 18 miles inland from Freemantle and is a very interesting run in the 'Chara'. We completed loading on October 14th and once more we were ready for a sea journey. We sailed away at noon for India. I was promoted from this point to 3rd Officer for the remainder of the voyage. We had a glorious trip, fine sunny weather and the sea was very calm. After 15 days at sea, we arrived at Columbo Ceylon, to bunker for the remainder of the voyage to India. We arrived in Columbo on October 29th after a distance of 3155 miles. After staying overnight, we sailed on the next day for Karachi at the North End of India. Again we had very fine weather and made a good voyage to Karachi arriving on November 6th

1939. The distance sailed from Colombo was 1537 miles. Here we discharged our cargo and loaded another for ENGLAND.

Reading Walter's diary/log, even now I find it surprising, why there is no mention at all of the war in Europe starting. As a ship's officer, I am sure it would have been discussed in the officers' quarters or dining area, but for some reason, Walter has decided not to comment. This is ironic considering the critically important role that the men and the ships of the Merchant Navy were destined to play in Great Britain's survival during the war years and especially in the early stages of the war. In England, during the first few weeks of the war, it was called, the 'phoney war'. And perhaps for those out in the Southern Oceans, the war was out of sight and out of mind. If that is the case, attitudes would soon dramatically change. Records have now been made available, which confirm that there was nothing at all phoney about the enemy action against merchant ships, which started almost immediately in the North Atlantic, and would continue to happen for most of the duration of the war.

After war was declared on 3rd September 1939, in the first month alone, thirty-one British merchant vessels were sunk and two others badly damaged as a result of torpedo attacks by German submarines(U-Boats). The SS Athenia was sunk with heavy losses on the actual day war was declared, which indicates that German U-Boats and surface raiding battleships were already out at sea patrolling the shipping lanes prior to the declaration of war. What Walter and his fellow officers were not to know, during the early months of the war, the German pocket battle ship Admiral Graf Spee was raiding and sinking merchant shipping in the Indian and Southern Atlantic Oceans. This was the route that the SS Antigone had to take to return home safely to England. Luckily they were not spotted by the Admiral Graf Spee; they managed to get home safely. Others were not so lucky; the Admiral Graf Spee sank many ships before it was scuppered during the Battle of the River Plate on 13th December 1939.

The monthly total of merchant ships sunk by the U-Boats was to rise considerably during the next four years. One particular convoy, referred to in the television documentary I watched, comprised thirty-four merchant ships and four escort vessels; a 'wolf pack' of seven German U-Boats was waiting for them. After the attack was over, seventeen (half of the convoy) merchant ships had been sunk, all the U-Boats escaped without damage.

Another incident that is much closer to home relates to Walter, who as we now know from his own words in his diary/log, was promoted to 3rd Officer on the 12th October 1939, as a result of the tragic accident when the Second Officer of the SS Antigone fell into the hold and died. What Walter wouldn't know as he was celebrating his promotion in the sunshine of the Southern Oceans was that, the very next day, on the 13th October 1939, the SS Heronspool, in which he had happily served two years of his apprenticeship (1929 - 1931), was sunk and all hands perished in the North Atlantic after being attacked by torpedoes from a German submarine. It is most likely that some of the sailors lost on the SS Heronspool would have been known to Walter. Further examination of the records that are now available of merchant ships that were sunk in the war reveals Sir R. Ropner & Company Ltd. – steamship owners and brokers, with whom Walter was apprenticed, lost many of their ships.

Despite the continuous threat from the U-Boats and the surface battleships, the SS Antigone managed to return home safely to England and arrived in Liverpool on the 4th January 1940. Walter took some shore leave to marry his sweetheart, Grace Mary, in Grimsby on 20th January 1940. The officers of the SS Antigone bought Walter and Grace Mary a silver-plated fruit dish, which they had appropriately engraved for a wedding present. Walter and Grace Mary didn't have long to honeymoon though, as he immediately signed back on to the SS Antigone on 23rd January 1940; by which time, Captain Beddie McDonald Stephen had married Walter's mother. Walter sailed for ten months until 17th October 1940, as the 3rd Officer on the SS Antigone with Captain Stephen, who was now his second stepfather; and made several crossings in the North Atlantic convoys. He eventually left the SS Antigone to study and sit for his 2nd Officer's certificate. This would be his second attempt to get his 'ticket'; this time he was successful. Fatefully, Captain Stephen also signed off from the SS Antigone to join the SS Antar, the vessel of which he was the Master when he was murdered in Israel in 1942.

Several of the convoys that Walter sailed in during the early part of the war, were designated with the prefix HX (Home from Halifax), meaning that they were east- bound from Halifax, Nova Scotia to the UK (Great Britain). Before the United States entered the war, the main port of assembly for the North Atlantic convoys was the Canadian city of Halifax. After the United States joined the war, many of the east-bound convoys started to assemble and depart from New York. The designation ONF signified convoy vessels that were 'Outward to New York – Fast'. Later in the conflict, Walter sailed on ships that were part of the MKS convoys: from Sierra Leone, Gibraltar and the Western Mediterranean to the UK. The significance of the 'S' in the designation meant it was a slow convoy, which obviously made them more vulnerable to attack.

The most vital convoy supply routes were those from the United States and Canada to Great Britain and to Murmansk in Russia, which is where most of the U-Boat attacks took place. It was not unusual for a dozen convoys with more than 20,000 men to be crossing the Atlantic at the same time, at speeds of between seven and nine knots. Bad weather and fog were a blessing for the convoys, as it made U-boat operations very difficult. On the other hand too much smoke from the ships' funnels was a dead giveaway, especially on the older coal-burning vessels. And a lot of these ships had to slow down and even drop out of the convoys altogether because of this, which left them in greater danger. In perilous waters the convoys sailed in zig-zag patterns to be less vulnerable to attack. Sometimes it worked, sometimes it would not.

Inevitably, the threat of sinking finally caught up with the SS Antigone during one of the convoys bound for Great

Britain. Death, destruction and terror came like a ghost out of the dark. The SS Antigone, which was built in 1928, was sunk just north of the Azores, at 10 o'clock at night on the 11th May 1943, along with a Norwegian ship 'Grado' whilst in convoy SC-129 on route from St Johns, New Brunswick to Halifax, Nova Scotia and then onwards to Avonmouth. Torpedoes from U-Boat U.402, which was commanded by Baron Siegfried von Forstner, sank these two ships. The SS Antigone was carrying a cargo of 7,800 tons of grain, 250 tons of general cargo and 250 trucks. The crew had to abandon ship into the icy waters of the North Atlantic; there were 43 survivors and 3 fatalities, who may have been Walter's shipmates from the time when he sailed on the SS Antigone. The survivors were picked up by the British rescue ship Melrose Abbey and landed at Gourock on the River Clyde on 25th May 1943. These were the last of fifteen ships sunk by Baron Siegfried von Forstner and the U-Boat U.402 before it too was sunk by depth charges.

After marrying Grace Mary, Walter lived for a short while with his mother-in-law in Victor Street, Grimsby until, like his mother Alice, he too wanted to move out of town to the suburbs. In 1940, Walter and Grace Mary moved to a semi-detached bungalow at 283 Louth Road, which was on the outskirts of the town and was where my sister, Pamela Diane was born. Many of the family photographs I found appear to show this was a happy home. However, with Walter away for months on end on wartime sea service, Grace Mary and baby Pamela spent a lot of time on their own. In the night, with the imposed blackout as protection against air-raids, not being able to see a soul and not having a telephone, which we take for granted today, to contact her family and friends, Grace Mary felt totally isolated and extremely lonely. And so, several times a week she used to walk, pushing baby Pamela in a pram, a distance of about nearly five miles each way, to her mother's house in Victor Street.

At the age of 29, from 13th March 1941 until 8th November 1941, Walter sailed on the North Atlantic convoys as the 3rd Officer on SS Esturia. By then he had successfully passed his examinations for the Second Officer's Certificate of

Competency. However, before he could actually sail as a Second Officer he needed to obtain a 'Certificate of Watch-Keeping Service', which he duly received on 6th November 1941, whilst serving on the SS Esturia. His Certificate of Competency as Second Mate of a foreign-going steamship, number 47933, was issued on 14th February 1942.

After a short period of shore leave, he was soon back at sea when he joined the SS Pennington Court, which was owned by Court Line. He originally signed on as the 3rd Officer from 6th - 21st March 1942, and was then promoted to 2nd Officer from 22nd March until 20th May 1942. Like all the other ships Walter sailed on during this stage of the War, the SS Pennington Court was also operating in the North Atlantic between Canada and Great Britain. According to a letter, dated 21st July 1942, regarding his status as a Second Officer, which he received from the Ministry of War and Transport, the SS Pennington Court was supposedly 'wrecked' in May 1942 at St. John, New Brunswick, Canada. Walter was subsequently returned to Great Britain on the convoy ship, SS Fort Senneville, where he remained as Junior Second Officer until the 5th September 1942. As I discovered with all the previous ships in which he served, Walter earned a fulsome reference in September 1942, from L Fraser the Master of the SS Fort Senneville.

Regarding the ultimate end of the SS Pennington Court, there is a strange contradiction between what the wartime maritime records says and the letter Walter had received from the Ministry of War and Transport. Something is not quite right! It is possible that the Ministry letter contained deliberate mis-information or was just plain wrong, particularly as it refers to the SS Pennington Court being wrecked. Whereas, the records of merchant ships lost in the North Atlantic indicate that it was sunk by a German U Boat. I can only conclude that if it was indeed wrecked, it must have been salvageable and returned to service. According to the records of lost shipping, just four months after Walter had left to join another ship, the SS Pennington Court, *'a straggler from the convoy, was struck by three torpedoes from the U Boat [U-254] on the 9th October 1942 and sank South East of Cape Farewell with the loss of 40 crew members and 5 others'*. There were no survivors! It was the third victim of U-254 in just a few days.

From a German perspective, the promising career of U-254 was almost cut short on this patrol, when the Norwegian Flower Class Corvette HNoMS *Eglantine* damaged her with depth charges during an attack on a convoy in the same area where it had sunk the SS Pennington Court. Although it was not sunk on that occasion, it was not long before this U-Boat met its fate. After repairs, U-254 returned in November 1942 to her old 'hunting' grounds of the North Atlantic routes. In December, the weather in that region is atrocious and visibility practically nil. As U-254 manoeuvered to attack Convoy HX-217, which she had been directed to on 8th December 1942, in those conditions, it is perhaps unsurprising that she failed to see another U-Boat [U-221] come steaming out of the gloom and straight into her broadside. Both submarines had become lost in the dark and collided with one another in a freak accident, which claimed 41 of U-254's crew, who were spilled into the ocean as the boat heeled over and sank. Sailors from U-221 dived into the turbulent sea tied to ropes, and succeeded in rescuing only four bedraggled survivors of the sinking. U-221 was badly damaged and being unable to dive, aborted the patrol and returned to its base at St. Nazaire in Western France

Walter's responsibilities while serving in the North Atlantic took on a new emphasis after he attended a three-day Merchant Navy Defence Course Part 2 in Hull in December 1942. He received a Certificate of Proficiency and was judged as, *'capable of taking charge of the armaments of a defensively equipped Merchant Ship'*. This new capability and additional responsibility would put him on the 'front line' as it meant when any ship in which he was serving, came under attack, from aircraft, surface submarines or any other hostile enemy action; he would be manning and taking charge of the armaments to defend the ship. Being on the open deck(s) of the ship, he would have been exposed to hostile fire. I have previously mentioned how Walter's Sunday School Bible saved his life; this, fortuitously, actually happened during one of these encounters with the enemy.

Not many years before she died, my mother gave me the bible and told me the story, but could not remember which ship Walter was serving on when the incident happened. She explained that during one of the convoys, his ship had come under enemy fire; she was not sure whether it was from aircraft or a surface raider. Walter was on deck as one of the officers in charge of the defence. According to my mother, he always carried his bible in his breast pocket during these encounters. In a fearfully dangerous situation like this, I suppose, being a Christian, one would draw mental comfort from doing so. In the course of this particular hostile engagement, Walter was struck by a bullet or a piece of shrapnel, which hit the bible. Fate had intervened; the bible had saved his life. I still have the bible. The damage is covered by a sailcloth dust jacket cover which Walter made. However, when the bible is opened, the bullet or shrapnel hole is plain to see. God certainly moves in mysterious ways.

The Bible and the bullet hole

According to his Continuous Certificate of Discharge Book, after completing the Gunnery course, on the 15th December 1942 Walter joined the SS Elizabeth Dal, as the 2nd Mate. He signed on to the ship for 'foreign' voyages in Hull and, was discharged from the vessel four months later on 3rd March 1943, also in Hull. Other than that, I could initially find no record at all for the SS Elizabeth Dal in registers of British shipping. It was a complete mystery, what the vessel was and where it went. I then discovered that the SS Elizabeth Dal came to an inglorious end, before the war was over. On the 3rd August 1944, whilst manoeuvring in the River Mersey, near the Port of Liverpool, it was in a collision and sank. With regard to the bible saving Walter's life; most likely it would have been during his service on this ship or his next berth, the SS Baron Douglas when fate was so kind to him. It is ironic though, exactly five years to the day that he signed on to the SS Elizabeth Dal, when the country was no longer at war, he would get killed.

A month after leaving the SS Elizabeth Dal, Walter journeyed to Cardiff and, on the 8th April 1943, joined the SS Baron Douglas, which was owned by H. Hogarth and Sons of Glasgow, as the 2nd Mate. He served on this vessel making foreign voyages until 11th June 1943. Whilst serving on this ship, on the 4th June 1943, he attended another Merchant Navy Anti-Aircraft Gunnery Course at Barrow and was awarded a 'Certificate of Proficiency'. He became qualified, *in the firing and cleaning and oiling of Machine Guns and Anti-Aircraft Devices*. Before he did that, I managed to find one of the convoys the SS Baron Douglas sailed in whilst Walter was the 2nd Mate. The SS Baron Douglas, with its cargo of iron ore, which was vital for steel-making, was one of thirty-four ships in convoy MKS 013G that left Gibraltar on the 22nd May 1943. The convoy, which was designated as slow, was escorted by HMS Anthony, an A – Class Destroyer, and four Bangor Class Minesweepers, HMS Fast York, HMS Parrsboro,

HMS Qualicum and HMS Wedgeport. Although the convoy arrived in England on the 24th May 1943, I could not establish whether all thirty-four ships made it safely.

On the home front, by 1943, Walter, Grace Mary and baby Pamela moved back into town to live at 181 Cooper Road, Grimsby. This would be Walter's last home, as we have known since this story began, he died in 1947. I was born in this house in 1946. Before then, whilst Walter was away on service, this house received a direct hit from an 'incendiary bomb' during the German air raid on Grimsby on the 14th June 1943. Both Grace Mary and Pamela, who was then only three years old, were in the house during the air raid; they were sat terrified and huddled together for safety on the staircase between the living room and the front room. They didn't have an Anderson air raid shelter. Fortunately both survived and the damage to the house was later assessed as repairable. Pamela tells the story of our mother, dressed only in her nightgown, carrying her to her mother's house, about two miles away, for shelter.

Walter's general health by this time had started to deteriorate. I was aware, from what my mother had told me, that at some stage of his Merchant Navy career, during a voyage down to West Africa, he had contracted malaria. Although, how severe the incident of malaria was, is not clear. In addition, he also started to suffer badly from pyorrhoea, a very debilitating disease of the gums, which affects the ability to eat. In June 1943, Walter wrote to H. Hogarth and Sons, asking for extended shore leave to deal with the problems he had been having with his gums and teeth. He pointed out that the problem was getting worse and had started to have a detrimental effect on his stomach and his general health and well-being. He persevered for several more months, but on the 13th March 1944, when aged 33, Walter's health had badly deteriorated and he was consequently discharged from the

Merchant Navy Pool as 'unsuitable for sea service'. His Merchant Navy career was finished.

Discovering that this was how his Merchant Navy career had ended made me extremely sad. Walter had faithfully served his country for approximately four and a half years in what was one of the most dangerous theatres of war during that terrible conflict. I have tried to estimate, from his Certificate of Discharge Book records and, knowing roughly how long each crossing would have taken with the ships averaging about 10 knots, how many North Atlantic convoys he must have sailed on. I believe it to be in excess of twenty-five. Was it just by fate and providence, he had not been killed in action; three ships on which he had served, the SS Heronspool, the SS Pennington Court and the SS Antigone, were all sunk by enemy action, with the loss of many sailors, after he had left them. Not to mention the sinking of the SS Elizabeth Dal. In addition, the SS Baron Douglas, the last ship on which he served, had also been badly damaged by a mine and had incurred casualties, only a short while before he joined it. And, not forgetting, he had been struck by a bullet or shrapnel during one enemy engagement, only for the bible to save his life. How mocking that his war service and career as a Merchant Navy officer was to end in this ignominious manner; general ill health making him *unsuitable for sea service*. But, I can now proudly say Walter had done his duty.

It must have been a very bitter blow to him to be declared unfit for sea service, something he had trained for and desired, for most of his adult life. Having a wife and a young child, he had to take a new career path. And in this respect, Walter's career after his War service was quite short and unremarkable. He raised the financial capital; his mother Alice may have helped him do that, to establish a greengrocery business; initially setting up a shop at the junction of Weelsby Street and Durban Road in Grimsby. As this was proving to be successful, he expanded the business by buying an old van and setting up a mobile Greengrocery and Fish mongering round. For this part of his enterprise, his clients would be the R.A.F. bases and the outlying villages in the undulating countryside of the Lincolnshire Wolds. Although the war still had another year to go before it finally ended, Walter's life with his family took on an air of domestic bliss and normality. He was re-admitted to the Freeman roll on 5th October 1944 and just fifteen days later on the 20th October 1944, Walter was initiated into the King Edward VIII Lodge of the Royal Antediluvian Order of Buffaloes (RAOB). The RAOB is a Fraternal, Benevolent and Social Organisation in the United Kingdom, open to any male over the age of 18, provided he is a *"true and loyal supporter of the British Crown and Constitution"* and he *"enters of his own free will and consent"*. Part of the organisation's raison d'étre is to aid members, their families, those left behind by deceased brethren (widows/orphans) and other charitable organisations.

The only anecdote I could find relating to this period of Walter's life occurred during the dreadful winter in the early months of 1947. Walter was out in the Lincolnshire Wolds with his van delivering food and supplies, when along with other motorists he got caught in a violent snowstorm. A local farmer gave them all shelter, for how long is not quite clear. My mother, who told the story to my elder sister, indicated it was more than just a day. The farmer, his family and the other trapped motorists were all sustained by the food that Walter had in the van. According to mother, when the road was finally cleared enough for people to continue on their journey, no-one offered to pay Walter for what had been eaten. How rude; but he was a generous man and most likely would not have cared less. Even so, the business was growing and starting to be very successful, enough for him to take possession on the 11th December 1947, of a brand new Bedford Van.

Just four days later on the 15th December 1947, that new van would crush him to death.

Walter shortly before he died

Chapter Fourteen

And, Finally – The Story Draws To A Close

The story of my search for Walter I now draw to a close. When I started out on this journey of discovery, similar to the explorer Christopher Columbus, I wasn't quite sure where the journey would take me. And now that this part of my metaphorical travels has come to an end, I am actually amazed at where I have been. Never, within my wildest imagination, did I expect to find all the interesting individual stories that I have. What started out as a simple piece of work in gathering the information and evidence required to claim Walter's medals, for his service and doing his duty in the Merchant Navy during World War 2, expanded into a far more rewarding and enlightening exercise that is rich in content and characters. Not only did I find the information that was required to be able to claim Walter's medals, which I have now done; I unearthed a wide range of fascinating facts about both sides of Walter's extended family.

I have spent many hours at my kitchen table sorting through the masses of documents, photographs and other information that the few remaining members of my immediate family had kept. In addition, I also sought out the support of other family members, some of whom, (my cousins), I had not spoken to for several years. Researching Walter's story has had the added bonus of bringing people back into my life from whom, whilst not estranged, I was certainly distant.

From all this wealth of information supported by materials from, *inter-alia* the reference libraries, council archives and the internet, I have strived to produce a narrative that reflects the social conditions prevalent at each stage of the family timelines I have explored. Not only have I uncovered a wealth of information about my family's history, I have also developed a more comprehensive understanding of aspects of our country's history that hitherto I had never previously considered. For example: the hiring fairs, the mass movement of people during the industrialisation of society, the desperate distress and struggles of Irish immigrants, Victorian criminal justice and how the insane were treated, are just some of the facts I can now talk about with some authority. Furthermore, as I am personally interested in societal history, especially the local history of Grimsby, I found the linking of my family to the manner and circumstances in which many people had to live in the 19th century extremely fulfilling and worthwhile, because now I was relating history much closer to home.

During my journey, which at times I must confess, was quite stressful and emotional, there were many surprises along the way; some happy, others not so happy. I unearthed some very distressing revelations, the knowledge of which had long been lost to the family. How can I, or anyone else who reads this story, forget that Walter's Great-aunt Grace Mabel burnt to death, at the age of two and was buried in the Ainslie Street cemetery. I can picture her quite clearly screaming her little lungs off with the pain. What I did not mention when discussing the death of Grace Mabel and the other infants, is that for four years during the 1990s, my office actually overlooked the Ainslie Street parkland that the cemetery has now become. Little did I know then, when I was daydreaming and gazing out the window, that I was overlooking an area where several of my ancestors, including Grace Mabel, had been buried. How ironic!

If that wasn't distressing enough, only one generation before Grace Mabel's tragic death, Walter's Great-uncle David had been incarcerated into a Criminal Lunatic Asylum for committing a 'murder' at the age of 16. And his brother (John), a thoroughly evil person, was also committed to a series of Lunatic Asylums. I still feel angry about the unjust treatment that David Bloy had received. Nowadays, his mental condition (epilepsy) would be dealt with very differently and the wound that he inflicted on Simon Cote would be dressed and cleared up in a few days with antibiotics. There was no real intent to murder. Whilst I am not an expert in the law, it is my contention that today, David would face the charge of 'grievous bodily harm' or, 'assault with a deadly weapon'. John, on the other hand, I am sorry to say, was a depraved villain!

Although I had a suspicion that some of my forebears came from the Fenland area of Lincolnshire, I had no real inkling at all about their circumstances. Truth be told, it hadn't occurred to me that, not many generations ago, they would be 'illiterate paupers' experiencing and suffering the real hardship, deprivation and desolation that abject poverty brings. Moreover, I had never ever considered that many of my ancestors were agricultural labourers having to take their chance of employment through the 'hiring fair' system. Not only can I now relate this aspect of our country's socio-economic history to my family's history, it has also broadened my perspective of how uncertain life would have been for those that depended on the land for their living. Discovering that members of both the Bloy and the Nelson families left the countryside and moved to the towns for a better life, which I then related to the social circumstances and inequality of Victorian England, was an real eye opener for me.

Although I was born and bred in Grimsby and had served the town during the 1980s as a local councillor, I had no idea or appreciation of how bad the East Marsh of Grimsby was in the mid to latter part of the 19th century, primarily because I had never sat down and thought about it. Why would I need to? It was a shock to discover that my extended family just 120 years ago lived in such squalor and had to contend with the frequent incidences of infant mortality so often associated with social deprivation. Perhaps more importantly, it made me appreciate, all the more the value of what they had achieved. Amongst all the despair and distress there had been strength. Ultimately they had triumphed over adversity.

While I was writing this story, an old friend of mine said that to be 'poor' has almost been redefined. He maintained: to be poor in the United Kingdom today is measured mainly in terms of material wealth and possession of items one has or doesn't have, such as a car, satellite TV, mobile phones, DVD player and the likes. Whereas to be poor in the Victorian period being considered in this story and on through the first half of the 20th century until after the Second World War had a totally different meaning – it was one of human rights. In which case, we are talking about basic living conditions such as sanitation, clean water, sufficient food to eat, not being overcrowded, clean clothes to wear and adequate welfare and medical attention. With the exception of the homeless and the people, who for whatever reason live on the streets, these are the things we now take very much for granted. He further argued that there has been a shift in societal values and a changing emphasis of what's important in life. What I discovered, in researching the story and talking to others, encourages me to have considerable empathy with his point of view.

To recap and conclude my story - I don't think it is unreasonable to suppose, whenever anyone starts researching their family history, that they would be disappointed if they didn't find something out of the ordinary, particularly from a few generations ago. Do people really want to discover that their family was an uninteresting bunch of bland, faceless nonentities who had achieved very little? In our desire to discover our roots, are we secretly hoping to turn up some unknown unknowns such as, great-great-uncle 'whoever' was a highwayman and was caught, tried and hung for his crimes? Or that we had relatives who at one time were very rich landowners, and someone had squandered away the family fortune and perhaps lost it gambling or playing cards! Relating stories of scoundrels and rascals appears to have broad appeal.

Uncovering something unsavoury or better still, scandalous; even sensitive subjects such as illegitimacy and stillbirths at 13 years old, if they were sufficiently far enough in the past, to be able to socially distance oneself from it, would make for stimulating conversations over a pint of beer, or at the dinner table. There must be a point in time when the shame of an incident and a reluctance to talk about it turns to 'ah well, that's family history' and it becomes an acceptable topic of conversation. Once we start researching our family history, I think most people are hoping to find something quite out of the ordinary. I'm not sure though, that the discovery of an alleged murderer in the family would sit comfortably with all!

In 'Searching for Walter', and exploring the history of the extended family, I was not to be disappointed; many interesting facts, relating to the extended family, which I can now socially distance myself from and relate as anecdotes for others, were discovered. On a pleasant note, the family connection to Admiral Viscount Horatio Nelson, which I and I suspect others, when told of it by my granny, dismissed as fanciful nonsense, proved to be correct. Her father (John Nelson), who made the claim, was indeed related to the great man, albeit, not as closely as he would have liked. They shared a common ancestor; John Nelson's five-times great grandfather was Lord Nelson's great-great-grandfather.

I was also astounded and delighted to discover a direct ancestor, my great-great-great-grandfather Henry Kiddle, who fought in the Napoleonic Wars as a Queen's Dragoon Guardsman. Being interested in English history, I have always found the paintings, of which there are many, in museums and galleries, of dragoons and guardsmen riding gallantly into the fray, quite emotionally stirring. Especially as the battle, when the opposing forces engaged, would be mainly hand to hand fighting, cutting and slashing with sabres inflicting terrible injuries. Even now as I write this paragraph, I can picture the horrendous carnage and hear the screams of injured men and horses. I have to admit this discovery was not only a surprising revelation but a source of immense pride, which allows me to say my great-great-great-grandfather was one of those brave men.

On the paternal side of Walter's family, (the Bloys), as well as now being able to tell Walter's life story, including his service in the war, within his ancestry, I uncovered, illiteracy, infant mortality, insanity, murder and committal to a lunatic asylum. And, although I cannot prove it, the truth being lost in the mist of time, I am still convinced that John Bloy had something to do with the death of his mother. In addition to all that, abject poverty, serving time in prison for '*Fagin*' type behaviour, i.e. encouraging young people to steal, contributed to shaping the family through the 19th century, as they strove to rise above their hopeless circumstances to be successful. More recently, the fact that Walter's grandfather, who arrived into the East Marsh of Grimsby during the 1870s, outlived his wife and all his children conveys all too clearly what families had to face. Overcrowding, poor sanitation and communal 'thunder-box' toilets all played a part in creating in my mind a ghetto of despair. Consequently, deaths from illnesses such as measles, whooping cough and bronchial-pneumonia were commonplace. Gladly, not so commonplace now! And against all these odds, succeed they did. Although in the case of Walter's grandfather, his business was forced into liquidation and evidence suggests that he lived the last few years of his life as a lonely old man.

Exploring the maternal side of Walter's family, the Smiths lineage, I found that the picture was considerably different, but no less remarkable: they were not as impoverished as the Bloys and, being Freemen of the borough, they would have played an important part in the development of Grimsby during the 19th century. My investigation revealed how the family had by and large prospered. Although, I did find that Walter's maternal grandfather, had lived for a short while in a home for paupers in Leeds. In general terms, the family did not appear to have struggled financially as much as the Bloys. It was also surprising to find that the Freeman status, which some male members of the Smith and the Bloy families, myself included, latterly enjoyed, had only come to the family through the marriage of George Smith to Eleanor Jewitt, in the early part of the 19th century. Further research revealed that Jewitt was an important family name of early medieval origin, which derives directly from the Middle English male given name Juwet or Jowet, in the feminine Juwette or Jowette. The Jewitt family, being Freemen by birth and with the surname that can be traced back in a direct line to 13th century England, one could therefore safely assume, would have been important members of the local community.

When I researched and discussed the multiple marriages of Alice Smith, my paternal grandmother, further surprises were in store, including the social embarrassment and scandal of her being seven months pregnant when she married her first husband; and then the fact that after he died, she allowed her youngest daughter to be brought up by her sister. Grandma's fortunes changed considerably for the better with her second marriage to a man 15 years her senior. Further exploration also revealed that during the Second World War, her third husband had actually been murdered in 1942 whilst his ship was docked in Haifa in Israel, although nobody was ever bought to trial for his killing. Despite all these setbacks Grandma managed to advance herself through property and became quite a wealthy woman at a time when so many others were barely managing to survive on the 'breadline'.

During this roller-coaster personal journey, when I focused on the paternal, (the James's) and maternal, (the Nelsons) history of the family of Grace Mary, Walter's wife, further surprising revelations were found. These included: a possible bigamous marriage, financial riches from the ill-gotten gains of cheating at cards in Hong Kong, which resulted in a curse, the unexplained loss of the money, industrial accidents, more hardship, deprivation and struggling to make ends meet, and the very poignant image of an impoverished father burning the numbers off old police boots for his children to wear. I also discovered that both Grace Mary (my mother) and my granny, had survived separate German bombing raids on Grimsby during the summer of 1943.

With respect to the Kiddle family, which are Grace Mary's maternal grandmother's antecedents, in addition to the old soldier Henry Kiddle, I discovered that her grandmother, Mary Ann Cullum (nee Kiddle), had had four of her children, the first when she was just 13, before she got married in 1873 at the age of 18. And her father and at least one other close relative on this side of the family, served prison sentences with hard labour. In one case, in 1830, the family ancestor was actually deported to Australia for seven years for the crime of stealing a coat. I still find it amusing to picture, John Kiddle (Mary Ann's father), who was sent to prison in the 1860s for stealing a duck, striding into Louth after the theft with the duck hidden away under his frockcoat and trying to sell it at the local butchers. John Kiddle was a scoundrel and a petty thief rather than a hardened criminal.

This brief recap has been as much for my benefit as well as for those that read this account of my family's history. Peeling my metaphorical onion has provided revelation after revelation, not only with who my family were, what they did and how they fared, but also within the context of the society in which they lived. My family were just bit players on a much wider kaleidoscopic canvas; I am now more enriched from mapping one over the other. And if nobody, other than my siblings and son, read this story, it has still been a worthwhile and rewarding thing to do.

Although I never found a 'highwayman', my research revealed several incidences and unsavoury characters about whom I am happy to talk openly, because they died over 100 years ago. Time can be a great distance when telling family stories without feeling any sense of shame or embarrassment. Time can also distort or skew, depending on your perspective, how those stories are 'remembered' and told. In fact, I believe that most of what I have discovered: the inequality of Victorian society, infant mortality, insanity, destitution, bigamy, pregnancy before marriage, murder and cheating at cards for high stakes, prison sentences and deportation, provides for interesting reading. And I am certain that these very personal, and often poignant stories, will serve me well, without any embellishment, when telling anecdotes at dinner parties and to grandchildren!

With regard to Walter, I pointed out in the introduction and throughout this story, that I never knew my father nor my father's family and I had no attachment to him at all. This has totally changed; I think I now know my father. By exploring his life and developing an understanding of what he had done, and what he had been through and experienced, I feel a real emotional connection to him. Relating my own personal experiences of life to what Walter had done, I began to identify with the highs and lows of his life. For example, as a young man, I once experienced the acute disappointment of failing an important examination, which I never re-sat. My subsequent personal drive to study and succeed at both Master's and Doctorate degree level was essential catharsis for me to balance out this earlier failure. It was therefore easy for me to comprehend and appreciate how Walter must have felt when he failed his Second Officer's Certificate so spectacularly.

Unexpectedly, the photograph of the very vulnerable boy sailor that hangs in my living room has, for me, become Walter's version of Oscar Wilde's portrait of Dorian Grey. Although he is the young boy and will never grow older, when I look at it now I see the man. He is no longer a stranger. It is impossible to glance at that photograph of the boy sailor without thinking about how he served his country, and the fears he must have had each time he set out across the North Atlantic. Although the bible that saved Walter's life has been in my possession, stored away in an old shoebox for quite a long time, through undertaking this research, I was able to place it within context of his young life. It fits within the story like the missing part of a jigsaw. I now wonder how many other families have a life's history stored away in a dusty old shoebox in the attic, in cupboards or under the bed. 'Searching for Walter' became something far greater than was originally planned, the whole of which, for me, was a very enriching and at times a poignant and touching experience. This has been a journey of discovery that, I am thankful I had both the time and capability to undertake. Writing this story has been so cathartic and satisfying. I am also sure that Walter would enjoy reading it.

I set out to search for the boy sailor and finally found my father.

Reference And Sources Of Information

Much of this story has been developed from family records such as; marriage, birth and death certificates, diaries, letters, wills, employment records and family photographs. Anecdotes and recollections have all been used to build up the story and bring some of the principal characters to life, to put flesh on the bones and to try and understand their personality and motivation. Furthermore, the notes that I made nearly forty years ago when talking to my granny, and Walter's diary from 1939, are actual voices from the past and added to the story. In addition to complete the picture, the following sources of information have been used:

Ainslie Street Cemetery, Grimsby – Register of Burials

Battle of the Atlantic 1940-1945: www.rhiw.com

Berkshire County Council Records Office

Chapman, P. (2002) *Grimsby – The Story of the World's Greatest Fishing Port,* Derby: Breedon Books

Community Fishing Heritage UK – timeline

Crime and Justice – Trial Verdicts: www.oldbaileyonline.org

Daniels, B. *Poverty and Families in the Victorian Era,* accessed on-line May 2010

Dowling, A. (2007) *Grimsby – Making the Town*, Chichester: Phillimore and Co Ltd

Edinburgh Gazette 1923/24: edinburgh-gazette.co.uk

Farming and Agriculture: www.familytreeforum.com

General Register Office - England

Grimsby and Cleethorpes Trade Directories – various, between 1870 – 1906

Grimsby and District Archive Club: www. GYCODHEAD.co.uk

Grimsby Evening Telegraph – Archives

Grimsby Registry Office

Grimsby Register of People Entitled to Vote in the 19th Century

Kelly's Trade Directories of Grimsby and Cleethorpes – various

Lawrence-Hamilton, J. (1893) *Foul Fish and Filth Fevers*, paper presented in Seattle, USA

Lincolnshire County Council Archives

Lincolnshire and Kiddle Family History – http://firefoxhole.weebly.com/age-two-html accessed on-line 4th December 2012

London Gazette 1923/24: london-gazette.co.uk

Mayhew, H. Article on poverty in Victorian Times – appeared in the Morning Chronicle in September 1849

Mingay, K. Archivist- Great Grimsby Guild of Freemen

National Archives – Nelson Family Facts

National Census Records, 1841, 1851, 1861, 1871, 1881, 1891, and 1901

North East Lincolnshire Library Services

North East Lincolnshire Council Archives

Old Liverpool Historical Time-line: www.old-liverpool.co.uk

Reflections: Grimsby, 800 Years of History in the Making, Grimsby: Marketing Publications

Register of Admissions – St John's Hospital and Lunatic Asylum, Bracebridge Heath, Lincoln

Register of Enrolled Freemen of Grimsby

Register of Shipping and Seamen

Register of Merchant Navy shipping sunk 1939 -1945

Register of Merchant Navy shipping that was damaged 1939 - 1945

Scartho Road Cemetery, Grimsby – Register of Burials

St Mary's Church, Tydd St Mary's – Parish Registers

The Burke's Peerage World Book of Bloys

The Family Tree Forum – On-line Magazine accessed 9th May 2012

The Grimsby Chums: www.rootsweb.ancestry.com

The Grimsby News – Archives

Types of Punishment –Victorian Crime and Punishment://vcp.e2bn.org/justice/page1361

War Graves Commission Website

Whites Lincolnshire Directory (1872)

www.ancestry.co.uk accessed between April –June 2010

www.ancestrylibrary.com accessed between April –June 2010

www.battleships-cruisers.co.uk/merchant_navylosses.htm

www.genesreunited.co.uk/records

www.nmm.ac.uk/researchers